AFTER IDENTITY

EDITED BY **ROBERT ZACHARIAS**

AFTER IDENTITY

MENNONITE WRITING IN NORTH AMERICA

PUBLISHED BY THE PENNSYLVANIA STATE UNIVERSITY PRESS
AND, IN CANADA, THE UNIVERSITY OF MANITOBA PRESS

Library of Congress Cataloging-in-Publication Data

After identity : Mennonite writing in North America / edited by Robert Zacharias.
pages cm
Summary: "An interdisciplinary reappraisal of the field of Mennonite writing in Canada and the United States. Essays explore the unique configuration of religious and ethnic cultural difference"—Provided by publisher.
Includes bibliographical references and index.
ISBN 978-0-271-07037-7 (cloth : alk. paper)
1. Canadian literature—Mennonite authors—History and criticism.
2. American literature—Mennonite authors—History and criticism.
3. Identity (Psychology) in literature.
I. Zacharias, Robert, 1977– , editor.

PR9188.2.M45A35 2015
810.9'9212897—dc23
2015014640

Published 2015 by The Pennsylvania State University Press in association with The University of Manitoba Press

Printed in the United States of America
Published by The Pennsylvania State University Press, University Park, PA 16802–1003

The Pennsylvania State University Press is a member of the Association of American University Presses.

It is the policy of The Pennsylvania State University Press to use acid-free paper. Publications on uncoated stock satisfy the minimum requirements of American National Standard for Information Sciences—Permanence of Paper for Printed Library Material, ANSI Z39.48–1992.

This book is printed on paper that contains 30% post-consumer waste.

CONTENTS

ACKNOWLEDGMENTS

All books are shared efforts in one sense or another, and collections of essays are unavoidably so. Nonetheless, *After Identity* was an especially collaborative project, and I am happy to acknowledge the many capable hands that helped to craft it. In the fall of 2012, following a Mennonite/s Writing conference at Eastern Mennonite University, Julia Spicher Kasdorf invited me to help organize a symposium exploring the role that identity was playing in the critical conversation about Mennonite writing in North America. We invited five Canadian and five American scholars of Mennonite writing to join us at Penn State University for an intensive four-day symposium entitled After Identity: Mennonite/s Writing in North America. In May 2013, Julia hosted ten of us—Di Brandt was unable to travel but participated via email—for a week of productive and occasionally heated discussions about the state of the field. Early drafts of the papers included in this collection were circulated in advance, and each paper was given an hour's focused consideration. These conversations were deepened by the participation of scholars from the Penn State Department of English, who joined us for sessions connected with their own areas of considerable expertise. To Hester Blum, Tina Chen, Chris Castiglia, Toni Jensen, and Benjamin Schreier: my sincere thanks for your time, your insights, and your hospitality. This collection is much stronger because of your engaged participation. Thanks, too, to Henry James Morello, of the Department of Comparative Literature and the Department of Spanish, Italian, and Portuguese, for hosting a viewing of Carlos Reygadas's *Stellet Licht* (Silent Light), and to Stephen Byler, author of *Searching for Intruders,* who joined the symposium to read from a remarkable memoir in progress.

The critical discussions at the After Identity symposium constituted the first round of editing for these essays; as such, they were foundational to the final shape of the *After Identity* book. I remain most grateful to each of the symposium participants—Ervin Beck, Di Brandt, Daniel Shank Cruz, Jeff Gundy, Ann Hostetler, Julia Spicher Kasdorf, Royden Loewen, Jesse Nathan, Magdalene Redekop, Hildi Froese Tiessen, and Paul Tiessen—for their time, efforts, and critical generosity throughout that week and for their patience and efforts throughout the substantial revision process that followed it. Thanks, in particular, go to Julia, for her generosity in inviting me to join her in planning the symposium, for her deft organizing, able hosting, and insight throughout the week, and for her encouragement to take on the editing of this volume. I also want to acknowledge and express my appreciation to the following Penn State partners for their generous support of the symposium: the Max Kade German-American Research Institute; the Center for American Literary Studies; the Institute for Arts and Humanities; Mark Morrisson and the Department of English; the Department of History; the Latin American Studies Program; and the University Libraries. I also want to express my sincere thanks to Kathryn Yahner, Charlee Redman, and the rest of the editorial team at Penn State University Press, who responded enthusiastically to the original book proposal, championed the collection through its early stages, and ably guided it through production. I am also grateful to Glenn Bergen and the University of Manitoba Press, who partnered with us to complete the book and distribute it in Canada, and to Dallas Harrison for his careful copyediting. The remarkable image on the cover of this collection is *Saving Private Ryan* (2003), a painting in the Green Zone series by Wanda Koop, a Canadian artist of Mennonite descent. The portrait at the center of the painting can be viewed as either coming into focus or expanding into pieces, a productive ambiguity that I find most fitting for the essays collected here.

During the time between the symposium and this publication, my research has been enabled by two generous postdoctoral fellowships: I held a Social Sciences and Humanities Research Council of Canada Postdoctoral Fellowship in the Centre for Diaspora and Transnational Studies (CDTS) at the University of Toronto, and a Banting Postdoctoral Fellowship in the Department of English Language and Literature at the University of Waterloo. I want to thank Dr. Ato Quayson, director of CDTS, and Dr. Winfried Siemerling at Waterloo, who supervised these fellowships, for their encouragement of my work on this project. I also want to thank the anonymous readers who read the manuscript and offered valuable feedback on how to improve it; Kit Dobson for his generous and timely feedback on early versions of my introduction and chapter; and Hildi Froese Tiessen for her translations of German passages in the collection.

Finally, thank you to my family: to Arvelle, for her ongoing support of my academic journey, and to our children, Adiah, Samuel, and Talia, for loving books as much as I do. As much as a collaborative project such as this is mine to dedicate, I offer it to my parents, Les and Marrian Zacharias, who taught me that after two thousand years the light still shines, and continue to demonstrate this to be true.

Introduction

After Identity: Mennonite/s Writing in North America

ROBERT ZACHARIAS

This is why we cannot leave the beliefs,
or what else would we be?
—Julia Spicher Kasdorf, "Mennonites"

The first Mennonites arrived in the British colonies of North America in the middle of the seventeenth century, with permanent settlement beginning several decades later in Germantown, Pennsylvania. It took roughly 250 years, until the start of the twentieth century, before the first authors of Mennonite descent began publishing literary texts in what had become Canada and the United States. "Mennonite/s writing," as a recognizable body of texts, is a much more recent phenomenon still, emerging over just the past thirty-five years: first in Canada, where a surprising burst of fiction and poetry by Russian Mennonite writers during the 1980s garnered national attention and was christened "the Mennonite miracle," and next in the United States, where poetry and life writing by Mennonites began landing on awards lists with regularity in the 1990s.[1] An increasingly vibrant critical conversation has emerged alongside the literary tradition, primarily in academic venues such as the *Mennonite Quarterly Review, Journal of Mennonite Studies, Conrad Grebel Review, Mennonite Life,* and, more recently, the online *Center for Mennonite Writing Journal.* The rising interest in Mennonite literature in the United States, coupled with ongoing interest in Canada, has sparked calls for a widespread reassessment of the field as a focus of criticism. Given that "Mennonite/s writing" is much more a critical construct than a transparent body of literary texts, *After Identity: Mennonite Writing in North America* seeks to turn the field's critical gaze back on itself. More specifically, the chapters in this volume aim to interrogate what is at stake in—and potentially to initiate a move beyond—the field's ongoing preoccupation with Mennonite identity itself.

Post-Identity

The Mennonites of North America are descendants, by faith or birth, of the sixteenth-century Christian dissenters collectively referred to as Anabaptists. Stressing adult baptism, nonconformity, and nonviolence, the diverse Anabaptist movements that sprang up in Europe during the early sixteenth century were subjected to widespread persecution. The first large migration of Mennonites to North America occurred as part of William Penn's "holy experiment" in Pennsylvania around the turn of the eighteenth century. Many of the descendants of these Mennonites, often called Swiss Mennonites or Pennsylvania Dutch, later established the first Mennonite presence in Canada when they emigrated from the United States following the American Revolutionary War. The second major cultural or ethnic group of North American Mennonites, often referred to as Russian Mennonites, arrived from their once-prosperous colonies in present-day Ukraine in three mass migrations (1870s, 1920s, and 1940s).[2] The larger Mennonite faith, however, has spread around the world through missionary efforts, and today there is a global Mennonite religious community of more than 1.5 million baptized adults, with the largest population in Africa. There are roughly 500,000 baptized members of Mennonite churches in North America, scattered broadly across some 150 different groups and denominations. Although the majority of North American Mennonites are assimilated into mainstream culture, others—especially those from Old Order or related Amish and Hutterite traditions—continue to live separated from "the world," maintaining distinct ethnoreligious traditions with conservative dress, unique dialects, and a reluctance to embrace modern technologies.

The brief history recounted above—as inadequate as it is necessary[3]—reflects the center of what Calvin Redekop has called the "Mennonite identity crisis," in that it is split between a narrative of a religious community expanding across the globe, on the one hand, and a narrative of two related ethnic communities migrating to North America, on the other. Although the division between faith and ethnicity has a long and contentious history in the broader field of Mennonite studies, Mennonite literary critics have rarely been willing to restrict their engagement with Mennonite literature to faith-based writing. In fact, many scholars in the field have expressed their disinterest in explicitly "religious literature," and few have engaged the details born of the community's denominational diversity beyond the broad Swiss/Russian divide.[4] Although this has certainly left some unanswered questions about who, exactly, the Mennonites are in Mennonite/s writing, critics have consistently responded to problems of definition by outlining the parameters of the field as broadly as possible.

Al Reimer's "wide-angle lens" is exemplary in this regard, encompassing "the work of writers who spent at least their formative years in a Mennonite milieu–family and / or community and / or church—regardless of whether they now consider themselves 'Mennonite' in a religious sense, or in a purely ethnic sense, or in both senses, or in neither sense" (*Mennonite Literary Voices* 2). In the introduction to her landmark anthology *A Cappella: Mennonite Voices in Poetry,* Hostetler similarly wrestles with the challenge of definition before settling on one meant to reflect "a diverse spectrum of sensibility informed by Mennonite experience—from outright rejection to vibrant and ongoing faith" (xviii). When she goes on to claim that her anthology can "represent the full range of North American poetry by writers of Mennonite origin" because, for Mennonites, "religious, ethnic, and linguistic criteria cross national boundaries" (182), she expresses a well-established principle in the field.

As admirably inclusive as such a critical tradition might be, it is worth taking note of a few of its implications. First, though it defines "Mennonite" in broad terms, it remains fairly narrow in its strict devotion to authorial biography. In this, the field is closer to nationalized literary studics, in which borders are conventionally drawn along the lines of an author's citizenship, than to fields in which the focus reflects the contents of the texts themselves—as in, say, many genre studies.[5] Second, it is worth recognizing that the field's "wide-angle lens" has quietly worked to downplay a host of significant religious, cultural, political, and historical differences among Mennonite communities across North America. And third, the North American frame itself has tended to gloss over the ways in which the field has been structured differently in Canada and the United States.[6] The state-supported rise of multicultural literature in Canada, for example, framed the study of Mennonite writing through the concept of ethnicity, enabling Russian Mennonite authors to figure prominently in Canadian literary discussions of "ethnic literature."[7] In the United States, where discussions of ethnic difference historically have been linked more closely to the discourse of race, Mennonites have more often been understood as "one of many hundreds of Christian sects vying for attention" (Hostetler, "Bringing" 149). As valuable as Mennonite/s writing continues to be as a longstanding project of inter- or transnational writing—indeed, the field offers a rich archive ripe for consideration through the non-national critical paradigms that have arisen in literary studies over the past two decades—scholars have yet to fully explore the ways in which questions of Mennonite identity and cultural difference, especially those surrounding language, faith, ethnicity, and race, have been negotiated through starkly different regional, denominational, and national contexts.

In asking questions about the enduring role of identity in the field of Mennonite/s writing, this volume participates in a much larger reconsideration of cultural identity currently under way in contemporary literary studies. Although notoriously slippery as a critical concept, Charles Taylor's broad definition of identity as "a person's understanding of who they are, of their fundamental defining characteristics as a human being" (25) has proven sufficient to ground an ongoing debate about the interplay between individual and collective identities in contemporary multicultural societies.[8] Yet critical discussions about identity have changed dramatically since Taylor was writing in the early 1990s, when it was conventional practice to classify minoritized literatures by racial or ethnic identity markers and position them in straightforwardly supplemental (if often antagonistic) relation to national narratives. Since then, a multifaceted critique of identity from across the humanities and social sciences has thoroughly undermined the notion of stable and homogeneous cultural groups, while the transnational turn in literary studies has made a parallel interrogation of the link between nation-states and cultural production. As the radical contingency of identities both cultural and national was increasingly accepted in North American scholarship, sweeping appeals to broadly defined communities such as "Asian American" or "Jewish Canadian" were rightly called into question.

Some scholars, including sociologists Rogers Brubaker and Frederick Cooper, advocated an outright rejection of identity as a critical term on the grounds that it was irredeemably "riddled with ambiguity, riven with contradictory meanings, and encumbered by reifying connotations" (34). At the same time, however, many of the concerns addressed by conventional identity politics are far from resolved, including not only the racialized inequalities that continue to mark North American society but also the larger discursive structures that facilitate their persistence. It may have been possible to posit a fully post-national or even post-identity future at the turn of the millennium, but the dramatic rise of economic and security concerns in North America over the past decade has occasioned a forceful reassertion of the nation-state and a racialized politics of identity. It is in this context that questions of identity—of communal history and cultural memory, of collective action and individual agency, and of race, ethnicity, and the politics of belonging—remain pressing but conflicted areas of critical concern.

In literary studies, debates over the prospect of moving "past" or "beyond" identity remain closely entwined with the politicized study of minoritized literatures. In *The Semblance of Identity: Aesthetic Mediation in Asian American Literature,* for example, Christopher Lee begins by pragmatically defining identity as "a means to conceptualize the relationship between an individual and the historical, cultural, and social conditions that situate his or her life circumstances" (2). Whereas Taylor, writing in the early 1990s, emphasized the complex role of "authenticity" in the construction of identity, Lee's description of the "'post-identity' turn" succinctly describes the fundamental ambivalence of more recent engagements with identity:

> [W]e can conceive identities as providing a form—a grammar as it were—for making sense of and representing the relationship between the subject and the social. Post-identity marks the breakdown of this grammar and unfolds as an inherent and integral dimension of identitarian thinking. Understanding post-identity in this manner allows us to account for why, despite frequent declarations about the constructedness and/or incoherence of identities, aspects of identitarian thinking continue to persist as affective investments, means of knowledge production, and modes of ethico-political engagement and imagination. (8)

Rather than understanding the drive toward post-identity in temporal terms as a reaction against identity, Lee suggests that it reveals the contradictions always already inherent in identitarian logic. His overview of the conundrum of identity politics in Asian American studies suggests that the field has widely acknowledged the superficiality of its identitarian frame yet continues to insist on its ongoing value in mobilizing collective agency and antiracist action.

Remarkably similar arguments have been made in Canadian literary studies, including by Roy Miki, who has called "Asian Canadian" a "double-edged site" that provides the vocabulary necessary for collective political action even as it risks reinscribing the essentialist logic that makes such action necessary (31). In their introduction to *Asian Canadian Writing Beyond Autoethnography,* Eleanor Ty and Christl Verduyn place contemporary Asian Canadian writing within a larger movement of writers who are "[n]o longer . . . identifying simply with their ethnic or racial background in opposition to dominant culture" and who "consciously attempt to question or problematize the link between ethnic identity and literary production, while still recognizing the racialized context in which they write" (3). Ty and Verduyn go on to insist that their interest in moving "beyond autoethnography" is not meant to disparage the gains made through past autoethnographic gestures or to discredit its potential value in the present. Instead, using language that parallels Lee's description of the "'post-identity' turn" as marking the instabilities of identitarian thinking, they argue that to go "beyond autoethnography" is simply to "characterize and highlight texts that refuse to be contained simply by their ethnographic markers" (4–5).

Although the history, form, and function of Asian North American studies are clearly incommensurable with Mennonite North American studies, the larger scholarly context outlined in *Semblance of Identity* and *Asian Canadian Writing Beyond Autoethnography*—in which scholars of minoritized literary traditions search for ways to build on earlier identity-based critical studies while taking seriously their limitations—offers an apt description of how and why scholars of Mennonite writing are currently working to reconsider their own field. Indeed, Ty and Verduyn's description of the state of contemporary "ethnic writing" in Canada has clear parallels with Hildi Froese Tiessen's recent account of what she calls the "new Mennonite writing," in which, Tiessen suggests, "history and tradition are no longer authoritative" and authors seem to be "less concerned . . . with group history than with individual becoming; less compelled by essential identity than by multifaceted identifications" ("Homelands" 14–15). In such a context, the enduring emphasis on reading Mennonite literature as the expression of a distinct ethnoreligious heritage feels increasingly outdated and reductive, one that risks practicing, as Anthony Appiah warns of group identities more generally, a "politics of compulsion" (163).

At the same time, Mennonite writing occupies a very particular position in the racialized tradition of area studies and multicultural literature, one that may further help to explain why the exploration of Mennonite literary identity has become an ambivalent project for many critics. The first major surge of Mennonite writing in North America came in a period dominated by identity politics and postcolonial critique, both of which mobilized minoritized communities in the name of social justice, often contrasting racialized or ethnic communities against a privileged majority culture. Given the conventional markers of historical North American Mennonite identity—as inheritors of a white, patriarchal, European, heteronormative, and conservative Christian tradition—there are legitimate questions about the position of Mennonite writing within the genealogy of North American identity politics. The shifting position of Mennonite literature in Canadian criticism, in which the conversation on cultural difference moved from ethnicity to race in the 1990s, helps to make clear what is at stake. When Mennonite literature emerged as a distinct body of writing in the 1980s, religious difference was largely understood in ethnic terms, and Mennonite writing was commonly discussed alongside other ethnic literatures, including Jewish, African, Asian, and Ukrainian literatures. By the late 1990s, however, critics were pointing directly to Mennonite literature as part of an argument that "white" cultural difference ought not to be uncritically collapsed into the same tradition as racialized literary studies.[9] The critical conversation in the United States, by contrast, has been more attuned to the role of religion in Mennonite writing. In the United States as in Canada, however, an enduring emphasis on Swiss and Russian Mennonite histories and concerns has meant that both popular and literary-critical conversations about Mennonites routinely evince an assumption of whiteness that does not reflect the growing racial and ethnic diversity of the broader Mennonite faith community in North America.[10] There is no question, then, that Mennonite identity has signified as a form of cultural difference in North America but it is far from clear just what that difference is or that it is in line with the larger activist projects that have characterized identity politics as a whole.

Indeed, critics from Stuart Hall to Slavoj Žižek have critiqued the aestheticization of difference in contemporary multiculturalism as a way of depoliticizing material and racialized inequalities by redefining them as the realm of culture and the arts. To the extent that the identity politics of the 1990s was focused on antiracist advocacy, critical discussions about traditional Mennonite literary identity have been running the risk of looking like they were advocating for their own privilege, or practicing what Richard Dyer, writing in the context of the rise of whiteness studies, has called "me too-ism." "We are often told that we are living now in a world of multiple identities, of hybridity, of decentredness and fragmentation," writes Dyer. "Yet we have not yet reached a situation in which white people and white cultural agendas are no longer in the ascendant" (541). In such a context, for critics of Mennonite literature to announce that concerns regarding identity are somehow passé, or to advocate for Mennonite studies to move "beyond" identity, risks implicitly endorsing the larger social, critical, and institutional infrastructure within which a still-normative form of Euro-Mennonite identity continues to operate from a position of relative privilege. Such claims risk projecting (and implicitly affirming) a uniform, status quo subjectivity onto the increasingly diverse and deeply unequal experiences of Mennonites across the continent, including many for whom basic identity claims continue to be necessary as means of coming to voice within communities that have rarely afforded them such authority. Moreover, there are key discussions about state and domestic violence, physical and sexual abuse, sexual diversity, and mental health currently taking place in Mennonite communities, churches, and institutions. Many of these concerns have been, and continue to be, powerfully explored in Mennonite literary texts, yet few have been meaningfully engaged by Mennonite literary criticism. As such, the critical urge to move "after identity" must itself be called into question, and needs to be contextualized within the particular critical history in which it is being expressed.

Chasing Identity

Where to begin when introducing Mennonite/s writing in North America—a field of study whose clear investment in the concept of identity is flagged through its very disciplinary signature—as being somehow "after identity"? One place, less obvious than it might appear, is with the term "Mennonite/s writing" itself. Contemporary Mennonite literary studies can be said to have begun in the late 1970s, but the emergence of this term in 1990 suggests a strain of critical thought through which a productive ambivalence was inscribed into the larger field. Following the first Mennonite/s Writing conference, held at Conrad Grebel University College in Ontario in 1990, Hildi Froese Tiessen reported that, though it was clear that Mennonite literature in Canada had coalesced into an important body of work worthy of further study, serious questions remained about the viability of Mennonite literary studies as such. "[T]o speak of writing by Canadian Mennonites is to speak of a tangible literary force in this country," she notes in the introduction to *Acts of Concealment: Mennonite/s Writing in Canada,* the collection that emerged from the conference. "Yet, for every word or gesture that spoke of something that one could call a coherent 'tradition' of Mennonite writing, another denied that any such thing does—or should—exist" (21). In the term "Mennonite/s writing," a large measure of this self-consciousness had already been stamped onto the conference's organizing theme, reflecting a desire to mark an interest in a wide variety of texts (hence *writing* rather than *literature*), along with a desire to trouble, or perhaps simply to double, its attachment to Mennonite identity as such. The term frames the field in both literal terms (as a description of *Mennonites* who happen to be *writing*) and more conventional but also more nebulous terms (as something called *Mennonite writing*). Very much a product of its moment in Canadian literary criticism,[11] the somewhat awkward term—how does one pronounce "Mennonite/s writing" anyway?—quickly became a key organizing concept for Mennonite literary studies, adopted as the title for a series of ongoing international conferences.

By the time that the second Mennonite/s Writing conference was held at Goshen College in Indiana seven years later, the viability of the field no longer seemed to be in question. In fact, conference organizers John D. Roth and Ervin Beck could confidently suggest that "the event represented a kind of coming-of-age for Mennonite creative writing and literary criticism" (v). However, to judge by their *Migrant Muses: Mennonite/s Writing in the U.S.,* the edited collection that emerged from the conference, it seems clear that Mennonite literary criticism continued to struggle with its relationship to

Mennonite identity. Although their contributions differ in important ways, for example, both Ann Hostetler and Hildi Froese Tiessen drew on Stuart Hall to argue that Mennonite writing was actively challenging the idea of a clear and coherent Mennonite identity that had been constructed by the "official" narratives offered by the church and literary critics alike. Focusing on Mennonite poetry in the United States, Hostetler engaged the long-standing debate about Mennonite ethnicity and faith to suggest that poetry can offer a "more complicated portrait of Mennonite identity" precisely because of its "unofficial character" ("Unofficial Voice" 41). Tiessen, meanwhile, suggested that the field's enduring focus on a series of binary tropes that turned on the hinge of identity—including the individual versus the community, the ethnic experience versus the religious vision, and the artist versus the church—had meant that literary critics were failing to keep up with the complexities of the literature itself. "The fixed categories of identity that Mennonites once believed they could slip into unproblematically are no longer useful," Tiessen warned. "The binary oppositions inscribed in their literary-critical writing and thinking over the past century serve them ill. Those who talk about Mennonite cultural identity must now learn to read the expanded text (or 'assemblage of texts') that creative writers have begun to inscribe" ("Beyond" 20). Along with Jeff Gundy's article positioning Mennonite poets as "lurkers" on the edge of the community ("In Praise"), and the opening article by Denise Levertov exploring the benefits and challenges of writing free from the "claims of the collective" (9), the essays in *Migrant Muses* seemed to be set on exploring the borders and exposing the limits of Mennonite cultural identity in North America.

I began this section with Mennonite/s writing rather than Mennonite literary studies more generally not because there is a clear distinction between the two (there isn't), but to trace the emergence of a critical strain marked by a self-conscious concern with the central claims of the larger field. Although the term "Mennonite/s writing" was coined in 1990, commentary on North American Mennonite literature began in earnest in 1977, when American critic John L. Ruth published a thin booklet with the title *Mennonite Identity and Literary Art.*[12] Gesturing to the burst of interest in "group-identity" occasioned by the "Black story *Roots*" and the "sugar-coated Jewish *Fiddler on the Roof*" (10), Ruth calls on Mennonite authors to contribute to the formation and maintenance of Mennonite identity by writing the history of Mennonites "in such a way that the over-arching Salvation-story in which it participates may be grasped" (70). Ruth emphasizes the Swiss Mennonite tradition in the United States to make a forceful argument for the cultural and religious significance of a dynamic literary tradition. If his study has often served as a foil for the less theologically engaged critical discussion that followed, it has also established many of the concerns that have come to dominate the field, including, most prominently, its central focus on the relationship between "literary art" and "Mennonite identity."[13]

Fifteen years later, in 1993, Canadian critic Al Reimer published a second influential booklet on Mennonite writing, *Mennonite Literary Voices Past and Present.* His book emphasizes the Russian Mennonite tradition in Canada, but its argument reflects many of the same concerns as Ruth's study, and, as Reimer acknowledges elsewhere ("Coming" 267), it is similarly invested in what Ruth identifies as "the holy meaning of our identity" (53). Reimer's booklet, however, moved the critical conversation away from Ruth's focus on history and toward a thematic critique. In the process, it formalized many of the identity-based concerns that were coming to dominate the field, including those reflected in chapter subheadings positioning religion against ethnicity ("Anabaptist Writing and the Russian-Mennonite Tradition"), insiders against outsiders ("One Foot In, One Foot Out"), individuals against the community ("Writing from Outside the Inside"), and the role of women writers in a patriarchal community ("The Re-Membering of the Mennonite Woman").

Together, Ruth's *Mennonite Identity and Literary Art* and Reimer's *Mennonite Literary Voices Past and Present* helped to establish Mennonite literary criticism within the larger scholarly field of Mennonite studies. In a 1992 review essay entitled "Mennonites, the Mennonite Community, and Mennonite Writers," however, Elmer Suderman warned that both Ruth and Reimer seemed to tie their critical concerns too tightly to the community itself. Suderman's essay is valuable not only because it marks one of the earliest metacritical moments in the field, in which a critic directly addresses something that he calls "the Mennonite critics" (25), but also because it implores those critics to focus on the literature itself. "I worry," he writes, "that a preoccupation with the writers and their context runs the great risk of ignoring the text" (25). The subsequent scholarly discussion has not always heeded Suderman's warning, but it has succeeded in constructing a vibrant critical discourse surrounding Mennonite writing, thoroughly exploring many of the tensions that mark the fraught relationship between "literary art" and "Mennonite identity."

Given that the field of Mennonite literary studies is quite literally defined by its connection to something broadly understood as "Mennonite," it is hardly a surprise to find that much of the critical discussion that has followed Ruth's and Reimer's booklets has remained closely tied to questions of identity. Although too numerous to cite individually, key essays exploring Mennonite writing and cultural identity can be found in journals such as the *Conrad Grebel Review,*

Journal of Mennonite Studies, Center for Mennonite Writing, Mennonite Life, and *Mennonite Quarterly Review,* in edited collections such as Harry Loewen's *Mennonite Images: Historical, Cultural, and Literary Essays Dealing with Mennonite Issues* (1980), Harry Loewen and Al Reimer's *Visions and Realities: Essays, Poems, and Fiction Dealing with Mennonite Issues* (1985), Hildi Froese Tiessen and Peter Hinchcliffe's *Acts of Concealment: Mennonite/s Writing in Canada* (1992), and John Roth and Ervin Beck's *Migrant Muses: Mennonite/s Writing in the U.S.* (1998). In addition to Ruth's and Reimer's studies, valuable single-authored studies that include explorations of Mennonite identity and writing include Di Brandt's *Dancing Naked: Narrative Strategies for Writing Across Centuries* (1996) and *So this is the world & here I am in it* (2007), Julia Spicher Kasdorf's *The Body and the Book: Writing from a Mennonite Life* (2001), Douglas Reimer's *Surplus at the Border: Mennonite Writing in Canada* (2002), Jean Janzen's *Elements of Faithful Writing* (2004), Jeff Gundy's *Walker in the Fog: On Mennonite Writing* (2005) and *Songs from an Empty Cage: Poetry, Mystery, Anabaptism, and Peace* (2013), and my own *Rewriting the Break Event: Mennonites and Migration in Canadian Literature* (2013). Although the primary concerns of these many texts are obviously wide and varied, a vital and occasionally heated debate about the relationship between literature and Mennonite identity can be traced through them all.

In the discussion that followed the sixth Mennonite/s Writing conference in 2012, several critics and authors took note of the field's enduring focus on identity and wondered if the time had come to move on to new concerns. In the opening essay to the *Mennonite Quarterly Review*'s special issue on the conference, for example, Julia Spicher Kasdorf confesses a growing weariness with the conventional narrative of Mennonite writing and wonders "what new histories of this literature can we tell" ("Sunday" 10). Hildi Froese Tiessen expresses similar frustrations in the next essay, reporting that "identity politics often runs [the field] aground," even as she wonders what will happen if and when the Mennonite text "is in effect no longer recognizable as a 'Mennonite' text" ("Homelands" 21). In the next essay, Ann Hostetler makes the case for a multiple and contradictory understanding of identity in the context of Mennonite memoirs, and tosses a challenge directly to Mennonite readers and scholars alike: "[W]hat if the 'self' doesn't particularly care about the project of preserving Mennonite identity?" ("Self" 33).

After Identity grew out of this shared frustration with the direction of the field, which must be understood within the longer critical context outlined above. What might it mean for critics of Mennonite writing to seriously interrogate the ways in which the critical field of Mennonite/s writing has relied on the notion of identity to date? Which histories and contexts have informed the shape of this focus, and what are its gaps? Has a focus on identity furthered the field by drawing attention to literature by Mennonite authors, or has it undermined the field by privileging ethnographic value over literary value? This volume's title, *After Identity,* is meant to reflect precisely such questions, signaling not only a call to move the critical discussion beyond a reductive autoethnography in its various manifestations, but also a recognition of the deeper complexities of such a request. Is it truly possible to talk of Mennonite writing or literature while setting aside the concerns of "group-identity," to move beyond identity and still retain coherence as a field? Or is it rather a question of thinking differently about identity, of reconsidering how it has functioned in the field to date, and how it might function differently in the future? Has the time come for Mennonite/s writing to move on, or will it always be (chasing) after identity?

After Identity

I have divided the twelve chapters of this volume into two parts. The chapters in the first part, "Reframing Identity," seek to reassess and reframe the role that Mennonite identity has played in literature and literary criticism to date. In "The Autoethnographic Announcement and the Story," Julia Spicher Kasdorf considers the shifting function of the conventional declarations of identity in literary texts engaging Mennonite concerns, those charged and increasingly self-conscious moments in which authors attempt to summarize Mennonite history or culture for their implicitly non-Mennonite readers. Royden Loewen's chapter, "A Mennonite *Fin de Siècle:* Exploring Identity at the Turn of the Twenty-First Century," complements Kasdorf's interrogation of the relationship between history and literature with a provocative reading of the late-century blooming of Mennonite writing in North America as evidence of the broader Mennonite community's belated entrance into modernity. The stern critique of community offered in many of the field's canonical texts, Loewen insists, is best understood as a rejection not of the traditional Mennonite community itself but of its turn toward conventional bourgeois values. Ervin Beck offers an alternative perspective on such community critiques in the next chapter, "Mennonite Transgressive Literature," in which he catalogues the field's key "transgressive" literary texts and identifies a marginalized strain of scholarship that has contested their portrayals of the community. Drawing on the tenets of reader-response theory to broaden the conversation on such texts to "include and respect resistant readers' understandings," Beck introduces the concept of "folk literary criticism" to engage the informal but often informed concerns persistently raised by nonacademic Mennonite readers.

Just as Loewen and Beck move beyond the text in their explorations of Mennonite writing, Paul Tiessen, in his chapter "Double Identity: Covering the *Peace Shall Destroy Many* Project," explores the archival history behind the publication of Rudy Wiebe's seminal first book. Revealing how deeply the editorial process shaped the content of Wiebe's novel and exploring how its iconoclastic cover shaped its reception, Tiessen encourages critics to better recognize the "vast horizon of literary and other events"—many of which have little to do with Mennonites themselves—that informs the circulation of even the most canonical of "Mennonite" texts. Ann Hostetler's comparative chapter, "After Ethnicity: Gender, Voice, and an Ethic of Care in the Work of Di Brandt and Julia Spicher Kasdorf," pairs the work of two major Mennonite poets to explore parallel trajectories in their poetry and nonfiction writing. Arguing that the role of "ethnic woman author" at once enabled and confined the early work of Brandt and Kasdorf, Hostetler suggests that both poets self-consciously broadened their work before returning to reimagine and recuperate key aspects of their Mennonite heritage. The first part closes with my own chapter, "The Mennonite Thing: Identity for a Post-Identity Age." Although many contemporary Mennonite texts explicitly challenge an essentialized understanding of Mennonite identity, I caution that this should not be taken as evidence that the field is no longer invested in such an identity. To the contrary, I argue that many of these texts mobilize an essentialized Mennonite identity strategically, routing their engagements through a variety of distancing gestures that enable the "Mennonite Thing" to continue serving as an animating force in the field.

The chapters in the second part, "Expanding Identity," argue for a broader critical engagement with Mennonite literature beyond—but perhaps not entirely past—conventional identity-based concerns. If the chapters in the first part collectively look back to argue for a critical reassessment of the way that identity has circulated in the field to date, the chapters in the second part collectively look forward to new methodologies and alternative avenues of critical thought. Di Brandt's chapter, "In Praise of Hybridity: Reflections from Southwestern Manitoba," begins with an intimately local discussion of the Manitoba Mennonite experience before opening into a broad mythopoetic invitation to radically expand our understanding of Mennonite identity. What might happen, she asks, if we sought to appreciate and celebrate the points of connection across communities, both historical and contemporary, rather than emphasize and reinscribe the divisions between them? In "Queering Mennonite Literature," Daniel Shank Cruz offers one answer, exploring the rising genre of queer Mennonite fiction. Calling on critics to actively participate in the genre's challenge to Mennonite heteronormativity, Cruz draws on queer theory to reimagine "community" as an open, dialogic space rather than one defined by homogeneity and firm borders. Paralleling the expansive gestures of Brandt and Cruz, Jeff Gundy, in his chapter "Toward a Poetics of Identity," argues for a fuller recognition of the always dynamic, contingent, multiple, and shifting nature of identity. Conceding his weariness with an enduring emphasis on the most narrow elements of Mennonite concern, Gundy calls for a faith and a writing practice that draw more generously on a broader array of concerns and influences.

While Brandt, Cruz, and Gundy call for a broadening of the parameters in which the field engages identity, the chapters by Jesse Nathan and Magdalene Redekop mark a methodological shift in emphasizing the formal and aesthetic elements of poetry by authors of Mennonite descent. Nathan's contribution, "Question, Answer," listens for echoes of the catechistic call and response through Mennonite American poetry, moving across generations of poets to initiate a promising turn to form as a means of tracing a Mennonite literary tradition. Redekop's chapter, "'Is Menno in There?': The Case of 'The Man Who Invented Himself,'" encourages a focused return to the literary texts themselves, offering an extended reading of a poem by Patrick Friesen as a way to both outline and demonstrate a criticism that acknowledges the "aesthetic accent" of work by Mennonite authors while carefully unpacking and appreciating its broader aesthetic achievements. The second part, and the volume, closes with Hildi Froese Tiessen's contribution, "After Identity: Liberating the Mennonite Literary Text." Tiessen argues that the firmly historicist, identitarian logic that has dominated the field has endured beyond the initial contexts that established its validity. Although not advocating a complete dismissal of identity-based readings, Tiessen urges critics to continue searching for broader critical perspectives through which to engage the writing—not to stop reading literary texts by and about Mennonites but to consider setting aside, perhaps only temporarily, the desire to read such texts as specifically Mennonite literature.

Individually, each chapter in *After Identity* engages the question of identity in some distinct way; collectively, they show something of the range in tone, methodology, and perspective that characterizes the broader field of Mennonite literary criticism today. Although the part titles that I have offered might appear to signal a progression, as if the chapters in "Expanding Identity" are the natural culmination of the efforts at "Reframing Identity," I want to close this introduction by cautioning against such a reading. Because of the dialogic structure of the larger After Identity project,[14] I suggest that the chapters here are best read as reflecting an ongoing debate that folds back on itself as the volume progresses, ultimately opening, I hope, toward future and further conversations.

NOTES

1. Andris Taskans, editor of the Winnipeg-based literary journal *Prairie Fire,* was the first to use the phrase "Mennonite miracle" to describe this unlikely flowering of literary writing from Manitoba's Mennonite community. The chapters in this volume provide a targeted introduction to many of the key authors and texts in the broader field of Mennonite/s writing, but the focus of this introduction is on the critical study of Mennonite literature rather than the literature itself. For readers interested in a broader survey, the most recent and comprehensive is Ann Hostetler's entry on Mennonite literature in North America (1960s–2010s) in the *Global Anabaptist and Mennonite Encyclopedia Online* (www.gameo.org). Ervin Beck maintains extensive bibliographies of Mennonite literature and criticism, separated into Canadian and American lists, at https://www.goshen.edu/english/ervinb/bibliographies/can-biblio.html and https://www.goshen.edu/english/ervinb/bibliographies/menno_us_bib/BeckBib.html.

2. Descendants of the first two of these waves of "Russian" Mennonite migration are often further differentiated as the *Kanadier,* or "Canadian" Mennonites, who arrived in the 1870s, and the *Russländer,* or "Russian" Mennonites, who arrived in the 1920s.

3. Descriptive paragraphs like this are the critical equivalent of what Julia Spicher Kasdorf identifies in this volume as the "autoethnographic announcement" so common in literary texts engaging the Mennonite tradition. Although it is likely true that the general lack of knowledge about Mennonites makes such paragraphs a necessary part of critical writing aimed at a broad reading audience, it is also true that providing them seems to affirm an implicitly sociological frame for the field, one of the assumptions that this volume seeks to question. The historical literature on Mennonites in North America is extensive, but those interested in a thorough yet readable account might consider Royden Loewen and Stephen M. Nolt's *Seeking Places of Peace in the* Global Mennonite History Series.

4. Jeff Gundy is most clear in marking this distinction, emphasizing his interest in "Mennonite writing" in general rather than "Mennonite literature" in particular, the latter of which he defines as "work that seeks self-consciously and more or less directly to promote Anabaptist faith and practice" (*Walker* 32). John Ruth, whose work is discussed later in this introduction, is a clear exception in his sustained focus on theologically engaged literature.

5. Valerie Weaver-Zercher's valuable study, *The Thrill of the Chaste: The Allure of Amish Romance Novels,* is a notable exception, focusing on novels written *about,* rather than *by,* the Amish in the United States.

6. The convention of understanding writing by Mennonites in "North America" as referring primarily to English-language literature published in Canada and the United States (but not Mexico) follows the history and geography of Mennonite literary publishing, as very little creative writing has yet to be published by Mennonites in Mexico. This bi-national understanding of North America is common in broader discussions of global Mennonites (see, for example, the Mennonite World Conference "maps" at https://www.mwc-cmm.org/maps/world), though it, too, is a subject of debate among scholars of Mennonite history.

7. See Tiessen, "Homelands," and the introduction to my study *Rewriting the Break Event.*

8. Taylor's definition goes on to stress the dialogic nature of contemporary identity claims, and the need for political recognition of cultural difference. For a critical discussion of Taylor's argument, see Amy Guttman's edited edition of his essay, which includes responses from Jürgen Habermas and K. Anthony Appiah, among others. For a critique of Taylor's argument specifically in the context of multicultural literature, see Smaro Kamboureli, *Scandalous Bodies: Diasporic Literature in English Canada,* esp. 113-29.

9. See, for example, the article by Daniel Coleman and Donald Goellnicht on race in Canadian literary studies, in which they argue that it is a mistake to position "authors of Asian, African, or Aboriginal descent . . . alongside authors of Czech, Mennonite, or Italian descent as if the differences of religious or cultural background are equivalent to those of 'race'" (n. pag.).

10. For a valuable recent discussion of the ongoing racialized politics of Mennonite identity in the United States more generally, see Felipe Hinojosa's study, *Latino Mennonites: Civil Rights, Faith, and Evangelical Culture*, especially chapter 7, "'Remember Sandia!': Meno-Latinos and Religious Identity Politics," and the conclusion, "Latino Mennonites and the Politics of Belonging."

11. The primary and deeply intertwined concerns of this period in Canadian literary criticism were identity politics, postcolonial criticism, and poststructural theory. These overlapping concerns resulted in a widespread ontological suspicion of language and identity claims, even as such claims were being mobilized as part of both the "appropriation of voice" debate and the larger interrogation of a state-sponsored discourse of multiculturalism and its attendant "ethnic" cultural production.

12. There are a number of earlier essays scattered across the preceding decades. Of these earlier discussions, the *Mennonite Life* special issue on the arts (volume 20, 1965) stands out in both breadth and quality.

13. Interestingly, the surging field of theopoetics heralds a renewed interest in the overlap between the religious and the literary in Mennonite studies. For a brief introduction to the debates surrounding theopoetics in the context of Mennonite/s writing, see *Mennonite/s Writing: Poetics and Theopetics,* a special issue of *Conrad Grebel Review* 31.2 (2013).

14. In May 2013, Kasdorf and I organized After Identity: Mennonite/s Writing in North America, a four-day symposium at Pennsylvania State University, to explore these and related concerns. Early versions of these chapters were circulated ahead of the gathering, where they were subjected to extended critiques by the contributors to this volume and a number of invited guests from Penn State's Department of English—Hester Blum, Tina Chen, Chris Castiglia, Toni Jensen, and Benjamin Schreier—each of whom joined us for sections of the symposium. For more on this event and its relation to this volume, see my remarks in the acknowledgments.

WORKS CITED

Appiah, K. Anthony. "Identity, Authenticity, Survival: Multicultural Societies and Social Reproduction." *Multiculturalism: Examining the Politics of Recognition.* Ed. and intro. Amy Gutmann. Princeton: Princeton UP, 1994. 149–63.

Brandt, Di. *Dancing Naked: Narrative Strategies for Writing Across Centuries.* Stratford, ON: Mercury, 1996.

———. *So this is the world & here I am in it.* Edmonton: NeWest, 2007.

Brubaker, Rogers, and Frederick Cooper. "Beyond 'Identity.'" *Theory and Society* 29 (2000): 1–47.

Coleman, Daniel, and Donald Goellnicht. "Race into the Twenty-First Century." *Essays on Canadian Writing* 75 (2002): n. pag. Web. 5 Feb. 2010.

Dyer, Richard. "The Matter of Whiteness." *Theories of Race and Racism: A Reader.* Ed. Les Back and John Solomos. New York: Routledge, 2000. 539–48.

Gundy, Jeff. "In Praise of the Lurkers (Who Come out to Speak)." Roth and Beck 23–30.

———. *Songs from an Empty Cage: Poetry, Mystery, Anabaptism, and Peace.* Telford: Cascadia, 2013.

———. *Walker in the Fog: On Mennonite Writing.* Telford: Cascadia, 2005.

Hinojosa, Felipe. *Latino Mennonites: Civil Rights, Faith, and Evangelical Culture.* Baltimore: Johns Hopkins University Press, 2014.

Hostetler, Ann, ed. *A Cappella: Mennonite Voices in Poetry.* Iowa City: University of Iowa Press, 2003.

———. "Bringing Experience to Consciousness: Reflections on Mennonite Literature, 2004." *Journal of Mennonite Studies* 23 (2005): 137–50.

———. "'New' Mennonite Voices in Poetry." *Center for Mennonite Writing Journal* 1.6 (Nov. 2009): n. pag. Web. 25 Apr. 2012.

———. "The Self in Mennonite Garb: Or, Where Does the Writing Come From?" *Mennonite Quarterly Review* 87.1 (2013): 23–40.

———. "The Unofficial Voice: The Poetics of Cultural Identity and Contemporary U.S. Mennonite Poetry." Roth and Beck 31–48.

Janzen, Jean. *Elements of Faithful Writing.* Kitchener, ON: Pandora Press, 2004.

Kamboureli, Smaro. *Scandalous Bodies: Diasporic Literature in English Canada.* Don Mills, ON: Oxford UP, 2000.

Kasdorf, Julia Spicher. *The Body and the Book: Writing from a Mennonite Life.* 2001. University Park: Pennsylvania State University Press, 2009.

———. "Mennonites." Hostetler, ed. 129.

———. "Sunday Morning Confession." *Mennonite Quarterly Review* 87.1 (2013): 7–10.

Lee, Christopher. *The Semblance of Identity: Aesthetic Mediation in Asian American Literature.* Stanford: Stanford University Press, 2012.

Levertov, Denise. "The Migrant Muse: Roots and Airplants." Roth and Beck 1–9.

Loewen, Harry, ed. *Mennonite Images: Historical, Cultural, and Literary Essays Dealing with Mennonite Issues.* Winnipeg: Hyperion, 1980.

———, ed. *Why I Am a Mennonite: Essays on Mennonite Identity.* Kitchener, ON: Herald Press, 1988.

Loewen, Harry, and Al Reimer, eds. *Visions and Realities: Essays, Poems, and Fiction Dealing with Mennonite Issues.* Winnipeg: Hyperion, 1985.

Loewen, Royden, and Stephen M. Nolt. *Seeking Places of Peace.* Global Mennonite History Series, North America. Intercourse, PA: Good Books, 2012.

Miki, Roy. *In Flux: Transnational Shifts: Asian Canadian Writing.* Edmonton: NeWest Press, 2011.

Redekop, Calvin. "The Mennonite Identity Crisis." *Journal of Mennonite Studies* 2 (1984): 87–103.

Reimer, Al. "Coming in out of the Cold." Loewen, *Why I Am a Mennonite* 254–67.

———. *Mennonite Literary Voices Past and Present.* North Newton, KS: Bethel College, 1993.

Reimer, Douglas. *Surplus at the Border: Mennonite Writing in Canada.* Winnipeg: Turnstone Press, 2002.

Roth, John D., and Ervin Beck, eds. *Migrant Muses: Mennonite/s Writing in the U.S.* Goshen, IN: Mennonite Historical Society, 1998.

Ruth, John L. *Mennonite Identity and Literary Art.* Kitchener, ON: Herald Press, 1978.

Suderman, Elmer. "Mennonites, the Mennonite Community, and Mennonite Writers." *Mennonite Life* 47.3 (1992): 21–26.

Taylor, Charles. "The Politics of Recognition." *Multiculturalism: Examining the Politics of Recognition.* Ed. Amy Gutmann. Princeton: Princeton UP, 1994. 25-73.

Tiessen, Hildi Froese. "Beyond the Binary: Re-Inscribing Cultural Identity in the Literature of Mennonites." Roth and Beck 11–21.

———. "Homelands, Identity Politics, and the Trace: What Remains for the Mennonite Reader?" *Mennonite Quarterly Review* 87 (2013): 11–22.

———. "Introduction: Mennonite Writing and the Post-Colonial Condition." Tiessen and Hinchcliffe 11–21.

Tiessen, Hildi Froese, and Peter Hinchcliffe, eds. *Acts of Concealment: Mennonite/s Writing in Canada.* Waterloo, ON: University of Waterloo Press, 1992.

Ty, Eleanor, and Christl Verduyn. *Asian Canadian Writing Beyond Autoethnography.* Waterloo, ON: Wilfrid Laurier University Press, 2008.

Weaver-Zercher, Valerie. *Thrill of the Chaste: The Allure of Amish Romance Novels.* Baltimore: Johns Hopkins University Press, 2013.

Zacharias, Robert. *Rewriting the Break Event: Mennonites and Migration in Canadian Literature.* Winnipeg: University of Manitoba Press, 2013.

PART ONE REFRAMING IDENTITY

1

The Autoethnographic Announcement and the Story

JULIA SPICHER KASDORF

I'm not a historian or sociologist or theologian. I'm only a fiction writer.
—Miriam Toews, "A National Literature"

Isn't storytelling always a way of searching for one's origin, speaking one's conflicts with the Law, entering into the dialectic of tenderness and hatred?
—Roland Barthes, *The Pleasure of the Text*

During the summer of 1990, as a fellow at the MacDowell Colony, I showed Jerome Badanes the MA thesis that I was revising. The novelist and writing professor prided himself on being able to spot beginners who would "make it," and he predicted success for the collection of poems that I had called *Sleeping Preacher,* but he advised me to draft endnotes or write a brief introduction to Amish and Mennonite culture as a preface or afterword. The suggestion confounded me. In addition to writing poems, had it also become my job to write prose that would explain my background in rational sociological or anthropological or theological language? Eventually, I drafted a few endnotes that provide translations of Pennsylvania Dutch idioms and an explanation of the *Martyrs Mirror* and the trance preacher phenomenon.

It had not occurred to me to think of *Sleeping Preacher* as a work of autoethnography, though of course it would be read that way, and its reception would later lead me to write essays that take up cultural concerns. Back then, I considered poetry an essentially self-expressive genre, and my poems attempt to make beautiful solutions to personal problems using the most immediate materials at hand: memory, experience, curiosity, confusion. But who can write from her life apart from its context? Indeed, I had ordered a copy of John A. Hostetler's

Amish Society from the tiny bookshop in Peterborough to keep me company that summer while I drafted poems from family memories, including the one titled "*Freindschaft.*" Hostetler was born in the old Amish settlement in the Kishacoquillas Valley of central Pennsylvania, where my parents grew up, and he returned there to conduct fieldwork as a doctoral student in rural sociology at Penn State. Had the term been available in the 1950s, he might have called himself an "autoethnographer."

Autoethnography and Mennonite Literature in the Contact Zone

Anthropologists and sociologists have talked about "autoethnography" since the 1970s, and from the start the term has pulled in several directions. In one early article, the prefix "auto" signified "autochthonous" (indigenous) as well as "automatic," denoting the ease with which native Dani children replied to a researcher's question, "What do Dani do?" This image of revelations easily springing from the native informant brings to mind the figure of the ethnic author who simply recounts details from home to produce the next mediocre literary hit, as imagined by critics such as Harold Bloom during the heyday of multiculturalism.[1]

Later the "auto" in "autoethnography" came to refer more conventionally to a professional's insider status and the work of researchers, like Hostetler, who study "their own people" (Reed-Danahay 4–5). In the 1980s, experts in the field of anthropology became increasingly skeptical about the insider/outsider dichotomy, recognizing that neither is an entirely fixed or clear position. Who, after all, are "my people" for a researcher like Hostetler: those Amish relatives still living in his community of origin or the colleagues in his academic field with whom he could discuss his findings and test his formulations? Moreover, as authenticity claims became increasingly suspect, attention shifted to the position of the researcher. Autoethnographic writing in anthropology came to refer to those texts about others that include elements of the researcher's own experience or context (Reed-Danahay 6).

The term finally entered literary discourse in the early 1990s when Alice A. Deck identified works in which the writer's perceived knowledge of her own culture grants sufficient authority without reference to outside sources, such as Zora Neale Hurston's *Dust Tracks on a Road.* Around this time, Mary Louise Pratt introduced an explicitly political inflection by using the term "autoethnographic text" to name writing "in which people undertake to describe themselves in ways that engage with representations others have made of them" (35).

Such writing occurs in "the contact zone," the social space in which "cultures meet, clash, and grapple with each other," usually in unequal power relationships (34).

Twenty years have passed since Pratt introduced the phrase in her discussion of a seventeenth-century multilingual Peruvian text protesting colonial abuses, yet her ideas have helped me to think about Joseph W. Yoder's *Rosanna of the Amish* and other kinds of writing that explicitly engage with images of Mennonite identity. Consistent with her initial characterizations of the autoethnographic text, these pieces resist, collaborate with, or mediate between the dominant discourse and the minor culture. Their authors often move between cultures and speak several idioms. The tone of the text can be ironic, parodic, or sincere and incorporate local as well as metropolitan idioms. Such projects typically draw on resources beyond the individual writer's experience, including traditional or scholarly sources. Because they attract audiences from within and outside Mennonite contexts, they suffer "highly indeterminate" receptions, for what satisfies outsiders might not please insiders and vice versa. Nonetheless, as Pratt observes, autoethnographic texts "often constitute a marginalized group's point of entry into the dominant circuits of print culture" (35).

In 1940, *Rosanna of the Amish* entered the contact zone between Amish and mainstream cultures in the United States. Although its title aligns it with the regionalist women's coming-of-age tales popular in the nineteenth century and early twentieth century—and it certainly attracted their readers—*Rosanna of the Amish* emphatically announced itself to be a work of nonfiction with an explicit autoethnographic agenda. Drawing on cultural material that Yoder gathered in his home community as a college student at the turn of the twentieth century, his book follows the story of his mother's adoption into an Amish family, her childhood and growing up, her choice to remain Amish rather than join her Irish American siblings, and her experiences of motherhood, aging, and death. An anti-assimilationist narrative, thick with descriptions of Amish customs and everyday practices in the late nineteenth century, it was written from memory by a native son who roved on the margins of his home culture working as an itinerant singing instructor and college recruiter.

At the age of sixty-eight, Yoder published *Rosanna of the Amish* through his own means to confront the unflattering and inaccurate representations of plain people common in national magazines and novels published by major presses. He states his intention in the book's preface: "Instead of holding the Amish, a very devout people, up to ridicule as some writers apparently delight to do, the author desires to tell the truth about them, setting forth their virtues, and they have many, as well as their peculiarities. The fact is that what seems like a peculiarity to the outsider becomes a virtue when one's experience enables him to understand the underlying motives and principles" (25). Resisting portrayals of Amish people in a number of novels, including *Straw in the Wind,* a contemporary, celebrated literary work, *Rosanna of the Amish* is framed as a nonfictional work that draws on Yoder's "experience" as an Amish insider. As such, it bears many of the characteristics that Pratt identifies with autoethnographic works. The book attempts to correct the mistaken perceptions of metropolitan readers. It employs a linguistic range: standard English, vernacular English inflected with Scotch-Irish localisms, and fragments of Pennsylvania Dutch, translated or not. It is grounded in personal memory as well as scholarly and local research that Yoder conducted among song leaders and other elders in his home community. Visits from Rosanna's urban Catholic siblings provide occasions in the book for dialogue that mediates religious, historical, and cultural differences, seeking affinities. When it first appeared, *Rosanna of the Amish* was read differently by those who were differently positioned: it was praised for its authenticity by academic and "worldly" readers, and pronounced an unbelievable boast, an idealized Amish "Never-Never Land situated in a Valley of Paradise," by the local newspaper, and by oral and written responses from Amish people in Rosanna's home community, as I have shown in *Fixing Tradition: Joseph W. Yoder, Amish American* (151–58).

Yoder's claim to have finally presented a "factual" account of Amish life—and the book's function as a "true story"—prompted minor editorial interventions in a 1995 edition produced by Herald Press, a Mennonite publisher that assumed publication rights from Yoder's widow. In 2008, S. Duane Kauffman revealed departures from the historical record significant enough to cast the first quarter of the book into the realm of fiction. Nonetheless, *Rosanna of the Amish* has sold nearly 500,000 copies to date, and it continues to circulate within and outside Anabaptist communities as an authentic representation of Amish life long ago, largely marketed in shops that cater to tourists.

The Autoethnographic Announcement

Pratt's characterization and Yoder's example from earlier in the twentieth century have led me to recognize the persistence of an autoethnographic impulse in Mennonite writing. Since the Second World War, Mennonite people have entered the North American mainstream in large numbers and in various ways, even taking up the production of culture and literature. At the same time, the most conservative groups continue to increase their numbers at rates that surpass the outward mobility of the most ambitious assimilationists. No matter how far "beyond the binary" an intellectual Mennonite might improvise a metropolitan life, the farm village or horse-drawn buggy remains in her background—or in the foreground of the mainstream imagination.[2] Whenever the term "Amish" or "Mennonite" is raised, those inscrutable, sectarian communities require some kind of explanation.

In this chapter, I tag that explanation, what I call the "autoethnographic announcement," in several works—"tag" meaning to identify for further study, and referring to the children's game that selects the next active agent: "You're it!" The autoethnographic announcement is primarily a declaration of identity: I'm it, we're it, you're not it, but here it is: the real story about who we are! Whether the announcement was drafted under editorial direction or as a self-conscious riff on conventional Mennonite identity scripts, it always erupts as an instance of *apparent* nonfiction, even in fictional works. The announcement steps back and temporarily sorts insiders from outsiders, facts from fictional misrepresentations, and tells the truth. Yet, even at their most careful or sincere, these blurbs invariably get it wrong—as Yoder's *Rosanna of the Amish* did—because it is impossible to pin down a complex and diverse people. Nonetheless, they persist, poised as extraliterary supplements or as deftly integrated elements of the story, strange occasions of authorial engagement with forces beyond the immediate literary project.

The announcements function like flash forms composed in response to outsider ignorance or insider expectations. They might simultaneously placate insider anxieties about Mennonite misrepresentation and construct a temporary fiction of identity that serves the purposes of the story at hand. The autoethnographic expectations of Mennonite readers might now vex Mennonite authors more than the distorted mainstream representations that prompted Yoder to write *Rosanna of the Amish.* In an article about Mennonite memoirs, Ann Hostetler has asked somewhat desperately whether this kind of work "must always be measured against an insider's standard for historical and sociological accuracy before the individual story is heard" (28). Alternatively, the announcements can create a space in which to resist the identity scripts that the community circulates about itself. As I examine some examples of autoethnographic announcements, I will highlight the ways in which these moments enable writers to negotiate among various audiences, to perform ethnicity or play the identity game, and to assert the interests inherent in their own stories.

Discussions about Mennonite literature in North America usually begin with *Peace Shall Destroy Many* (1962). Regarded as the first serious work of Mennonite writing in English, and a foundational novel in western Canadian literature, it also remains one of Rudy Wiebe's bestselling books. At the same time, memory of the novel's traumatic reception in Mennonite Brethren church circles has long haunted conversations about the place of literary writing in Mennonite communities in North America.[3] *Peace Shall Destroy Many* was initially written as a thesis in creative writing at the University of Alberta. In 1960, Wiebe's adviser, F.M. Salter, asked Wiebe to write a foreword to the novel for the MA exam because his examining faculty knew little about Mennonites. In three dense paragraphs, Wiebe's foreword summarizes Mennonite beliefs and history following the genealogy that originates in Zurich with Conrad Grebel, which H.S. Bender plotted out in *The Anabaptist Vision* (1940). Wiebe also mentions Menno Simons, naming only two figures: an urban intellectual humanist from Switzerland and a former Catholic priest from Friesland who published theological writing and gave his name to the group. Grebel and Simons established a useful intellectual tradition for the generation of mid-twentieth-century Mennonites who—like Wiebe or John A. Hostetler or my own father—turned for the first time from farming to higher education.

The foreword to *Peace Shall Destroy Many* narrates the story of a persecuted remnant that has survived from several European origins. Its identity coheres around distinctive scriptural principles: "believers' baptism, a life of discipleship, separation of church and state, non-participation in war or government" (7). Because of these identifying beliefs, Wiebe writes, Mennonites were "savagely martyred by Catholic and Protestant alike" and "driven" to Russia and the New World. Consistent with the circumstances of the immigrant settlement depicted in his novel, the foreword stresses violence, persecution, migration, and faith: "Wherever they went they carried peculiar customs, a peculiar language, a peculiar faith in the literal meaning of the Bible" (7). As in Yoder's foreword to *Rosanna of the Amish,* distinctive cultural features are described as "peculiar," but they would seem so only to outsiders in the contact zone. Mennonites understand their "peculiar" aspects to be marks of righteousness, an allusion to 1 Peter 2:9: "But ye are a chosen generation, a royal priesthood, a holy nation, a peculiar people."

The editors at McClelland and Stewart in Canada, and later Eerdmans in the United States, retained the autoethnographic announcement as a separate yet essential element of the text. The final sentences of the foreword signal the conclusion of the generalizing, apparently factual announcement and prepare readers for the "fictional" novel that follows: "The Mennonites portrayed in this book belong to no particular faction; they could belong to any one of several groups that came to Canada from Russia in the 1920's. All characters and situations are fictional" (7). Despite this disclaimer, Mennonite readers would likely identify the Krimmer Mennonite Brethren group from the baptism scene in the book. As for the autoethnographic announcement, several details fail to align precisely with the historical record.[4] But I am concerned with the perceived need for a nonfictional introduction to the people depicted in the novel, as if they were too strange to be comprehended through their embodiment in the text. What is more, Mennonites living in Canada in 1962—or in the 1940s, when the novel takes place—had little in common with the Anabaptists of sixteenth-century Zurich or Friesland mentioned in the foreword, except in the most ideologically idealized way. The novel builds upon the community's struggle to maintain the Anabaptist ideal of "defenselessness" or nonparticipation in war and their inability to maintain peaceful relations within their group and between themselves and neighboring Métis and Cree people.

Published nearly a half century later, Rhoda Janzen's memoir *Mennonite in a Little Black Dress* (2010) seems to have little in common with the serious Mennonite literary novel, except that the author's father attended Mennonite Brethren Bible College in Winnipeg with Wiebe in the early 1960s. Yet the next-generation memoir also contains an autoethnographic announcement that was not the author's idea. A poet and professor at Hope College in Holland, Michigan, Janzen wrote the book for a broad, commercial audience.[5] An early website and the back pages of a later edition explain that the project began as email messages sent to non-Mennonite friends after the author returned to her parents' place to recoup from a divorce and injuries sustained in a car accident. The memoir neatly fits the "chick lit" formula: smart, self-deprecating gal overcomes hardship through her irrepressible capacity to laugh and love. The "memoir of going home" spent thirteen weeks on the *New York Times* bestseller list. Breezy, gossipy, and vulgar in a flirtatious feminine way, the book is also intelligent, irreverent, and very funny, in part because of Janzen's break-neck switches in diction. The wisecracking prodigal daughter engages in a kind of white ethnic minstrelsy that renders (Russian) Mennonite stereotypes explicit—and therefore nearly harmless—through repetition and exaggeration in a carefully constructed contact zone. Her current website quips that "Rhoda's good-natured mother suggested she date her first cousin—he owned a tractor, see."

The book was enthusiastically reviewed in the *New York Times* but received tortured responses from Mennonites who praised Janzen's wit but faulted the edgy caricatures, inaccurate representation of her Mennonite Brethren church, and appropriation of identifying practices from more conservative groups. In her investigation of the book's reception, "The Self in Mennonite Garb: Or, Where Does the Writing Come From?," Ann Hostetler points out that *Mennonite in a Little Black Dress* was never intended for Mennonite insiders who would be troubled by imprecise representation. Contemporary memoirs, she argues, are valued not so much for their accuracy of portrayal as for the author's ability to create a compelling voice that renders and interprets transformative episodes in a life.

In an interview that appeared around the same time, Janzen said much the same thing about her own book. When asked why she framed her story as a memoir instead of a novel, she said that her agent had recommended it, presumably for marketing reasons. "Memoir is especially tasty to Americans. Our passion for it devolves from a cultural emphasis on self-reinvention," she said. "So, to sum it up: memoir isn't the story of our life. It's the story of our change. We have conversion, and epiphany, a moment of confrontation with some jawdropping reality. And then we are never the same. Christianity and memoir! Made for each other!" ("Interview" 52).

Why, then, in the age of Wikipedia and other forms of instant information, would an editor at Henry Holt ask Janzen to add an autoethnographic appendix to the memoir, particularly given her detailed description of her family and its context? I can only guess that the announcement offered another opportunity to stage the drama of the dissenting daughter caught in the contact zone between tradition and the broader culture. Janzen rose to the occasion, exploding the short form into seventeen pages of rambling self-conscious parody before concluding that "[t]he above summary of Mennonite culture is probably much more to the point than whatever's on Wikipedia" (*Mennonite* 241). The "Mennonite History Primer" begins by slyly mocking the presumed appetite for ethnography: "If you're like most folks, you may still have some pressing questions about the Mennonites." Swiftly sweeping aside the most common fetishistic and consumptive confusions, she asks, "Are they Amish? What do Mennonite women wear under those dresses? How much do quilts fetch on E-bay?" Then she turns to the past for a quick identity lesson, as flip and ironic as the rest of the book: "Before all Mennonites in Western Europe could meet their Maker in this rather spectacular fashion [martyrdom], Catherine the Great saved the day in 1789 by inviting them to settle her weakest border spot, the land that would one day become Ukraine. They came; they saw; they planted" (229).

Like Wiebe's foreword, Janzen's "appendix" grounds Mennonite identity in history and belief, but her postscripted autoethnographic announcement overturns the narrative of persecution and purity, the story valued by her father's generation. The age of martyrdom is followed not by migration and enduring faithfulness but industry, prosperity, Mennonite cultural supremacy, and arrogance toward Jewish, Russian, and indigenous Nogai neighbors, a picture that draws on the research of James Urry and other recent historians. Wiebe and

Janzen come from the same Mennonite Brethren denomination—a church that did not officially ordain women until the twenty-first century—and differences in gender and generation naturally shape their representations of the group. In her memoir, Janzen portrays herself as more at ease at a cocktail party of academics than at a conservative church service.

Her selection of details from Imperial Russia enables a rigorous critique of the community, past and present. Mennonites are portrayed not as a persecuted remnant but as materialist oppressors and czarist collaborators: "Mennonite superiority wasn't about what we believed. It was about what we did. It turned on demonstrable things like work habits and hygiene. It wasn't our fault that the entire native population was shiftless, unmotivated, and blighted by poor economic judgment, but we could fix that shit!" (231). The collective point of view and particular phrases that Janzen uses to describe indigenous people in this sentence invite comparison with Mennonite settlement in North and South America and lingering attitudes toward Indian and other non-Mennonite people. With a poet's instinct for synecdoche, Janzen reproduces illustrations from a nineteenth-century historical text to demonstrate Mennonites' pride in the superior design of their wagons. The autoethnographic announcement turns from dispensing information to an ignorant public to accusing the smug Mennonite choir of hypocrisy. Like Wiebe's portrayal of the imperfect community in *Peace Shall Destroy Many,* however, her sharp critique of history implies a fundamental commitment to the Mennonite ideals of peace, justice, and humility. Janzen concludes that "[f]or hundreds of years Mennonites had a teensy ego problem" (231).

Her historical narrative skips the destruction of the Mennonite colonies in Russia and subsequent migrations to North America and resumes with her own childhood of cultural marginality—"long skirts, tight braids, and Borscht in your thermos" (234). In keeping with chick lit's selectively bright tones, the violent demise of the Russian colonies occurs out of sight, like her abusive marriage, only briefly mentioned in the memoir. The wheel of fortune spins, she bouncily concludes: "History reminds us that there are highs and lows on any ethnic journey" (233).

Now a practicing Pentecostal, Janzen published a second memoir, *Does This Church Make Me Look Fat?,* in 2012. In the final chapter, titled "Double Dip," she narrates her baptism in the Mennonite church and a recent rebaptism. Rather than write about Pentecostalism, she directs readers who might be curious about her Mennonite background to the "helpful appendix" in her first book. For those who find such research daunting, she cheerfully offers to sum up Mennonite praxis in the form of "a pleasant haiku." After all, she asks with a characteristic sense of the absurd, "[w]hat's more fun than trying to squeeze five hundred years of Anabaptist theology into a poem the size of a Chiclet?" (232). Then Janzen reduces Mennonite identity to a perky celebration of the biblical position on peace sustained by peculiar, ethnic food:

> Mennonite Haiku
>
> Jesus lived in peace.
> Let's give it a try! It helps
> to have hot prune soup. (232)

Janzen's first book was a volume of poetry that employed traditional forms. It is no surprise, then, that she expands and contracts the autoethnographic announcement, making the imperative an occasion for innovation and play. Partitioned from the main body of both of her memoirs, it is transformed in her hands into other genres altogether: appendix and haiku. The unmitigated celebration of the gospel message of peace in both books suggests that pacifism is the one distinctive mark of Mennonite identity that—for her at least—resists irony and play.

Although they work in different genres and live in different countries, Rhoda Janzen and Miriam Toews occupy similar positions in Mennonite literature: their writing and its worldly success still rankle in their traditional home communities. Both authors write from a female first-person singular point of view, and both have adapted the autoethnographic announcement for their own purposes.

In two of Toews's most recent novels, autoethnographic announcements appear to be embedded within the story as charged spaces that integrate historical fact and fiction to advance the plot. Both books are narrated by teenaged, dissenting daughters who come from troubled homes. Like verbose, autochthonous subjects, the speakers describe their peculiar communities and recount Mennonite history as means of revealing and understanding their own experiences. The first novel, *A Complicated Kindness* (2004), won the Governor General's Literary Award, one of Canada's most esteemed prizes, spent over a year on the Canadian bestseller lists, and has been translated into many foreign languages, but it earned Toews a reputation for reinforcing negative stereotypes of Mennonites as narrow-minded, uneducated, intolerant people. The second novel, *Irma Voth* (2011), set in an Old Colony Mennonite farm community in Mexico, adds "abusive" to the unflattering list of adjectives. In a 2012 address at an international writers' conference, Toews responded to the expectation that Mennonite writers reiterate the group's "epic tale of persecution, exile, and hard-won religious independence."

The writer must resist pressure to tell communal or national identity stories, she advised, and tell only the stories that are truly hers. In both of her books, an individual character's story determines the revelation of communal history.

In the most-often quoted passage from *A Complicated Kindness,* Nomi Nickel makes a highly idiosyncratic autoethnographic announcement that frames Mennonite identity in terms that have become so familiar that they almost constitute a cliché: history and theology, persecution and migration. But unlike Wiebe or Janzen, Toews presents this ethnographic announcement as an integral part of the literary work, continuous with Nomi's voice and shaped by her personal urgencies. Neither her desire for "the world" nor the crises in her fractured family can make any sense unless Nomi steps back from the immediate details of her situation and describes the "peculiar" context in which her story unfolds. (Imagine Holden Caulfield pausing his rant against the grown-up phonies to offer a historical and theological survey of WASP culture.) For a sixteen-year-old girl trapped in a small-town Manitoba Mennonite community in the 1980s, the autoethnographic announcement provides a stage on which to personify and complain about her culture's joyless constraints. "Menno" is the patriarch who "set off to do his own peculiar religious thing" and ended up naming "the most embarrassing sub-sect of people to belong to if you're a teenager." Nomi figures Menno as "the least well-adjusted kid" in school who forms a "breakaway clique" that prohibits "media, dancing, smoking, temperate climates, movies, drinking, rock 'n' roll, having sex for fun, swimming, make-up, jewelry, playing pool, going to cities, or staying up past nine o'clock. That was Menno all over. Thanks a lot Menno" (5).

Her rant goes on to reckon the wages of the martyr memory and to articulate the profound critique of conservative Mennonite culture that lies at the core of the novel: "We are supposed to be cheerfully yearning for death and in the meantime, until that blessed day, our lives are meant to be facsimiles of death or at least the dying process" (5). The only industries in Nomi's hometown are a chicken evisceration plant and a Mennonite heritage visitor's center, both grimly tainted by death and sacrifice. If the chicken plant is the more obvious site of violence, the heritage center is defined by martyrdom and migration in the past and shunning (or the voluntary withdrawal) of dissenters to preserve the peace in the present. Excommunication—a fate that drove Nomi's sister away, caused her mother to abandon the family, and eventually befalls Nomi—is an absolute form of social exclusion, the violent dismemberment of the religious community figured as the Body of Christ.

Similarly in *Irma Voth,* elements of nineteen-year-old Irma's story determine the autoethnographic announcement. Early in the novel, Irma explains that her father does not like her husband because he is a "non-Mennonite." This term of non-belonging triggers the announcement, which begins with the 1920s migration of Mennonites from Manitoba to Mexico, "where they wouldn't have to send their kids to regular school or teach them to speak English or dress them in normal clothing." Flight from the broader culture is seen in relation to the long history of Anabaptist migration. After Menno in Holland five hundred years ago, "they started to move all around the world in colonies looking for freedom and isolation and peace and opportunities to sell cheese." Irma's narrative names refusals to comply with military conscription and tax laws as reasons for Mennonites to "pack our stuff up in the middle of the night and move to another country where we can live purely but somewhat out of context" (12). Later we learn the real story: a crime that was also a grave sin forced Irma's father to suddenly move the family from Canada to Mexico.

Clues to her future are subtly woven into the history that Irma tells about her sect early in the novel. Her marriage breaks with the practices of endogamy and collective separation held by her Mennonite group. Like her community, she will also make a fugitive migration, fleeing an abusive Mennonite father and her Mexican husband, a drug runner who eventually abandons her. With two of her sisters, she will travel to Mexico City, where the murals of Diego Rivera will enable her to think about history differently. Conversations with compassionate, worldly people will help Irma to begin to narrate and understand her own experience. Her autoethnographic announcement concludes with an authoritative affirmation of separation: "Our motto is from the 'rebuke of worldliness,' which is from the Biblical book of James: *Whosoever will be a friend of the world is the enemy of God*" (12). Yet her story will lead her out into the world and back home again, redeemed for having transcended those oppositions. The embedded autoethnographic announcement articulates one of the central themes in *Irma Voth* as it destabilizes fact and fiction, inside and outside, us and them, friend and enemy.

Let us turn to one final example. In *Shaken in the Water* (2013), Jessica Penner makes no attempt to represent fact in a literary text, but she seems nonetheless to be mindful of autoethnographic pressure. Her first novel deploys a two-page announcement poised at the back of the book like a defensive fact-checker hired to correct the author's deliberate misrepresentations. In an essay about her writing process, Penner admits that her novel-in-stories is grounded in Mennonite family tales and history, but she did not conduct much historical research because she "was afraid the facts would get in the way of making the story [her] own." The pivotal tale, "Tarred," shows a Mennonite family threatened by bullies for refusing to buy bonds during the First World War. Throughout the twentieth century and into the twenty-first, the stories follow three generations of Kansas Mennonites as their ethnic and religious identity becomes less legible. The novel incorporates magical elements, the appearance of a white tiger and a mysterious Voice, and these "Russian" Mennonites observe some peculiar religious practices more commonly practiced by the "Swiss" Mennonites in the United States, such as the selection of leaders by "the lot" and mandatory head covering and long hair for women.

After reading reviews of Janzen's memoir, Penner, also of Mennonite Brethren background, anticipated resistance from readers who would recognize her appropriation of emblems of "Swiss" Mennonite identity, so she created an afterword to sort fact from fiction and deflect critique.[6] Her autoethnographic announcement, simply titled "Mennonites," notes the difficulty of defining such a diverse people: "The Mennonites are a complex people with different interpretations of faith and cultural heritage. . . . Amish, Old Order Mennonite, and Holdeman Mennonite, Mennonite Brethren and Mennonite Church USA" (375). Presumably, readers curious about Mennonite history or sociology would seek information from sources more reliable than a fantastical novel, and these pages offer more information than outsiders will ever want or need—but of course they might not be her primary audience.

Next, Penner turns to the sixteenth-century Anabaptist movement, Menno Simons, and various migrations, following the pattern established by Wiebe. Like his, her announcement signals the relationship between fact and fiction in the book: "Although there is a real Ulysses, Kansas, the Ulysses and its particular breed of Mennonites in this novel exist on no map except that of the imagination. They will be recognized as the Russian Mennonites of the 1870s migration, with the exceptions of plain dress and selection of elders by lot." Penner discusses the head coverings worn by Holdeman women (depicted on the cover of her book) and the scriptural basis of the lot (376). She also includes a separate note about the use of Low German and other German quotations. The presence of former Mennonite languages in the text functions as a keeper of authenticity—and illegibility for outsiders—because the languages once functioned as signs of identity in the communities of Kansas Mennonites that she describes.

The Contact Zone Comes Home

Reading the writing of minority writers as ethnography has fallen out of fashion for good reason; it is neither fair nor reasonable to assume that the work of an individual imagination can represent an entire community or race. Yet what is a reader to do with these autoethnographic announcements that continue to erupt in even current works of Mennonite writing?

Slow down, exercise caution. These passages demand close readings because they are overloaded with significance. They are sites in which the conflicts of the contact zone become apparent, whether the announcements are crafted to provide information for metropolitan readers or to resist and revise the old Mennonite identity scripts. If my survey of autoethnographic texts from 1940 to 2013 suggests anything, it is that the contact zone is no longer out there somewhere. The contact zone has come home in the forms of cultural change and strategic assimilation, and autoethnographic announcements are now aimed as much at Mennonite insiders as they are at curious strangers. I do not expect the announcements to go away, given that stories about identifiable Mennonite subjects located in cultural contact zones still seem to stand the best chance of success in both the commercial and the critical spheres—and perhaps they hold aesthetic satisfaction for their authors. I do expect writers to continue to adapt new uses for the autoethnographic announcement. What once might have felt like a burdensome editorial or academic imperative placed on an obscure minority representative now opens a productive space for resistance or play in the identity game. "This is the real dope on Mennonites," Janzen promises in her first book, "the good stuff that you won't find in the academic works by Mennonite scholars" (*Mennonite* 234).

NOTES

1. During the early 1990s, Bloom launched an argument against enthusiasm for work by minority and ethnic writers, those who might not have been published or taught in university courses if there had not been an interest in reading multicultural literature. His dismissal applied to major African American and American Indian works as well as the sorts of minor literature discussed in this volume. *Sleeping Preacher* was published in 1992, and in 1993 I enrolled in a graduate course titled "The Western Canon" with Bloom at New York University, so the argument hit home.

2. I allude to Hildi Froese Tiessen's essay "Beyond the Binary: Reinscribing Cultural Identity in the Literature of Mennonites," which describes the tendency of Mennonites to understand their experience and identity in binary terms, such as center/margin or inside/outside, as do many minority groups. Although the critical writing of Mennonite writers has not escaped these cultural essentialisms, she notes that the literary work—given the nature of literature—often defies simple binaries, describing the "diverse, multiple, and unfixed" locations beyond or between identities that many Mennonite people now occupy.

3. In 1990, I attended the first Mennonite/s Writing conference as an unpublished writer on assignment for *Festival Quarterly* magazine. There I interviewed Canadian poets Di Brandt, David Waltner-Toews, and Patrick Friesen, who were ten, fourteen, and twelve years old, respectively, when the controversy over *Peace Shall Destroy Many* erupted. I asked them about

its impact on their imagination. "I remember it clearly," Brandt said, "that story about wicked Rudy Wiebe. In my village, the worst thing anyone could call you was a communist. So they said, 'Rudy Wiebe is a communist!' . . . I thought that would happen to me, that they would hound me out of the community" (cited in Kasdorf, "Making" 16). In 2001, in an essay titled "Writing Like a Mennonite," I animated the "myth" of Mennonite authorship: "Because she [Brandt] seized the authority of literature and persecuted her community by telling its secrets and exposing its shame, it must punish her in turn—as happened after Rudy Wiebe's first novel, as happened to the martyrs of old" (182). In 2005, American poet Jeff Gundy challenged the myth, pointing to Wiebe, Brandt, Friesen, and me as examples of only one way of being a Mennonite writer, a way that has not been his way: "This story seems to be the Ur-myth of the modern Mennonite writer, the agonistic story of how the most visible and prominent cried out against communal repression and endured the cost" (25). At the sixth Mennonite/s Writing conference, in a "Sunday Morning Confession" delivered from a pulpit, I owned up to my part in writing this myth and wondered whether the figure of the trickster or Richard Rorty's ironist might be a more sustainable role for the contemporary Mennonite writer.

4. At the After Identity symposium in 2013, historian Royden Loewen casually observed that Wiebe's "non-fictional" foreword is riddled with errors. When pressed, he provided an email on 19 June 2013 with a list of corrections. Menno Simons was not the sole early theological leader to survive persecution, as Conrad Grebel, Pilgram Marpeck, Dirk Philips, and Leonard Bowman all died natural deaths. Anabaptism began not in 1523 but in 1525, when Conrad Grebel, Felix Manz, George Blaurock, and about a dozen others baptized each other in the home of Manz's mother in Zurich. No Mennonite was "driven" to Russia or from there to the Americas; rather, they chose to migrate. The language spoken by Mennonite people is not a singular "peculiar language." The Swiss Mennonites who moved to Pennsylvania were only a few among many other Palatinate German speakers; the Dutch Mennonites moved to Prussia speaking Dutch, and some of them later migrated to Russia. The Anabaptists emphasized community cohesiveness, not individualism; schisms were the result of their democratic (sectarian) church polity and emphasis on ethics.

5. Rhoda Janzen, email to the author, 1 May 2013.

6. Jessica Penner, email to the author, 29 June 2013.

WORKS CITED

Barthes, Roland. *The Pleasure of the Text.* New York: Hill and Wang, 1975.

Bender, Harold S. *The Anabaptist Vision.* Scottdale: Herald Press, 1944.

Deck, Alice A. "Autoethnography: Zora Neale Hurston, Noni Jabavu, and Cross-Disciplinary Discourse." *Black American Literature Forum* 24.2 (1990): 237–256.

Gundy, Jeff. *Walker in the Fog: On Mennonite Writing.* Telford: Cascadia, 2005.

Hostetler, Ann. "The Self in Mennonite Garb: Or, Where Does the Writing Come From?" *Mennonite Quarterly Review* 87.1 (2013): 23–40.

Hostetler, John A. *Amish Society.* Baltimore: Johns Hopkins University Press, 1980.

Janzen, Rhoda. *Does This Church Make Me Look Fat?* New York: Grand Central, 2012.

———. "Interview with Rhoda Janzen." By Victor Enns. *Rhubarb* 32 (2013): 49–52.

———. *Mennonite in a Little Black Dress.* New York: Henry Holt, 2010.

———. "Mennonite in a Little Black Dress: About the Book." http://www.rhodajanzen.com/mennonite-in-little-black-dress. Web. 14 Nov. 2013.

Kasdorf, Julia Spicher. *Fixing Tradition: Joseph W. Yoder, Amish American.* Telford: Pandora/US, 2003.
———. "The Making of Canada's 'Mennonite' Writers." *Festival Quarterly* 17.2 (1990): 14–16.
———. *Sleeping Preacher.* Pittsburgh: University of Pittsburgh Press, 1992.
———. "Sunday Morning Confession." *Mennonite Quarterly Review* 87.1 (2013): 7–10.
———. "Writing Like a Mennonite." *The Body and the Book: Writing from a Mennonite Life.* Baltimore: Johns Hopkins University Press, 2001. 167–89.
Kauffman, S. Duane. "*Rosanna of the Amish:* Fact or Fiction?" *Pennsylvania Mennonite Heritage* 31 (2008): 2–11.
King James Bible. Cambridge ed. http://www.biblehub.com. Web. 1 May 2013.
Penner, Jessica. "Research Notes: *Shaken in the Water.*" *Necessary Fiction* 5 Mar. 2013. Web. 11 July 2013.
———. *Shaken in the Water.* Tipp City, OH: Foxhead Books, 2013.
Pratt, Mary Louise. "Arts of the Contact Zone." *Profession* 91 (1991): 33–40.
Reed-Danahay, Deborah, ed. *Auto/Ethnography: Rewriting the Self and the Social.* Oxford: Berg, 1997.
Tiessen, Hildi Froese. "Beyond the Binary: Reinscribing Cultural Identity in the Literature of Mennonites." *Mennonite Quarterly Review* 72.4 (1998): 491–501.
Toews, Miriam. *A Complicated Kindness.* Toronto: Knopf Canada, 2004.
———. *Irma Voth.* New York: HarperCollins, 2011.
———. "A National Literature." International Festival of Authors, Toronto, 25 Oct. 2012. Speech. Web. 11 July 2013.
Wiebe, Rudy. *Peace Shall Destroy Many.* Grand Rapids: Eerdmans, 1962.
Yoder, Joseph W. *Rosanna of the Amish.* Scottdale: Herald Press, 2008.

2

A Mennonite *Fin de Siècle*

Exploring Identity at the Turn of the Twenty-First Century

ROYDEN LOEWEN

Loss and Surprise at the End of the Century

It is a widely known fact that the 1920 census in the United States and the 1921 census in Canada indicated that, for the first time in these two countries' respective histories, more citizens resided in cities and large towns than in small villages and on farms. Sociologists have pointed out that the same statistic did not hold true for Mennonites until about 1975. Mennonites among long-settled North Americans were relatively late in their coming to the city. But when they came, they arrived as all such farm-to-city migrants did, with a sense of uprootedness and even loss. They experienced a bewildering reorientation that saw many abandon old ways and familiar churches and endure a radical restructuring of old life worlds, socially and ideologically.

In the final volume of the *Mennonites in Canada* history series, T.D. Regehr describes the years 1940 to 1970 as a "sea change that . . . took the [Mennonites] out of their former isolation and into the mainstream" (2). In the United States, Paul Toews writes in the final volume of the Mennonite Experience in America history series that the midcentury decades saw "pressures continually challenge . . . inherited ways of thinking and acting" (340). If this was true for postwar North American Mennonites, then it was doubly so in the following generation, the end of the century, the *fin de siècle*. Arguably, the last decades of the twentieth century and the first years of the twenty-first represented a vast redrawing of the Mennonite world in avenues such as economics, theology, gender relations, approaches to the arts, and certainly, as this chapter argues, literary expression. It was a wide-ranging transformation that only history will clarify for us. This is the period that I want to ponder here, for it seems to me that something profound was afoot in the Mennonite communities of both Canada and the United States during the past generation.

In many ways, the North American Mennonites did a marvelous job of plotting their mid-twentieth-century exodus from the farm and laying the foundation for late-century cultural and religious resilience. They succeeded in the project that we call modernization. Mennonites' claim on what Raymond Breton famously dubbed "institutional completeness," that requirement for newcomers to succeed in urban centers, for example, is without a doubt. Consider the cradle-to-grave Mennonite organizations that have made Winnipeg and Elkhart, Kitchener and Akron, Abbotsford and Fresno into household names among the North American faithful; these are places rich with universities, hospitals, businesses, professional offices, newspapers, and venues for performing artists specifically structured to serve their Mennonite communities. Signs abounded in the 1970s and 1980s that the transition to the city had been ideologically successful as well; Harold Bender's 1944 "Anabaptist Vision," or versions thereof, survived and spawned a sort of religious renaissance, one in which Mennonites were assured of their inherited faith's relevance in the city, especially in its promise to address the social ills of postwar North American society with its teachings on love, community, and nonviolence. Landmark sociological works in 1972 and 1989 that surveyed "Anabaptism four centuries later" suggested that some laudable values had died with the passing of the farmyard but mostly that four hundred years of rural isolation had stifled a once-vibrant Anabaptism (Kauffman and Harder) that could now be reclaimed in the city.

But other signs suggested that uprootedness and loss and worry infused the changing Mennonite world. Voices from several quarters noted that modernity had failed the Mennonites, and a certain foreboding, a mistrust of the future, lay just below the surface. Indeed, for every success, a new concern seemed to rise. It was as if, having come to the city late, fifty years after the majority of North Americans did so, the Mennonites also endured the famous fin de siècle era of psychological and cultural upheaval late. And, given the Mennonites' remarkable institutional strength and depth of collective memory, it stood to reason that their own fin de siècle came a hundred years after the Western world endured the radical cultural refashioning of the 1880s and 1890s, with spillover into the twentieth century. I want to suggest that a fin de siècle experience does indeed illustrate North American Mennonite culture, say from the mid-1980s until the present. It was a "moment" when modernity hit a high point among the Mennonites, but it was a high point that hid profound internal stresses and generated stiff criticism from a rising artistic community that looked to the future with a longing for a lost authenticity.

The fin de siècle period of the late nineteenth century and early twentieth century has generated much historical analysis, but generally it shows how the cultural terms of "modernism" and "romance" reflect a response to the social term of "modernization." A representative study, *Modernism, Romance, and the Fin de Siècle: Popular Fiction and British Culture, 1880–1914,* by literary scholar Nicholas Daly, argues that "romance," that search for authenticity in nature and the ancient past, did not precede "modernism" and its array of secular avant-garde abstraction. Rather, a hybrid of these two cultural forms contested the banality of "modernity": that is, the confining, individuating city, the life-snuffing factory, the self-serving political elite, the shallow media, and the materialistic middle class.

Historians have used the term "fin de siècle" at once more generally and in a more detailed way. Indeed, many use the term to mean any social consequences of urbanization and industrialization, including commercialization, rationalism, and consumer society. Period historians talk about a literary community with "a conflicted hatred of the bourgeoisie," reacting to a culture that they saw as barren and judgmental, and in their reactions fusing "sexual, political and writerly radicalisms," all amounting to "a millennial overture to the modern" (Maxwell 341–42). They even talk of working-class culture engaged in class struggle, more specifically an iconoclastic subversion, also driven by a sense of loss of authenticity, homing in on a class consciousness in a period of monopoly capitalism (Palmer). The most noted of these works, T.J. Jackson Lears's *No Place of Grace: Antimodernism and the Transformation of American Culture, 1880–1920,* describes it most generally: "Toward the end of the nineteenth century, many beneficiaries of modern culture began to feel they were its secret victims" (xiii). As a consequence, they "recoil[ed] from an 'over civilized' modern existence to more intense forms of physical or spiritual experience." These reactions, however, were never straightforward: "[I]t was ambivalent, often coexisting with enthusiasm for material progress, . . . a complex blend of accommodation and protest" (xiii).

So do these descriptions of the late nineteenth-century world really help us to understand Mennonite society a hundred years later? The late twentieth-century decades and the first decade or so of this century certainly marked significant social and cultural shifts among the Mennonites, perhaps more so than members of other cultural groups who had undergone their moments of urbanization earlier in the century. For the Mennonites especially, an old order seemed to be passing away. But it was not the passing away of what we might call "traditionalism," an old order that we associate with *Gemeinschaft* society, horse-and-buggy culture, for example; that transition had already occurred for most Mennonites in the early and mid-twentieth century. Being tested in unprecedented fashion was the established order of the modern Mennonites. From the 1980s well into the twenty-first century, indeed to the present, it seemed that the Mennonite "center," or the Mennonite "mainstream" if we can mix metaphors, came under particular strain. Ironically, perhaps, just as with the wider North American culture of the late nineteenth century, here in the late twentieth-century Mennonite world were all the signs of health and vigor but ones that might have hidden a certain kind of undoing.

Consider the social phenomenon of amalgamation, perhaps a mark of new toleration and growth but also, as history demonstrates, sometimes a sign of significant new challenges. Several institutional consolidations can be noted, but certainly the most significant one for North American Mennonites was the creation of a mighty new Mennonite Church (MC) in 2001, arising amid poetics of Christian love and unity from the bones of the General Conference and the Mennonite Church (formerly "Old" Mennonite Church). Still, the very coming together contained the seeds of division. The Canadians, for example, insisted on their own MC, and conservative members seemed to be profoundly worried that the new organism would be too liberal. Conrad L. Kanagy's 2007 *Road Signs on the Journey: A Church Profile of Mennonite Church USA,* reports that this concern with liberalism in part resulted in the loss of 11,000 members and a net loss of 150 congregations, with many citing the new united denomination as lukewarm on inerrancy, infallibility, homosexuality, and pastoral authority. A silver lining in this story, writes Kanagy, was the unexpected growth of minority churches. The MCs in the Pacific Southwest, for example, attracted 580 new members and associates between 2001 and 2007, especially in greater Los Angeles–area Hispanic congregations. But even then church officials readily acknowledged "declining denominational membership," albeit with the protest that being "faithful" was "not all about growth" but having "a much larger influence than the numbers suggest" (Schrag).

The large Mennonite Brethren (MB) denomination experienced similar seismic changes, albeit in a different way. The big change here came in a shifting public face, commensurate with a strong program of evangelicalism and a remarkable demographic growth that saw MB membership double to 72,000 between 1975 and 2010. At the same time, the number of MB churches that changed their names to community or theologically based names also grew rapidly. In his *A People Apart: Ethnicity and the Mennonite Brethren,* John Redekop reports that the first MB church in Canada to drop the name "Mennonite" did so in 1963 but that over the next two decades about one-third of all MB churches in North America followed suit. A quick search of MB church websites indicates that by 2013 about 50 percent of Canadian and 70 percent of American MB churches no longer used the name Mennonite Brethren. An MB missions agency official noted in 2012 that "looking back over the past 10 years . . . a majority of new US MB congregations . . . include 'church' in the name, but none in the same period use[s] 'Mennonite'" (Huber). The meaning of this penchant for name change has been debated, but a representative comment is BC MB pastor James Toews's 2009 observation that as Mennonite Brethren "we wrestle with what quality or quantity of Anabaptist, evangelical, and now emergent . . . lies behind our names" and that "the debate about what to do with our inherited and given names always creates a high level of energy."

In a way, the MCs and MBs shared in the relative decline of the public face of Mennonitism, the first through membership loss and the second by no longer using the "Mennonite" designation. Coincidentally, just as this realignment took place at the MC-MB core of the Mennonite world, the periphery of that world was growing more visible. Consider, for example, how the strict "horse-and-buggy" Old Order Mennonites, as well as the more moderate albeit still traditional or "plain people"—the Conservative Mennonites, Holdeman Mennonites, Amish Mennonites, Beachy Amish, Reinland Mennonites—more than doubled between 1975 and 2010 (Loewen and Nolt 339–40). Consider too the growth of Anabaptism in unexpected places. In a number of cases, Mennonites left Mennonite denominations only to reassemble with critical mass in competing denominations. A thesis on St. Margaret's Anglican Church in Winnipeg, for example, demonstrates that half of its attendees were "Manglicans," Anglicans in name but Anabaptists in theology (Fisher). In yet another development, the British Baptist church planter Stuart Murray's *The Naked Anabaptist: The Bare Essentials of a Radical Faith* caught North American Mennonites by storm, in part, it seems, because of the book's message that Anabaptism is most refreshing when it is delivered in a decidedly English tone, shorn of "ethnic" roots, and, just as importantly, presented outside traditional church structure.

What did these patterns mean? What was the significance that the public face of a modern Mennonitism was being challenged just as powerful institutions were poised for growth? Was this a sign that modernity was cutting the Mennonite populace off from a meaningful connection with the past and a confident march into the future? Was this evidence that "the Anabaptist Vision" paradigm had run its course, that a "naked Anabaptism," free of collective memory and ecclesiastical encumbrance, was the pathway of the future? Was there a certain disillusionment with a Mennonite modernity? Were the Mennonites enduring their own fin de siècle?

Learning History from the Mennonite Novel and Poem

Perhaps the clearest evidence that the Mennonite world at the end of the twentieth century was facing a moment of truth, however, lay in the surprising rise of another new Mennonite constituency, not a denomination or settlement but a loose collage of poets and novelists who burst onto the national scenes of both Canada and the United States in the late decades of the twentieth century. I want to argue that, notwithstanding the idea that the Canadians might have preceded the Americans in this literary florescence by a decade or so, the rise of writers in both countries was part and parcel of this fin de siècle paradigm and that they articulated the culture of this era with particular poignancy. Like the modernist artists and writers of the wider world who critiqued modernity in the late nineteenth century as vacuous and unrooted, these Mennonite writers critiqued modernity as they saw it expressed by the Mennonites around them.

Clearly, the past three decades have manifested a remarkable rise in the Mennonite arts, literature in particular. Mennonite writing had a specific beginning and a rapid rise against cultural obstacles, and, according to some observers, it will some day have an apex, for "the Mennonite ethos may fade with time" along with "intact" identities (Reimer 235). The beginning in Canada occurred around 1980, in the United States perhaps a decade later. When Harry Loewen launched the Canadian-based *Journal of Mennonite Studies* in 1983, he could still write that, "for all the skills they have shown over the centuries for practical arts, Mennonites have failed to develop among themselves an appreciation for the literary arts and more so for literary artists" (119). Over the next generation, that hope was met by a veritable florescence of Mennonite literature. Consider the seven international Mennonite/s Writing conferences—two in Canada and five in the United States—between 1990, when Hildi Froese Tiessen organized the first one at Conrad Grebel College, and 2013, when the Penn State workshop that gave birth to this volume took place. Take into account the increased number of books of fiction and poetry reviewed in the *Journal of Mennonite Studies* in each of the three decades since it was founded: eighteen for the first decade, thirty-nine for the second, and 109 between 2003 and 2013. Works by American writers—Dallas Wiebe, Julia Spicher Kasdorf, Jean Janzen, David Wright, Rhoda Janzen, and others—were among these reviews. More specifically, Ann

Hostetler's 2003 anthology, *A Cappella: Mennonite Voices in Poetry,* as well as the *Centre for Mennonite Writing Journal* that Hostetler began editing in 2007, attests to a groundswell of work south of the forty-ninth parallel. Jeff Gundy's comment in his 2005 *Walker in the Fog: On Mennonite Writing,* "I have heard it suggested quite openly that control of 'the' Mennonite narrative belongs with historians and theologians, who can be trusted to get the story right" (162), hinted at a growing defensiveness among an old guard to the rising dominance of the literati, a cultural phenomenon apparent in either country.

The surge of literary writing is significant, but for the historian in particular its meaning comes from what the texts say about the age that they describe. The literary critical community, of course, has often employed the "new historicism" of the 1980s, urging readers to recognize what David Richter calls a "closed circle of textuality" (qtd. in Brizee and Tompkins): that is, to "reconnect a work with the time period in which it was produced and identify it with the cultural and political movements of the time" (Brizee and Tompkins). More often, though, historians use texts such as novels and poems by employing methods of "thick description," to employ Clifford Geertz's terminology. We thus find here the symbols, nuances, psychological structures, and social meanings that make ordinary events into cultural moments, a nexus shaping an ethnoreligious identity, for example. Many historians recognize that they more fully learn how Mennonites weave their "webs of significance" (Geertz) through an interdisciplinary exchange with literature.

In approaching literature, historians can certainly be dismayed with poets and novelists, especially when they are seen to "make up" the facts. Historians, after all, insist that they constitute that craft based on the belief that "facts" somehow relate to "truth." A bus tour in October 2010 of "literary places" in southern Manitoba—in which, among several performances, Pat Friesen read from *The Shunning* on the front steps of the Steinbach farmhouse from which Bishop Loewen read his excommunication letter, and David Bergen pointed out the Niverville feedmill where Johnny of *A Year of Lesser* worked—could be tolerated as tour participants happily realized that these geographic sites were only imagined. But sometimes the novelists "make it up" without letting on. Miriam Toews seems to conflate Menno Simons and Claas Epp in *A Complicated Kindness,* for example, not caring that the historical Menno was patently anti-apocalyptic and never visited a desert, shrouded as he was in the rainy mist and verdant landscape of northern Europe his entire life. Similarly, Andreas Schroeder's statement of injustice—"according to Mennonite tradition, the first born son inherited the entire estate" (17)—might relate to primogeniture-practicing Germanized Mennonites from West Prussia but not to the vast majority of

European-descendant Mennonites with strong roots in Swiss, South German, and Dutch lands practicing bilateral and partible inheritance.

In another way, historians do embrace the role that novelists and poets play in shedding light on history, and on the late-century Mennonite mindset in North America, in particular. To illustrate this point, I want to focus on six recent novels and works of nonfiction by acclaimed western Canadian writers, not because they are unique or regional voices but because, in certain ways, they might be representative of this North American Mennonite fin de siècle. Writers such as Rudy Wiebe, Andreas Schroeder, Pat Friesen, Di Brandt, Miriam Toews, and David Bergen write about Manitoba, Saskatchewan, Alberta, and British Columbia geographies (prairie or mountainous), and local historical realities (often based in small denominations not known in the United States) and personalities (readily apparent to readers with local knowledge), but to my mind they can be seen to share a wider cultural phenomenon with their American counterparts. As Robert Zacharias points out in his recent *Rewriting the Break Event: Mennonites and Migration in Canadian Literature,* even writers who reference distinctive "Canadian" phenomena, such as the 1920s and 1940s arrivals of *Russländer* immigrants bearing wartime traumas and stories of dislocation, also butted up against the teleology of modernization. But because only Wiebe and Schroeder in my list of western Canadian writers concern themselves with themes of migration, their commonality with American writers seems to be especially apparent. That commonality is the theme of once-rural Mennonites negotiating middle-class and urban cultures, a common theme in the wider North American Mennonite world.

Significantly, each of these writers addresses the pitfalls of "modernity," and each "recoils" from a position of "beneficiar[y] of modern culture," to repeat Jackson Lears's terms. True, the protagonists in these works contest church authority and accepted religious understandings. But, most significantly, they do not ultimately challenge "traditional" religious authority: that is, the old communitarian, agrarian authority based on Anabaptist values of nonconformity, simplicity, and community. Usually, they do not even castigate rural Mennonite communities for their agrarian primitivism. Rather, they almost uniformly critique aspects of modernity: that is, small-town, bourgeois, materialistic, and evangelical binaries. And they tend to find salvation or liberation by simultaneously taking two somewhat contradictory pathways; just as Daly's late nineteenth-century fin de siècle critics did, most embrace the avant-garde literary form of the city at the same time that they romance an imagined rural past in search of authenticity.

One of the earliest works of this generation of writing, Patrick Friesen's award-winning book of poetry *The Shunning* (1980), captures this protest with special poignancy. It is a moving account, set in 1919, of a poor Mennonite man, Peter Neufeld, whose excommunication from the church and shunning by all, including his wife, leave a psychological wound that drives him to suicide. At first blush, it might appear that the poem attacks traditional Mennonite practices, but a closer look reveals something quite different and more complex. The lengthy poem in the form of a diary begins with a rather idyllic depiction of Mennonite farm life: on 12 August Helena says that she "Finished [canning] 12 quarts of yellow beans," and on 13 August "Abe Neufeld came with his buggy [for her, the midwife] in the night" (15). And this is followed by numerous highly sympathetic references to farm life—hard work, thrashing horses, land, and bush. Significantly, Peter's sin of "pride" (22) is referenced not to the lack of an old Anabaptist humility but to modern fundamentalist belief: Peter "said more than once that there couldn't be such a place as hell, not with a loving God," says Helena at one point, and "that's what started all the trouble with the church" (30). Under intense pressure from the church, Peter finds solace in connection to the land, "go[ing] into the bush when he felt too strong about one thing or another" (22). At the same time, though, he wants to "be left alone" (22), and he feasts on John Stuart Mill's 1859 *On Liberty,* that scathing critique of modernity, especially democratic principles that turn the "tyranny of the majority" against the individual (49). In the end, Peter celebrates not the modern Mennonite, like the missionaries, "those who went to Africa or Asia to save the souls of heathens," but "the quiet ones who live their faith so you never really notice until they're dead" (87).

More recent acclaimed works can be read in similar fashion, as attacks not on Mennonite tradition but on Mennonite modernity. In *A Complicated Kindness* (2004), Nomi Nickel finds salvation in the city and damnation in a small town. But she has no desire to become a member of suburban middle-class culture, not even of individualistic and secular New York, where the repressive preacher, the Mouth, would have no reach; Nomi wants to become a poet, a member of bohemian Greenwich Village. The Mennonites in East Village are evangelical moralists: they are "discouraged from going to the city . . . but are encouraged to travel to the remotest corners of Third World countries with barrels full of Gideon Bibles and hairnets" (7). They feed on newly introduced premillennialist ideas: "My mother's dream was to go to the Holy Land. She was very intrigued with the Jews" (8). Here religion closes "the bar and the bus depot and the pool hall and the swimming pool" but allows television shows: "Like it's theirs. Like my father owns *Hymn Sing*" (13, 85). Here commercialized farming has taken off with "giant semis filled with pigs and chickens whipping past at four thousand miles an hour" (136). Old-fashioned agraria is dead: "main street is bookended by two fields of dirt that never grow a crop" (47). Any semblance of Mennonite agrarianism is cocooned at the town's museum, where people "from all over the world [come] for a first hand look at simple living," in other words "backward Jesus freaks" (11). Nomi's world has long transcended the traditional agrarian Mennonite place; she is caught in an antiseptic, middle-class town.

None of these works feature a heralding of middle-class culture. Restless Peter in Andreas Schroeder's 2008 *Renovating Heaven: A Novel in Triptych* has no intention of becoming an entrepreneur or professional in Vancouver; he wants to be a writer. True, he wishes to shed a religion, that sad and outdated relic of peasant immigrants, countering everything beautiful, sensual, and liberating. And he is delighted when his family is forced to relocate to Vancouver, celebrating urban freedom: "On the farm we'd huddled together. . . . In Vancouver, this unity crumbled. . . . The resulting freedom hit us like a blast of oxygen" (128). But it seems that Peter dislikes farming as much for its financial instability as for its role as "sacred altar" (17), and "urban freedom" is as much liberty from bourgeois banality as from rural repression. Indeed, when his "Mennonite" father objects to his unorthodox vocation, it is in the language of the capitalist order, not rural parochialism. His father's objection is not only that "'writer' was virtually synonymous with 'liar' and 'rascal'" (108) but also that a writer is "sloppy, imprecise, hasty, shallow, . . . lazy" (109), emblematic of "a country where shoddy work is considered acceptable" (166). Peter rejects his father's middle-class penchant that insists on "order" and "discipline"; he wants his father to "accept me for who I am" (166), the slovenly poet.

In the most recent of these works, *The Age of Hope,* David Bergen presents the city as no great panacea for any social ill. The Mennonite town might possess a lethargic, arcane, and out-of-touch religiosity, but the city is capricious and alienating. And what is most overtly critiqued in the novel is not the traditional Holdeman church, where at a funeral men and women sit in opposite sides, or Roy's pacifism, which results in rather remarkable acts of charity, or the young Mennonite seminarian who uses the word *ennui.* Rather, the problem lies with middle-class conformity and hypocrisy; Hope is thoroughly middle class, the duty-bound housewife, escaping for weekly trips of consumption in the city, suffering a Betty Friedanesque postpartum sojourn at a mental institution, showing bourgeois charity by picking up a hitchhiker and cooking him dinner. Her family escapes not Mennonitism but small-town moralism, with one daughter living in Paris with a struggling writer and a son caught in a bizarre and hurtful marriage in which his wife surreptitiously bears another man's children. Hope's car-dealer husband faces the economic crisis of high interest rates in the early 1980s and endures a humiliating, emasculating bankruptcy; the traditional Mennonite social safety net is nowhere to be seen as his supposed friends at the local credit union parrot versions of Adam Smith's laissez-faire economics. Capitalism does have its check on greed, and that check is called bankruptcy. Eden is a small Mennonite town without any traditional Mennonite virtues.

Just as it seems to me that these writers are critiquing modernity, so too it seems that they romanticize the past—that is, the past beyond the immediate past. In this development, Mennonite writers turn the modernist spin on its head and invoke the romantic, bucolic, agrarian way of life and even early Anabaptism. Ironically, the most celebrated articulators of this return to the Mennonite farm village are writers in their fifties, sixties, and seventies, who burst onto the scene as angry young writers in their twenties and thirties. Among the recent second-generation writers who have muted their critiques of an immediate past and reached back beyond it to an idealized agrarian world are Di Brandt and Rudy Wiebe.

In his 2006 work *Of This Earth: A Mennonite Boyhood in the Boreal Forest,* Rudy Wiebe turns to yesteryear, to a time even before Mennonites hypocritically orchestrated that harmful, racialized, patriarchal "peace [that] shall destroy many" of his first novel, and here he finds genuineness on a Mennonite farm in the boreal forest of Saskatchewan, an "isolated," "physical spot": here is "the ground of whatever I was or would be, root and spirit" (3). Here Wiebe grows up, on a farm, a quarter-section graced with "tall trembling aspen[s]" and "small water sloughs hidden by willows that nubbled into silver pussy willows in spring long before leaves appeared; and also clumps of paper birch" (24). Here, on the mixed farm, children sing "Low German skipping song[s that] go . . . on for as many verses as you can invent" as they run "wildly down the slope of the yard toward the cattle corral, shouting, swinging the empty milk pails over our heads" (65). And here any vestige of evangelical wrath is negotiated by quotidian agraria: Wiebe comes to see his "mother's life as contradiction; her abiding fear at the immanence of divine, eternal wrath, yet she herself lived a life devoted to goodness and love" (364). She would hear the evangelists who "never talked about 'the wind blows where it wills,' or 'the light shines in the darkness'" (309), but she herself would sing in the wind, embrace light in herbs and gardens and tasks well done.

A year after Wiebe's book, poet Di Brandt, nationally acclaimed since her 1987 *questions i asked my mother,* by all reports a scathing, radical feminist, and iconoclastic attack on Mennonite patriarchalism, produced quite a different book. Her 2007 *So this is the world & here I am in it* revisits a Mennonite past when "the people of this land tried to live in harmony with its shifts and rhythms" (10) and understands that "the word 'wild' had a whole other meaning in our traditional Mennonite lexicon" (74). Brandt has come to admire Mennonite agraria where "'paganism' [. . .] was both greatly feared in the Mennonite community of my childhood and at the same time extensively, albeit covertly practiced" (120–22). Now the Mennonites of the past are said to have been "joyfully indigenous-minded" (129), profoundly "connected to the rhythms of the seasons" (107). The city might have spelled freedom in her earlier works, but her sojourn in the Windsor-Detroit region consisted of life in the "hyper-industrialized landscape of the Great Lakes region" amid "thick toxic fumes of factory smoke" (106). Anabaptism is now celebrated, for "at the heart of Mennonite culture lies a much older world view than the early modern" era that resembles "peasant-led resistance movements to corporate takeovers" (81). Brandt confesses that where she once "made an irrevocable break with my Mennonite heritage and deep-rooted prairie upbringing," she is now "trying to understand . . . that stern, proud, humble, retrograde, free-spirited heritage" (107). Yearning for a deep-rooted tradition now no longer contradicts literary license and genius.

The case studies of these six western Canadian writers point out a specific concern with "tradition" and "modernity." Certainly, regional and national differences in Mennonite writing exist, as do differences between nationally acclaimed writers and those with regional reputations. But where these writers critique a particular tradition that was not traditional at all, and long for a modernity that was not especially modern, they seem to me to reflect a larger phenomenon than one rooted in any one quarter of the Mennonite literary world. They observe a broader Mennonite accommodation with the modern and desire a sort of anti-modern authenticity absent in urbanizing, acculturating Mennonites. I have read less widely in American Mennonite literature than Canadian, but works that I have used in orientating myself to Mennonite history generally include nonfiction works by Jeff Gundy and Julia Spicher Kasdorf, both of whom quietly celebrate salt-of-the-earth ancestors even as they claim their own individuated artistic voice. Works that I have assigned in Mennonite history courses include fiction such as Dallas Wiebe's *Our Asian Journey: A Novel* and Rhoda Janzen's *Mennonite in a Little Black Dress.* Wiebe boldly confronts an embarrassing chapter in Mennonite history, the chiliastic millennial wanderings of Claas Epp, by finding his peasant, Low German soul and his connection to the land even as he rips his group from their Mennonite roots and takes them into strange and exotic lands. Janzen, in a sense, does the opposite as she finds the Mennonite maternal epitomized in borscht and *kartoffsalat* in her mother's kitchen, after life in the broader, secular world collapses in failed love, a traffic accident, and bankruptcy.

Both the Canadian writers considered in some detail, and the American writers mentioned here in passing, seem less to reject Mennonite religion than to celebrate its historical intersection with the sensuous and earthy; they also seem less critical of Mennonite history than of Mennonite acculturation. Indeed, they seem to celebrate the messy, quotidian process by which an older, quieter rurality has become mythologized, and they overtly criticize a cerebral, formulaic, antiseptic culture tied to a middle-class separation of the natural world and society.

Conclusion

The dominant Mennonite historical narrative of the twentieth century was one of Mennonites slowly modernizing, most dropping Old World dialects, shedding old cultural garb, building Protestant-looking church buildings, adopting church constitutions, and embracing town or city life. Along the way, they infused this process of accommodation with a "usable past," an Anabaptist vision for the twentieth century, one celebrating a particular "following" of Christ—community, love, and peace—the very antidotes that could save modernity from its own internal contradictions. As the twentieth century came to an end and another century dawned, something seismic seemed to be afoot. While the large, core modernizing groups—the Mennonite Church and the Mennonite Brethren—showed remarkable energy, growing and amalgamating, engaging the modern world, they also revealed a reorientation that resulted in an unprecedented strain on Mennonite identity. One denomination exhibited this change through remarkable membership decline following a historic amalgamation, another by a notable rebranding within a period of unprecedented growth.

Even as these bodies signaled the height of modernity, an array of anti-modern voices was expressed. One anti-modern refrain came from old order groups—including the Amish, Old Colony Mennonites, Old Order Mennonites, and other "plain people"—who, having stood up to modernity throughout the twentieth century, now defied sociological prediction and actually became a rapidly growing Anabaptist segment. But if this was surprising, so was the florescence of Mennonite literary writing, expressing its own poetics of anti-modernity. In both Canada and the United States, literary voices rose and contested a middle-class cosmology, institutionalized and acculturating Mennonite society, reaching back to the time before the hegemony of small-town Mennonitism while simultaneously moving well beyond it. It behooves historians to take note, not worrying that the literati are writing this story, but recognizing that it originated at a particular moment in Mennonite history. In this turn-of-the-century moment, these writers articulated what many readers already suspected, that a modernized Mennonitism was being severely tested, for in the very act of seeking greater social relevance it had strained its moorings. The Mennonite fin de siècle has been, among other things, a moment in Mennonite history that also anticipates the more pluralistic and innovative forms of identity.

WORKS CITED

Bender, Harold S. *The Anabaptist Vision.* Scottdale: Herald Press, 1944.

Bergen, David. *The Age of Hope.* Toronto: HarperCollins, 2012.

———. *A Year of Lesser.* Toronto: HarperCollins, 1996.

Brandt, Di. *So this is the world & here I am in it.* Edmonton: NeWest, 2007.

Brizee, Allen, and J. Case Tompkins. "New Historicism, Cultural Studies (1980s—Present)." Perdue Online Writing Lab. Web. 16 Mar. 2012.

Breton, Raymond. "Institutional Completeness of Ethnic Communities and Personal Relations of Immigrants." *American Journal of Sociology* 70.2 (1964): 193–205.

Daly, Nicholas. *Modernism, Romance, and the Fin de Siècle: Popular Fiction and British Culture, 1880–1914.* Cambridge, UK: Cambridge University Press, 1999.

Fisher, Susan. "'High Church Mennonites?' The Relationship Between Religion and Ethnicity Among Manitoba Mennonites at an Anglican Church." MA thesis, McMaster University, 2010.

Friesen, Patrick. *The Shunning.* Winnipeg: Turnstone Press, 1980.

Geertz, Clifford. "Thick Description: Toward an Interpretive Theory of Culture." *The Interpretation of Cultures: Selected Essays.* New York: Basic Books, 1973. 3–30.

Gundy, Jeff. *Walker in the Fog: On Mennonite Writing.* Telford: Cascadia, 2005.

Huber, Tim. "Church Name Trend: Less Is More?" *Mennonite World Review* 10 Dec. 2012. Web. 3 May 2013.

Janzen, Rhoda. *Mennonite in a Little Black Dress.* New York: Henry Holt, 2009.

Kanagy, Conrad L. *Road Signs on the Journey: A Church Profile of Mennonite Church USA.* Scottdale: Herald Press, 2007.

Kasdorf, Julia Spicher. *Fixing Tradition: Joseph W. Yoder, Amish American.* Telford: Pandora, 2003.

Kauffman, Howard J., and Leland Harder. *Anabaptists Four Centuries Later: A Profile of Five Mennonite and Brethren in Christ Denominations.* Scottdale: Herald Press, 1975.

Lears, T.J. Jackson. *No Place of Grace: Antimodernism and the Transformation of American Culture, 1880–1920.* New York: Pantheon Books, 1981.

Loewen, Harry. "Mennonite Literature in Canada: Beginning, Reception, and Study." *Journal of Mennonite Studies* 1 (1983): 119–32.

Loewen, Royden, and Stephen M. Nolt. *Seeking Places of Peace.* Global Mennonite History Series, North America. Intercourse, PA: Good Books, 2012.

Maxwell, William J. "Dunbar's Bohemian Gallery: Foreign Color and Fin-de-Siècle Modernism." *African American Review* 41.2 (2007): 341–46.

Murray, Stuart. *The Naked Anabaptist: The Bare Essentials of a Radical Faith.* Scottdale: Herald Press, 2010.

Palmer, Bryan D. "'Cracking the Stone': The Long History of Capitalist Crisis and Toronto's Dispossessed, 1830–1930." *Labour/Le Travail* 69 (2012): 9–62.

Redekop, John. *A People Apart: Ethnicity and the Mennonite Brethren.* Winnipeg: Kindred Press, 1987.

Regehr, T.D. *Mennonites in Canada: A People Transformed.* Toronto: University of Toronto Press, 1996.

Reimer, Al. Rev. of "Words from the West Coast," a special issue of *Rhubarb* 11 (2005), ed. Elsie K. Neufeld, Robert Martens, and Leonard Neufeldt. *Journal of Mennonite Studies* 24 (2006): 234–36.

Schrag, Paul. "Church Aims to Stop Membership Decline." *Mennonite World Review* 15 Oct. 2007. Web. 2 Mar. 2013.

Schroeder, Andreas. *Renovating Heaven: A Novel in Triptych.* Lantzville, BC: Oolichan, 2008.

Toews, James. "A Mennonite Brethren by Any Other Name." *Mennonite Brethren Herald* Jan. 2009. Web. 15 Feb. 2013.

Toews, Miriam. *A Complicated Kindness.* Toronto: Knopf, 2004.

Toews, Paul. *Mennonites in American Society, 1930–1970: Modernity and the Persistence of Religious Community.* Scottdale: Herald Press, 1996.

Wiebe, Dallas. *Our Asian Journey: A Novel.* Waterloo, ON: Mir Editions, 1997.

Wiebe, Rudy. *Of This Earth: A Mennonite Boyhood in the Boreal Forest.* Intercourse, PA: Good Books, 2007.

Zacharias, Robert. *Rewriting the Break Event: Mennonites and Migration in Canadian Literature.* Winnipeg: University of Manitoba Press, 2013.

3

Mennonite Transgressive Literature

ERVIN BECK

The "transgressive myth of origins" of Mennonite literature (Kasdorf, "Sunday" 8) assumes that the remarkable recent development of Mennonite literature began in 1962 with the publication in Canada of Rudy Wiebe's novel *Peace Shall Destroy Many,* which disturbed many Mennonite readers. The tradition of offense has continued through other major Mennonite writings, including in 2009 in the United States with Rhoda Janzen's bestselling memoir *Mennonite in a Little Black Dress.* Out of their Mennonite communal context, these writings do not seem to be very transgressive. In fact, their transgressive nature is mostly a matter of how they have been received and interpreted by Mennonite lay readers. Professional Mennonite critics either ignore the objections of many Mennonite readers or rationalize them away by citing literary theory and using interpretive strategies instead. The literary merits of these works will certainly outlast their initial reception and ensuing reputation among Mennonite readers. Yet if a literary culture is to be "Mennonite," it will also include and respect resistant readers' understandings of Mennonite texts.

Transgressive Literature

The *topos* of "transgression" entered literary discourse through discussions by Michel Foucault and, especially, Mikhail Bakhtin, whose notion of the "carnivalesque" asserted the creative renewal that "rites of reversal," including literature and other arts, could bring to individuals and cultures (Stallybrass and White). A similar view of literature as creative transgression is part of the theopoetics of Anabaptist scholar Scott Holland and others, who regard the arts and aesthetic experience as sources of a postmodern theology. However, my use of the term "transgression" in this chapter is related more to the discrete genre of "transgressive fiction," which continues in the tradition of the Marquis de Sade, William Burroughs, Henry Miller, and others by shocking, provoking, and offending many of its readers (Neeper).

Of course, what is transgressive is in the eyes of the beholder—in this case, in Mennonite readers—so it is not surprising that the offense in what we might call the canon of transgressive Mennonite literature is milder and different. In place of sadism and bodily functions, transgressive Mennonite literature most often offends through character defamation, negative stereotyping of Mennonites, or distortion of Mennonite history or theology. If such offenses are not immediately noticeable to non-Mennonite readers, they are disturbing to many Mennonites who, being deeply familiar with and invested in the history and values of the Mennonite community, are understandably concerned to find them misrepresented or held up to ridicule. It is this meaning of transgressive that both Julia Spicher Kasdorf (*Body* 182) and Di Brandt (*Dancing* 36) use in discussing their own early writing and that Kasdorf used recently in questioning the "transgressive myth of origins," as noted above. The first use of the term in Mennonite discourse, however, might be the comment made by Canadian writer and critic Robert Kroetsch as an observer at the first Mennonite/s Writing conference in 1990: "[T]he writer—in this culture—is, as I listen, a transgressor" (238).

Since the reaction by "lay" or nonprofessional Mennonite readers has mainly defined the transgressive nature of some Mennonite literature, I examine in this chapter the literary and cultural phenomenon of transgression from these often-ignored Mennonite readers' perspectives.

Texts

The canon of transgressive Mennonite literary works, as established by their reputations in Mennonite communities, probably consists of the following seven books.

- *The Flamethrowers* (Caxton, 1936) by Gordon Friesen (1909–1996), a novel in the naturalistic protest style of Theodore Dreiser and Sinclair Lewis, offended members of his Krimmer Mennonite Brethren communities in Gnadenau, Kansas, and Corn, Oklahoma, by depicting a dysfunctional Russian immigrant family as victims of the hypocrisy, individualism, and greed of fellow Mennonites and other capitalists. Elmer Suderman, a native of the Gnadenau area, said that Friesen's book depicts Mennonites as "peculiar, stupid, ignorant, and unworthy," "brutal, deceitful, vicious, despicable, contemptible, cynical, and inhuman," "degenerate," and "repulsive, sickening, and obnoxious" ("Pioneer" 106–08).

- *Peace Shall Destroy Many* (McClelland and Stewart, 1962) by Rudy Wiebe, a coming-of-age novel, offended members of his Mennonite Brethren community in Saskatchewan by depicting a closed community of Russian Mennonites rife with contradictions, hypocrisies, and latent violence. As Paul Tiessen's chapter in this volume points out, even the editors at McClelland and Stewart anticipated a negative reaction to its publication.
- *The Shunning* (Turnstone, 1980) by Patrick Friesen, a book-length narrative of poems and prose poems, offended his Evangelical Mennonite Conference (Kleine Gemeinde) church in Steinbach, Manitoba, by depicting the shunning, or excommunication, of a man who then committed suicide. Many readers regarded it as a betrayal of Friesen's family history and an overly negative depiction of church discipline.
- *questions i asked my mother* (Turnstone, 1987) by Di Brandt, a book of poems, exposes the physical abuse, misogyny, and religious fundamentalism found in her Evangelical Mennonite Mission Conference (Rudnerweide) church community and family in Reinland, Manitoba. She famously observed that Mennonite literature is "one of the ways of destroying [Mennonite] separateness. . . . I'm helping to kill it" (qtd. in Mierau 19).
- *Sleeping Preacher* (University of Pittsburgh Press, 1992) by Julia Spicher Kasdorf, a book of semi-autobiographical poems, mainly offended relatives and friends in her ancestral community of Swiss Mennonites and Amish in the Kishacoquillas (Big) Valley near Belleville, Pennsylvania, by depicting identifiable people and fictionalizing others' experiences.
- *A Complicated Kindness* (Knopf, 2004), a novel by Miriam Toews, offended her Evangelical Mennonite Conference (Kleine Gemeinde) church community in Steinbach, Manitoba, by dwelling on shunning and other fundamentalist practices, presenting negative stereotypes of Mennonites, and conflating experience in the Steinbach community with less fundamentalist Mennonite groups.
- *Mennonite in a Little Black Dress* (Holt, 2009) by Rhoda Janzen, a *New York Times* bestselling memoir, offended her Mennonite Brethren community in Fresno, California, by badly depicting some family members and friends and offended other Mennonite readers by conflating her Mennonite Brethren experience with that of more liberal Mennonite communities.

Readers

What is at stake for Mennonite readers of transgressive literature? For an individual reader, the use of Mennonite characters and milieus in fiction might seem to implicate the Mennonite reader in all generalizations about Mennonites. "But this does not represent me and my people" is a typical response to negative representations. For Mennonites as a group, transgressive fiction too often establishes negative stereotypes that can be used against them by the dominant culture. Even grave political issues might be at stake, as Paul Tiessen's chapter on *Peace Shall Destroy Many* in this volume points out, since some Mennonite leaders feared that the negative depiction in the novel of an immigrant community might prompt the government to refuse the immigration of more Russian Mennonite refugees. The organized church also shows concern, as indicated by the *Femonite* blog entry by Melodie Davis, an employee of Mennonite Church USA in its MennoMedia office, where she expresses concern about the negative stereotypes found in *Mennonite in a Little Black Dress.* Mennonite Church USA has officially defined itself as a "missional" church, meaning that it wants to be welcoming to new members. In her *Femonite* blog, however, Hannah Heinzekehr suggested that the book is "anti-missional." Who would join a church that is so darkly portrayed? Much is at stake.

In this era of cultural criticism, minoritized groups regularly express similar concerns about representations of them in literary works, which they think have consequences in real life. One thinks of African Americans, Native Americans, feminists, gays. If those groups' objections to fictive representations of their communities are respected and listened to, then Mennonites' concerns about their own representations should be too.

Pinning down the specific critique by Mennonites of transgressive literature is difficult because evidence of it is diffuse, ephemeral, and usually oral rather than in print. Written forms include personal letters, letters to the editors of local or church papers, and, more recently, blogs. An example of a personal letter comes from a relative of Kasdorf who grieves not for herself but for other acquaintances exposed in *Sleeping Preacher:* "It would have hurt me, too if a relative of mine had dug all that stuff into a book even if I know it happened. I'm not saying these things aren't true, but I am trying to point out to you that it was a bad enough hurt to have happened and then drag it into a book" (14 Sept. 1994, Kasdorf, email). Al Reimer ("Look") cites excerpts from several similar letters sent to editors regarding *A Complicated Kindness.* "Toews denigrates a religious faith and a thinly disguised prairie town," reads one. "The author is clearly attempting to cast out personal demons by herding them into unsuspecting people and traditional institutions," reads another. The book is "a continuing damning vendetta before an applauding audience" and reflects the "secular cultural elites' tortured image of Steinbach in particular, and of Bible-believing Canadian Christians generally," reads a third.

Mennonite book study groups often form consensus responses and repeat them to friends, who might then pass them on to others. At their best, such responses constitute valid and critical engagements with texts; at worst, they become rumors spread by people who have not read the texts, as in this response to Jessica Baldanzi's online review of *Mennonite in a Little Black Dress:* "I was excited to buy the book until I was told that the memoir might be better called fiction . . . and, at the very least, she twisted truth at others' expense. . . . I will not buy the book." Blogs are currently the most accessible source of informal comments on Mennonite writing. In their interactive nature, they become virtual book discussion groups. One of the best examples is the blog attached to the Baldanzi review cited above. The vigorous responses include positive and negative positions, of course, but highlights of the negative reviews include the following.

> [This is] a surprisingly provincial view of the Mennonite world. . . . [S]he commits one of my pet peeves which is to characterize widely shared experiences as uniquely Mennonite. . . . [H]er tendency to mock anyone or anything less sophisticated than she is (or thinks she is) often seems mean-spirited.

> It's not funny and it's way too self-absorbed. . . . [I]t has the tone of a teenager who just knows that she's cool and her family isn't so it's okay to make fun of them.

> Rhoda's statements concerning what a Mennonite is (or believes) should be prefaced by "in my experience a Mennonite is or believes."

Some blog entries, though highly personal responses, attain the quality of formal literary reviews, as in Heinzekehr's *Femonite* blog essay on Janzen's book. "I. HATED. This. Book," she writes in the midst of a thoughtful critique. She goes on to object to Janzen's depiction of Mennonite women ("plain and unattractive . . . ; uneducated and inept") and of Mennonites in general ("judgmental . . . ; sectarian and closed off"), as well as the way in which her generalizations about Mennonites also unfairly implicate Heinzekehr.

Mennonite literary critics have largely responded to such reader objections by ignoring the perceived transgressions or by using their professional skills to explicate the artistry and socially and morally redeeming value of such literature. Critics tend to write for each other, however, not for recreational readers, which means that critics' explanations do not reach the objectors. Mennonite literary critics tend to regard resistant readers as naive or reactionary. Kasdorf, for example, says that such readers illustrate a "defensive reading strategy" (*Body* 41).

Yet Mennonite critics also illustrate a defensive reading strategy when they object to the misrepresentation of Amish people in feature films such as *Witness* or in the television reality shows *Amish Mafia* and *Breaking Amish*. One scholarly analysis of Amish misrepresentation in fiction is Kasdorf's book *Fixing Tradition: Joseph W. Yoder, Amish American*, which analyzes early fiction that misrepresented the Amish and inspired Yoder to correct the record by writing *Rosanna of the Amish*. Another is Valerie Weaver-Zercher's *Thrill of the Chaste: The Allure of Amish Romance Novels*, a fine analysis of the representation of the Amish in the current craze for Amish-themed romances. One might expect Mennonites, readers and critics alike, to be similarly concerned about their representation in books by Mennonite authors. After all, the meaning latent in any use of the term "Mennonite" always implies the widespread community, or communities, to which an individual Mennonite belongs. The communal ideal in Mennonite culture could, and should, assume a role in the literary enterprise for the responses of readers in addition to the creativity of authors and the criticism of professional critics.

Critics should be able to perceive that this kind of nonprofessional textual interpretation is legitimized by the reader-response school of literary criticism that flourished in the 1970s and 1980s and is still relevant in postmodern discussions. Reader-response theory denies that a literary text contains an objective meaning or that a reader should search for the author's intention in order to understand the work. Instead, literary meaning occurs in the process of an individual's reading of a text, and a text's meaning comes partly, or even entirely, from the individual reader's identity and experience. As Jane Tompkins puts it, "Literary meaning is a function of the reader's response to a text and cannot be described accurately if that response is left out of the account" (xiii). "The reader must act as co-creator of the work" (xv). Just as authors impose an "identity theme" onto their writing, so too readers project an "identity theme" onto their reading. According to Stanley Fish, one reader's interpretation can become "knowledge" if it is negotiated with others' readings and the ensuing discussion yields a kind of consensus (Tompkins xxi). Such negotiation occurs in an "interpretive community," such as an academic classroom, a book club discussion, or, in the present case, communities of Mennonite readers. Both

Kasdorf and Gundy expand on this possibility of an interpretive community, Kasdorf by regarding literary creativity as a result of conversations in a community ("Genius" 287), Gundy by invoking Kenneth Bruffee on the community as "the prime location of all meaning and knowledge" (*Walker* 50).

In regard to Mennonite literature, the type of reader response that I am interested in here might be better described by the term "folk literary criticism" since it is performed by the particular religious-ethnic community of Mennonites. The term is a variation of Alan Dundes's "oral literary criticism," which denotes interpretations, often conflicting, given to folk tales, songs, and customs by folk performers and audiences. These community-oriented interpretations often differ radically from the meanings perceived in the folk materials by "objective" outsiders, such as professional folklorists who collect and study them. "Oral" might suffice for peasant cultures, but "folk" is better for Mennonite culture, intertwined with academic and pop culture in a high-tech society. Folk literary criticism circulates not only by word of mouth but also in writing, as in the letters and blogs noted above. Those media, like oral/aural, are not vetted by authorities and represent unofficial culture that circulates informally and conforms to the broader current understanding of folk culture in a high-tech society. The conservative nature of many Mennonite readers' understanding of literature also conforms to the culture-conserving function of most folklore.

Authors

Authors respond to folk literary criticism in various ways, including silence, but often by citing the autonomy of the author from communal restraints or the autonomy of the story, memoir, or poem that, during its writing, fulfills its own natural, almost compulsive, course of development, seemingly beyond the author's control. As Miriam Toews puts it, "Serve your story and you are doing your proper business" ("Is There").

Mennonite authors might sympathize with Philip Roth, the Jewish writer who was much taken to task by Jewish readers who objected to negative stereotypes of them in his *Portnoy's Complaint* and other early writings. "I write to a Jewish audience, not for it," he has said (168). That defense, however, poses several problems. First, an author does not control either the audience of a literary work or the meanings that readers find in it. Second, an author like Roth is read more by non-Jews than by Jews. And when readers from mainstream culture read literature by minority writers depicting minority experiences, they commonly regard it as a true depiction of that minority's experience. Here again arises the minority's dread of receiving a bad reputation in public discourse because of transgressive literature.

The production of canonical transgressive texts by Mennonite writers might be understood in a number of ways. Most of the texts represent the first books published by their young authors (for Patrick Friesen, Toews, and Janzen, their first Mennonite-themed books). As Paul Tiessen emphasizes, Wiebe, at twenty-eight years of age, was hailed as a "young theologian" on the first cover of *Peace Shall Destroy Many.* All of the books in question (except perhaps *Peace Shall Destroy Many*) are creative renderings of autobiographical experiences of their authors when they were teenagers or late teenagers. That includes Janzen's background account of leaving home as a young woman. Wiebe's book is presented from the point of view of a teenage boy. The books might reflect the process of individuation by their authors as they wrestle with questions of personal identity in relation to more traditional claims laid on them by their Mennonite communities. As is the case with Gordon Friesen, they might also spring from their young authors' shattered ideals regarding what a Mennonite community could become (Born 118).

In addition, most of the books seem to arise from experiences in dysfunctional families or from some other personally traumatic experiences of their authors, whether explicitly stated (Brandt, Janzen) or implied (Gordon Friesen, Toews). For them, writing the books might have been one way to creatively process and move beyond such traumas. The most sensational case in point is that of *The Flamethrowers* by Gordon Friesen. A grandson of Mennonites from the 1874 emigration from Ukraine, he grew up in a dysfunctional, destitute family, with a bitter mother and a feckless father. He wrote *The Flamethrowers* and the unpublished novel *Unrest* while "totally bedridden" (Teichrow 12) during a two- or three-year bout with anxiety disorder and severe depression (Born 118–19)—to the extent that his cousin had to trick him into driving away from home and moving to Oklahoma City.

Authors of transgressive literature from minority groups fit into a more general sociological framework. Kurt Lewin, founder of the discipline of social psychology, in considering his fellow Jews who strive for assimilation into mainstream society, said that they "will dislike everything specifically Jewish, for [they] will see in it that which keeps [them] away from the majority for which [they are] longing. [They] will show dislike for those Jews who are outspokenly so" (164). He added that this phenomenon in Jewish culture "has its parallel in many underprivileged groups" and cited African Americans as one of the "better known and most extreme cases." But it can also be found "among the second generation of Greek, Italian, Polish, and other immigrants" (189). Mennonites also seem to be a clear parallel with Jews since both are religious ethnic groups who historically have maintained a separatist stance toward mainstream culture. Although Wiebe is the only second-generation immigrant author, he and Patrick Friesen, Di Brandt, and Gordon Friesen learned Plautdietsch as a native language. Their movement into English-language culture might have had the same effect as with the assimilating immigrants referred to by Lewin. This is not to claim that the assimilative process and a resulting transgressive literature come from deliberate choices made by Mennonite writers—that is, to reject their Mennonite community in order to attain acceptance by the dominant culture—though this might have been the case with Gordon Friesen, who moved to New York City, became a blacklisted communist, and never returned to his home community. But to some degree, it might be inevitable that, when Mennonite authors write for a nondenominational press, hoping to attract mainstream attention, they consciously or unconsciously offer the exotic or sensational content that mainstream readers expect to find in minority literature.

Reader-response theory assumes that reading is "transactional": that is, a give-and-take process involving author, text, and reader, each contributing to the meaning of a text (Probst). The transaction sometimes goes one step further, when the reader's response prompts a response, in turn, from the author. Without claiming cause and effect, one can observe steps in some of the Mennonite authors' careers that perhaps were influenced by readers' reception of their writings.

Both Wiebe and Patrick Friesen have been generally silent in public about Mennonites' negative responses. As Friesen told Kasdorf, "Goes with the territory, doesn't it?" (*Body* 40). In Wiebe's second published novel, *First and Vital Candle,* the protagonist is named a Presbyterian, though he could as well be a Mennonite. Wiebe might have missed a chance to please his community with this decision, since that novel has a strongly Christian evangelical appeal. In his 1983 novel, *My Lovely Enemy,* James Dyck, the Mennonite professor protagonist, is unrepentant about committing adultery, and in one of a number of magic-realist scenes Jesus converses with Dyck, postcoitus, about sex and love. Negative Mennonite reaction was defused when his home congregation, Lendrum Mennonite Brethren in Edmonton, sponsored a program for release of the novel.

Negative criticism of their first books has served as the sand that generates a pearl for Kasdorf and Brandt, who have published elegant essays that respond to their Mennonite critics—especially "Bringing Home the Book" by Kasdorf (*Body* 39–47) and "Letting the Silence Speak" by Brandt (*Dancing* 18–31), as well as other essays in both books. Kasdorf has since written few poems about Mennonites and Amish, but she has become a prominent scholar of historical Mennonite culture with her books and essays on Yoder, *Martyrs Mirror,* and other Mennonite-related subjects. In recent years, Brandt has moved closer to her home community, both in geography and in appreciating the culture that she fled and that is now disappearing, especially as found in chapters 6, 8, and 12 in *So this is the world & here I am in it.* For both Kasdorf and Brandt, a kind of transaction between readers and authors, in the authors' minds, was present even prior to the publication of their first books. Having recently completed a course on reader-response theory (*Body* ix), Kasdorf suffered from migraine headaches as she imagined the possible consequences of publishing *Sleeping Preacher* (39). Brandt withheld publication of her first book of poems because she feared her community's reaction, even to the extent of writing, several times, that she thought someone from the community might come and kill her (*Dancing* 10).

Janzen and Toews have responded to their critics mainly in interviews. Janzen says that she will not write again about family members ("Interview"), while Toews says that, in the "middle of promoting" *A Complicated Kindness,* she decided that she would not write again about Mennonites. She changed her mind, though, calling it a "silly" decision (qtd. in Heidenreich 43), and wrote the novel *Irma Voth,* set in an Old Colony Mennonite community in northern Mexico—a Plautdietsch community whose members will probably never read it or respond to their representation in it. Most recently, in a high-profile address to the International Festival of Authors in Toronto, Toews said that she understands why Mennonites might object to her books but goes on to say that such criticism reflects "arrogance and embarrassment. And self-image."[1]

Literary Critics

The preceding discussion of Mennonite readers' informally stated reception of transgressive literature is complemented by a small but continuing discussion of that problem, in print, by professional Mennonite literary critics, usually academics with advanced degrees in literary studies from major universities. The main examples are Elmer Suderman (PhD, Kansas), John Ruth (PhD, Harvard), and Al Reimer (PhD, Yale).

In critiquing *A Complicated Kindness* in *Queen's Quarterly,* James Neufeld faults Toews for reducing "the complexities of faith to the simplicities of its prohibitions" and contenting "herself with superficial satire instead of sustained social commentary" (101). Most recently, Valerie Weaver-Zercher wrote a negative review of *Mennonite in a Little Black Dress* in *Christian Century*, criticizing the memoir for giving a reductive view of Mennonites by "treasuring their eccentricities and pointing out their provinciality" (54).

Such reviewing began in 1949 with a critique of *The Flamethrowers* by Elmer Suderman (1920–2003), whose list of negative descriptors of Mennonites in that novel was cited earlier. He added that "it is poor taste to use any particular religious, cultural, racial, or ethnic group for themes of this nature" ("Pioneer" 109). In 1967, he called Friesen's novel an "anti-Mennonite" work ("Character" 127). Suderman was apparently the first professional Mennonite literary critic in North America. Brad S. Born, a more generous critic of *The Flamethrowers,* nevertheless wrote recently that Friesen seems to "denounce his Mennonite community" and is "certainly bitter and perhaps unfair" (113). With the publication of Wiebe's *Peace Shall Destroy Many* in 1962, Suderman found that his judgment of *The Flamethrowers* had mellowed: "Let the Mennonite writers write and not worry too much about their audience, either Mennonite or Non-Mennonite, whether they will approve or object, but speak the truth in love—or, if need be, in anger—to all" ("Mennonites" 25).

A long, complex discussion of transgressive Mennonite literature is the 1998 forum in the journal *Preservings* sponsored by its editor, Delbert Plett (1948–2004), a lawyer (QC) and historian who wrote voluminously on his people, the Kleine Gemeinde, in order to rehabilitate their reputation in Mennonite historiography. The forum derives from Plett's sense that "the Russian Mennonite literary tradition [is] unique among the world's literature for being mainly obsessed with negating the validity of its own spiritual ethos and historical tradition as a culture of significance and worth" ("Russian" 110). The forum consists of his concluding essay, preceded by discussions by Ralph Friesen, a historian; Douglas Reimer, a lecturer at the University of Winnipeg and eventual author of *Surplus at the Border: Mennonite Writing in Canada* (2002); and my own review of Al Reimer's book *Mennonite Literary Voices: Past and Present* (1993). Plett, Friesen, and Reimer were all from the Kleine Gemeinde tradition (now the Evangelical Mennonite Conference church). Patrick Friesen (Kleine Gemeinde) and Di Brandt were the main authors discussed in the forum.

Although Friesen criticizes Plett for desiring a historiography that idealizes too much the Kleine Gemeinde tradition, he admits that "the positive aspect of our ancestors' lives remains, in terms of fiction or poetry, largely hidden in the shadows" (111). Reimer's discussion of Friesen and Brandt is nuanced and sympathetic, but Reimer makes shrewd observations about them as minority writers in English-dominant culture: "It does not surprise me that early Mennonite artists like Friesen and Brandt played to the powerful major group and in the process seemed to revile the communities which raised them. They did this partly because they felt rejected by their own non literary communities, and partly because of their own vain desire to be heard by as large and important an audience as possible" (review 114). He adds, "A major group commonly makes sport of minor groups. The major group finds minor groups queer, crazy, or even stupid, and by making this sort of sport they manage to get to look pretty good to themselves" (114). Plett, citing "the racist aspects of Anglo-conformity" in Canadian culture, claims that *The Shunning* catered to "audiences pleased to affirm their 'Anglo-conformist' view of minority and ethnic groups" ("Zen" 114). He thinks that the transgressive elements in Friesen's and Brandt's works were brought about by their reactions to their church communities' pursuit in the 1950s and 1960s of the theology of "Fundamentalists, Pietists and Revivalists" (115) in order to proselytize outsiders, in the process moving away from, even condemning, their Mennonite heritage.

The thoughtful work most often invoked in discussions of transgressive Mennonite literature is John Ruth's early pamphlet *Mennonite Identity and Literary Art* (1978). Ruth speaks from the Swiss Mennonite community in the United States, a perspective that sometimes marginalizes him in discussions of Canadian Mennonite literature. Mentioning only authors Rudy Wiebe and Warren Kliewer, Ruth worries about "the multifarious North American process of acculturation, the individual or communal abandonment of our identity, the absorption of our story by another story, so that we have no story" (20). He warns against the "suburban, socially and professionally upward-mobile Mennonites who find the peculiarities of their tradition embarrassing" (64). That cultural embarrassment, he writes, "pretends to be sophistication" (22). He is confident that Mennonite authors can match the creative imagination of Mennonite theologian John Howard Yoder in "releas[ing] the depth-meaning of what to some is an outworn traditional testimony" (56).

Ruth and the *Preservings* critics try to describe what a desirable Mennonite literature would be like. Ruth calls for Mennonite literature that "strikes a creative balance between critique and advocacy" (63) and is "an aesthetically serious representation of our ethos in its classic issues—obedience, simplicity, humility, defenselessness, the questioning of progress, the maintenance of identity" (23). Plett finds his model for a "more inclusive and holistic" literature in *Mirror of a People: Canadian Jewish Experience in Poetry and Prose* (1985; see Oberman and Newton), which, he suggests, presents prominent Jewish writers who are "confident enough in their minor voice to also portray the positive elements of their own culture (and by definition their own being)" ("Zen" 116).

Douglas Reimer says, "What we Mennonites need now is a deliberate, more mature art which understands the conventions of major literature but which subverts those conventions in order to show its support of the communities which raised them. We need artists who will take leadership roles in their communities, artists who will be thinkers within, not outside the community" (review 114).

Opposing these writers and, I think, contributing to the production of transgressive Mennonite literature is the position of Al Reimer, as articulated in his influential set of lectures *Mennonite Literary Voices* (1993). His is the stream of thought most often invoked in discussions of Canadian Mennonite literature, to the extent that Plett regards it as the "politically correct" position in Mennonite literary circles ("Zen" 115). As I characterize it in my 1993 review of Reimer's book, "[Reimer] defends . . . writers in their seeming battle with the Mennonite community, which they criticize and which, in turn, rejects them—to their dismay. . . . Reimer [gives] an impassioned plea for accepting the literary artist as a visionary prophet standing free at the edge of the community and speaking words that the community needs to hear in order to correct itself" (110). Just as Ruth gave a list of positive aspects of Mennonite experience that should be affirmed, so too Reimer gave a list of negative aspects of Mennonite reality that should be exposed: "religious traditions and long-accepted prejudices and practices, . . . pressures to conform, . . . ethnic complacency and a whole host of other issues" (70). In taking on the role of prophet, Mennonite writers of "the cultural elite" (65) should confront the "dead weight" (57) of Mennonite tradition, expose it to Mennonites and the world, and take the risk of "themselves contributing to the already ongoing disintegration of ethnic identity" (58).[2]

Most recently, Reimer rose to the defense of *A Complicated Kindness* during the initial Mennonite reaction to the novel. The thesis of his defense is stated in the subtitle of his essay, "Look Homeward, Nomi: Misreading a Novel as Social History." Reimer defends Toews's book by stating a classic defense of fiction:

> A novel makes an imagined world come alive as a fictionalized reality that deals with human experiences we all share. And because fiction sets up this alternative world of reality, controlled and directed by a creator who understands that fictive world, a novel can provide meanings and truths mythologized beyond the reach of history. But the reader can only enter that fictive world through "a willing suspension of disbelief," that is, by accepting that world as real in its own right and not as a falsification of the literal world.

Reimer admits that it is difficult to persuade recreational readers: "The temptation to misread a novel from a historical perspective is almost irresistible when the reader is personally familiar with its setting." He even admits that he had to read *A Complicated Kindness* a second time before being able to appreciate its merits.

Reimer's position here tends to support modernist, formalist approaches to texts as "well-wrought urns" whose meanings are to be found within their formal constructs and discovered through careful explication. No reader-response theory here. His thinking might fit Toews's novel *The Flying Troutmans,* for instance, which has only a generic historical and sociological setting in contemporary popular American culture. But it is disingenuous in regard to a text such as *A Complicated Kindness,* set in a thinly disguised Steinbach, Manitoba, with thinly disguised family and community members. As a result, the "social history" elements in it are equal to the fictive elements. *A Complicated Kindness* also becomes social history when its author discusses the novel, in frequent interviews, in relation to her historical home community and church and the historical problems that it is intended to expose. If the author thereby acknowledges the novel's "social history" relevance, then it is not surprising that Mennonite recreational readers do likewise.

As mentioned above, culturally mainstream readers typically regard works of minority literature as stereotypically representative of their authors' minority cultures—as social history, not as well-wrought urns. That includes educated literary reviewers in newspapers and other media. For instance, the interview of Toews by Terry Gross on National Public Radio in the United States did not discuss the coming of age of Nomi but the social history of Toews herself as a Mennonite. Gross especially probed excommunication, marriage of second cousins, and the banning of worldly pleasures in Mennonite culture. Toews laments that the same thing happened to her in Italy, where reporters and audiences were more interested in her identity as a Mennonite than in the fiction of her novel ("Is There"). Kasdorf reports a similar experience during her interview on National Public Radio (*Body* 50).

Consequences

Although the negative stereotyping in transgressive literature is most often applied at the level of the community, its effects are often felt at the individual level. For instance, the reception in England of *A Complicated Kindness* posed a personal problem for me regarding my reputation among English friends. The

Guardian published a long review by Zoe Williams, who visited Steinbach and interviewed Toews in Winnipeg. Williams pays tribute to the literary excellence of the book, but most of the review emphasizes the peculiar, undesirable aspects of Mennonite culture. It cites "how critical the book is of Mennonite ways" and indirectly quotes Toews as saying that, had she "been writing a factual essay about the Mennonites, she would have been far more critical and damning than her protagonist ever is" ("One"). The *Guardian* review essay is ethnic exoticism.

Having spent three sabbaticals in England, I have friends at the Universities of Warwick and Sheffield as well as in Friends Meetings in Coventry and Sheffield. They tend to be liberals who likely read the *Guardian.* The Mennonite culture depicted in the *Guardian* report absolutely does not represent me and my social history. How do my English friends now regard me? Even if I had the chance, how could I persuade them that my experience has not been like Nomi's, whether by invoking literary theory, by explaining the differences between Russian Mennonites and Swiss Mennonites, or by outlining the differences between the Evangelical Mennonite Conference in Canada and my own Mennonite Church USA? The reception of literary works is part of their accumulated meaning, and the transgressive aspect of Mennonite literature sometimes has social consequences.

In my 1993 review of Al Reimer's *Mennonite Literary Voices,* I said that the "adversarial, corrective and even angry" literature produced by some Mennonite authors "is so good that we would not want it to be otherwise." I still feel that way, even about *A Complicated Kindness,* despite my defense in this chapter of the other point of view in Mennonite folk literary criticism. Books in the transgressive canon have many literary excellences, and negative reputations tend to dwindle over time.

Yes, the dominant role of the "transgressive myth of origins" in Mennonite literary discourse needs to be reconsidered, as Kasdorf has suggested ("Sunday" 8). As an alternative to "transgression" as the originating impulse for Mennonite literature, Gundy suggests "desire" (40). Kasdorf suggests "irony" ("Sunday" 10).

Plenty of fine Mennonite writers do not perpetuate the transgressive tradition, and it is time that we appreciate equally those writers who have offered, as Ruth suggested, "an aesthetically serious representation of our ethos in its classic issues" (23). Gundy, poet and essayist, is one prominent example. As he says, "A necessary separation [from] and critique of 'home' has fueled much of the best Mennonite writing to emerge so far. . . . [But] the myth . . . is not *my* story" (26).

NOTES

This chapter also appears as Ervin Beck, "Transgressive Mennonite Literature," *Mennonite Quarterly Review* 89.2 (April 2015): 299-317.

1. Ironically, the photo that illustrates the abridged version of Toews's address is apparently of Beachy Amish women wearing their distinctive garb rather than the very different group of Mennonites who are the subject of Toews's book. It illustrates again popular stereotypes of Mennonites in mass media and the inability of reporters and researchers to "get it right" regarding the differences among Mennonite groups.

2. Rudy Wiebe's novel *Sweeter Than All the World* seems to satisfy the desiderata of both Ruth and Reimer. See their respective reviews of the novel.

WORKS CITED

Baldanzi, Jessica. Rev. of *Mennonite in a Little Black Dress,* by Rhoda Janzen. *Journal of the Center for Mennonite Writing* 1.5 (2009). Web. Blog responses 18 July 2013.

Beck, Ervin. Rev. of *Mennonite Literary Voices: Past and Present,* by Al Reimer. Plett, ed. 110.

Born, Brad S. "Writing Out from the Mennonite Family Farm: Gordon Friesen's Homegrown Grapes of Wrath." *Mennonite Quarterly Review* 82.1 (2008): 108–26.

Brandt, Di. *Dancing Naked: Narrative Strategies for Writing Across Centuries.* Stratford, ON: Mercury, 1996.

———. *questions i asked my mother.* Winnipeg: Turnstone Press, 1987.

———. *So this is the world & here I am in it.* Edmonton: NeWest Press, 2007.

Davis, Melodie. "Laughing at the Images." *Femonite* 10 May 2013. Web. 18 July 2013.

Dundes, Alan. "Metafolklore and Oral Literary Criticism." *The Meaning of Folklore: The Analytical Essays of Alan Dundes.* Ed. Simon J. Bronner. Logan: Utah State University Press, 2007. 77–87.

Friesen, Gordon. *The Flamethrowers.* Caldwell, ID: Caxton Press, 1936.

Friesen, Patrick. *The Shunning.* Winnipeg: Turnstone Press, 1980.

Friesen, Ralph. Rev. of *Rosanna of the Amish,* by John W. Yoder. Plett, ed. 111–12.

Gundy, Jeff. *Walker in the Fog: On Mennonite Writing.* Telford: Cascadia, 2005.

Heinzekehr, Hannah. "On Martyr Complexes, Memoir, and Misunderstanding." *Femonite* 8 May 2012. Web. 18 July 2013.

Holland, Scott. "Theology Is a Kind of Writing: The Emergence of Theopoetics." *Mennonite Quarterly Review* 71.2 (1997): 227–41.

Janzen, Rhoda. "Interview: Rhoda Janzen, Author of *Mennonite in a Little Black Dress.*" By Laurel Rhame. *Smith Magazine* 22 Apr. 2010. Web. 16 Aug. 2013.

———. *Mennonite in a Little Black Dress.* New York: Henry Holt, 2009.

Kasdorf, Julia Spicher. *The Body and the Book: Writing from a Mennonite Life.* Baltimore: Johns Hopkins University Press, 2001.

———. *Fixing Tradition: Joseph W. Yoder, Amish American.* Telford: Pandora/US, 2003.

———. "Genius and the Verbal Dance: A Conversation About Language, Writing, and Community with John Ruth." *The Measure of My Days: Engaging the Life and Thought of John L. Ruth.* Ed. Reuben Z. Miller and Joseph S. Miller. Telford: Cascadia, 2004. 273–89.

———. Message to the author. 7 July 2013. Email.
———. *Sleeping Preacher.* Pittsburgh: University of Pittsburgh Press, 1992.
———. "Sunday Morning Confession." *Mennonite Quarterly Review* 87.1 (2012): 7–10.
Kroetsch, Robert, et al. "Closing Panel." *Acts of Concealment: Mennonite/s Writing in Canada.* Ed. Hildi Froese Tiessen and Peter Hinchcliffe. Waterloo, ON: University of Waterloo Press, 1992. 223–42.
Lewin, Kurt. *Resolving Social Conflicts: Selected Papers on Group Dynamics.* Ed. Gertrud Lewin. New York: Harper, 1948.
Mierau, Maurice. "Rebel Mennos Move into the Arts." *Midcontinental* 19 (1987–88): 18–23.
Neeper, L. "On Teaching Transgressive Literature." *College English Forum* 37.2 (2008). Web. 18 July 2013.
Neufeld, James. "A Complicated Contract: Young Rebels of Literature and Dance." *Queen's Quarterly* 112.1 (2005): 98–107.
Oberman, Sheldon, and Elaine Newton, eds. *Mirror of a People: Canadian Jewish Experience in Poetry and Prose.* Winnipeg: Jewish Educational Publishers, 1985.
Plett, Delbert, ed. "Russian Mennonite Literature, a Great Tradition?" [Symposium.] *Preservings* 12 (1998): 110–16.
———. "Zen and the Art of Literary Portrayal." Plett, ed. 114–16.
Probst, R.E. "Transactional Theory in the Teaching of Literature." *ERIC Digest* 1987. Web. 18 July 2013.
Reimer, Al. "Look Homeward, Nomi: Misreading a Novel as Social History." *Mennonite Life* 60.2 (2005). Web. 18 July 2013.
———. *Mennonite Literary Voices: Past and Present.* North Newton, KS: Bethel College, 1993.
———. Rev. of *Sweeter Than All the World,* by Rudy Wiebe. *Journal of Mennonite Studies* 20 (2002): 227–29.
Reimer, Douglas. Rev. of *Rosanna of the Amish,* by John W. Yoder. Plett, ed. 112–14.
———. *Surplus at the Border: Mennonite Writing in Canada.* Winnipeg: Turnstone Press, 2002.
Roth, Philip. *Reading Myself and Others.* New York: Farrar, Straus and Giroux, 1975.
Ruth, John. *Mennonite Identity and Literary Art.* Scottdale: Herald Press, 1978.
———. Rev. of *Sweeter Than All the World,* by Rudy Wiebe. *Mennonite Quarterly Review* 77.4 (2003): 727–30.
Stallybrass, Peter, and Allon White. *The Politics and Poetics of Transgression.* Ithaca: Cornell University Press, 1986.
Suderman, Elmer. "The Mennonite Character in American Fiction." *Mennonite Life* 22 (1967): 123–29.
———. "The Mennonite Pioneer." *From the Steppes to the Prairies.* Ed. Cornelius Krahn. Newton, KS: Mennonite Publishing Office, 1949. 102–15.
———. "Mennonites, the Mennonite Community, and Mennonite Writers." *Mennonite Life* 47.3 (1992): 21–26.
Teichrow, Allan. "Gordon Friesen: Writer, Radical, and Ex-Mennonite." *Mennonite Life* 36 (1983): 4–17.
Toews, Miriam. *A Complicated Kindness.* New York: Counterpoint, 2004.
———. *The Flying Troutmans.* Toronto: Alfred Knopf, 2008.

———. "Fresh Air." Interview by Terry Gross. National Public Radio 5 Jan. 2005. Web. 18 July 2013.
———. Interview by Rosmarin Heidenreich. *Rhubarb* 31 (2012): 48–50.
———. *Irma Voth.* Toronto: Knopf, 2011.
———. "Is There Such a Thing as a National Literature?" *Guardian* 16 Nov. 2012. Web. 18 July 2013.
———. "A National Literature [abridged]." International Festival of Authors, Toronto, 25 Oct. 2012. Web. 18 July 2013.
———. "The One That Got Away." Interview by Zoe Williams. *Guardian* 23 July 2004. Web. 18 July 2013.
Tompkins, Jane P. "An Introduction to Reader-Response Criticism." *Reader-Response Criticism: From Formalism to Post-Structuralism.* Ed. Jane P. Tompkins. Baltimore: Johns Hopkins University Press, 1980. ix–xxvi.
Weaver-Zercher, Valerie. Rev. of *Mennonite in a Little Black Dress,* by Rhoda Janzen. *Christian Century* 20 Oct. 2009: 51–54.
———. *Thrill of the Chaste: The Allure of Amish Romance Novels.* Baltimore: Johns Hopkins University Press, 2013.
Wiebe, Rudy. *First and Vital Candle.* Toronto: McClelland and Stewart, 1966.
———. *My Lovely Enemy.* Toronto: McClelland and Stewart, 1983.
———. *Peace Shall Destroy Many.* Toronto: McClelland and Stewart, 1962.
Yoder, Joseph W. *Rosanna of the Amish.* Scottdale: Herald Press, 2008.

4

Double Identity

Covering the Peace Shall Destroy Many *Project*

PAUL TIESSEN

The dissonance between the book and its cover is startling in the case of Rudy Wiebe's first novel, *Peace Shall Destroy Many,* published by the venerable Canadian press McClelland and Stewart (M&S), on 13 October 1962. It is also instructive. Recent archival revelations suggest that, contrary to conventional presuppositions, the *Peace Shall Destroy Many* project—most noticeably at the moment of the book's first appearance—was not Wiebe's alone.[1] In particular, the cover design—in its brilliant swagger so at odds with the tone and timbre of Wiebe's text—must have induced shuddering among what became some of the book's most vociferous early readers. By extending our understanding of this urtext within Mennonite literary culture, I suggest, we are invited to understand "Mennonite" literary works more generally as the products of multiple, including particularly "non-Mennonite," hands. Hence, we are invited to regard

My sincere thanks to Rudy Wiebe for permission to quote from hitherto unpublished work, including our email correspondence, and to Frank Newfeld for permission to quote from our email correspondence and for permission to reproduce his *Peace Shall Destroy Many* cover design. Also, my sincere thanks to Suzanne McClelland Drinkwater for permission to quote from hitherto unpublished writings by Jack McClelland. Warmest thanks, too, to archivists in Winnipeg (Jon Isaak, Centre for Mennonite Brethren Studies), Calgary (Marlys Chevrefils, Special Collections, Libraries and Cultural Resources, University of Calgary), and Hamilton (Rick Stapleton, The William Ready Division of Archives and Research Collections, Mills Memorial Library, McMaster University) and their colleagues for their generous help and support. Thanks also to Sam Steiner, John Rempel, and Matt Tiessen, who made dust jacket copies available to me, to Frank Newfeld's publisher Tim Inkster, and to the press's readers of this chapter.

what we hitherto have come to know as "Mennonite" writers as, indeed, hybrid creatures, for in the making (as in the reception) of Mennonite texts many forces and factors, from the complementary to the contradictory, are at work. Indeed, we are reminded that a Mennonite writer—shaped by a vast horizon of literary and other events—is also always, already, a non-Mennonite writer.

For more than five decades, this foundational text for Mennonite literary studies, *Peace Shall Destroy Many*, has mapped out a prominent place by combining renown with notoriety. Its high visibility is a product more of the opposition that it generated as what Wiebe himself has called a "small explosive device" ("Afterword" 293) than its considerable achievement as a work of fiction. That is, its reputation is rooted in the "firestorm" (Kroeker 89) of negative reaction that it aroused among Mennonite readers in Canada, a reaction strong enough to force Wiebe (b. 1934) to step down by 30 June 1963 from his influential position as founding editor of the *Mennonite Brethren Herald*. American poet and essayist Julia Spicher Kasdorf argues that the brouhaha surrounding its reception has sent a message that "the publication of a work of literature by a big, worldly press . . . was so transgressive that Wiebe became an exile" (7). Over the decades, she says, his early troubles have become "a freighted myth of origins for Mennonite writers" (7).

The "uproar" in the fall of 1962 (Wiebe, "Afterword" 294), spilling over well into 1963, was a Mennonite phenomenon focused within the Canadian Mennonite Brethren denomination (concentrated in western Canada as well as Ontario) of which Wiebe was one of some 15,000 baptized members. Since January 1962, the religious-reform-minded Wiebe had been serving as a controversial editor of the denomination's English-language national magazine, but there his criticisms and proposals were contained within the religious readership to whom they were directed. That he held such an influential post so intensified Mennonites' responses to the novel that by early 1963 reactions mushroomed into an "inevitable explosion" (Wiebe, "Skull" 16), culminating in his departure from the position.[2] His co-religionists' sense—given shape and momentum, I will argue, by the novel's astonishing dust jacket—that his novel had been appropriated by a "big, worldly press" that had its eye on worldly (non-Mennonite) traffic put them on high alert.

The cover statement (or "blurb," as internal memos of the press referred to it)—making bold demands, like some public billboard, and with its claims about Wiebe's fictional world marked by "prejudice and bigotry"—left these Mennonites feeling betrayed (see fig. 1). Submerged within their persistent complaints about the content of Wiebe's work was a barely articulated accusation of his having given up sole ownership of his project. What Wiebe's

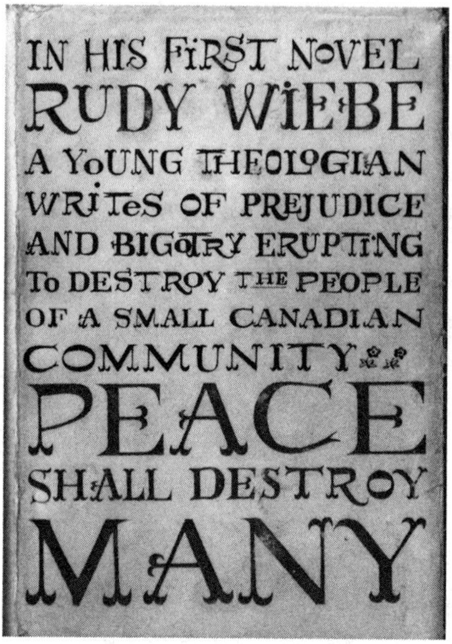

FIG. 1 Cover of *Peace Shall Destroy Many* (Toronto: McClelland and Stewart, 1962). Used by permission of McClelland & Stewart, a division of Random House of Canada Limited, a Penguin Random House Company.

accusers intuitively recognized, I would suggest, was that an important degree of control over his project had passed precipitously into unsympathetic hands whose fingerprints were all over the dust jacket. Of course, the Mennonites' accusations—"[i]n person and by letter and telephone, from ministers and lay people" (Wiebe, "Afterword" 294)—were directed not at M&S, within whose office and studio spaces the creators of the language and look of the cover were safely ensconced, rendered faceless, but at Wiebe. "You wash our dirty laundry in public—what will they think of us?" they charged, implying surveillance of their enclosed world by non-Mennonites. "If it was just written for church members [as in the case of the national magazine that Wiebe edited]—well, okay, but in English, spread all over Canada?" "It's like going to the bathroom with the door open," they claimed, squirming at things having gone out of their control. And from respected leaders anxious about their immigrant culture finding its way in Canada: "This book will make further immigration of our people into Canada much more difficult" (qtd. in Wiebe, "Afterword" 294–95).

Wiebe's detractors need not have read the book, of course. Indeed, often they did not. "Sometimes," as a Winnipeg-based literature professor, Herbert Giesbrecht, himself active in the Mennonite community, wrote in March 1963, "the most stringent and ready-made criticism [came] from folk who had themselves only heard of the novel or, at best, merely dipped into it here and there"

(51). For such folk, a glance at the shock tactics of the dust jacket—with its cocky brashness and sensationalism about a people unaccustomed to "public and not necessarily flattering scrutiny" (Kroeker 89)—would have confirmed that Wiebe's novel had been taken over and commodified by what Mennonites used to call "the English."[3] These early readers, however unintentionally, have helped us to see that the "Mennonite" literary text ought rightly to acknowledge multiple points of origin besides the purely "Mennonite."

For Wiebe, the "convulsion" that followed the publication of his first novel was difficult (qtd. in Keith 131). But at the same time, it was also the consequence of an energizing event. He had, after all, sought from the beginning "a non-religious publishing house,"[4] just as he would court non-religious (along with religious) reviewers, critics, honors, awards.[5] A close look at its production, promotion, and reception gives us some insight into the fascinating dynamic that transformed *Peace Shall Destroy Many* into a project that, more palpably than most books, dramatized its own hybridity, its multiple ownership.

My focus here is narrow: glimpses of the forces that led to the development of the dust jacket of the first edition. In its wording and design, the dust jacket—unique among dust jackets in Canada (or anywhere else, for that matter) in its address of and demands on its author/book and its readers—spectacularly showcased its own origins and ownership: that is, of its publisher and the designer rather than of Wiebe.

It was a non-Mennonite, Wiebe's creative writing teacher, Professor Frederick M. Salter, who in 1959 laid before Wiebe the "ultimate temptation" to write a novel about his people as his MA thesis (Wiebe, "Skull" 13). He convinced Wiebe to add the foreword concerning "Anabaptists of the sixteenth century" to the manuscript, so that people would have a rough historical/religious framework for the events of the novel—the coming of age during 1944 of Thom Wiens. Wiens, nineteen years old, seeks a means of overcoming rigid traditions within his prairie-based Mennonite community of Wapiti in light of larger demands both of an enlightened view of biblical teaching and of the war raging in Europe. Salter—recognizing the novel as a springboard for Wiebe's long-range ambitions—encouraged Wiebe to submit it to M&S (which he did, on 25 May 1960) and wrote a letter on 30 May in support of Wiebe to the president, Jack McClelland. McClelland, a scion of the "upper-middle echelons of Toronto's WASP society" (King xviii), and thus considerably removed from anything Mennonite in Canada, might have been struck by Salter's comment—was it commendation or warning?—that his prairie-based protégé was "a Mennonite" with a novel about "a Mennonite community" like those tradition-bound communities that Wiebe wanted to bring into "the modern world." Salter notified Wiebe that he had contacted McClelland (Wiebe, "Skull" 14–15) but avoided telling him that he had identified him as Mennonite.

In his own letter, addressed to "Dear Sirs" at M&S, Wiebe did not identify himself as Mennonite, perhaps imagining that such an identity might not stand him in good stead with anyone at the publishing heart of Anglo-Canada.[6] However—again without mentioning the term "Mennonite"—he drew careful attention to his historical foreword. The foreword was a detached statement bearing the tone of an encyclopedia entry rather than a personal confession, and it provided a historical frame for the novel, pointing abstractly to "peculiar" customs, language, and literal-minded faith in the Bible that these self-isolating German-speaking Mennonite people carried with them (7). Wiebe made it clear that the foreword gave enough explanatory material about these "peculiar" people, even though he did allow that it "could be changed or expanded on your advice" (letter, 25 May 1960). He seemed to imply that, should the daily customs of his characters require explanation, it could be added to the foreword rather than mixed into the main text, where he preferred a certain sparseness of description. He also seemed to imply in the letter that while a Mennonite society provided the occasion for the novel—which was "completely my own work and completely ficticious"—its circumstances might apply just as readily to some other cultural group.

However, M&S, as we shall see, wanted the texture of the everyday life of Mennonites *as Mennonites*—more and fuller descriptions of their clothing, housing, food—mixed right into the story itself. It wanted a fuller embodiment, too, of a normative Mennonite voice and of a resolution of that voice at the conclusion of the novel. But at the end of its substantial editorial interventions, and Wiebe's just as substantial responses, M&S remained uneasy. It decided to take the last word—and, looking ahead to a hoped-for readership, the first word—into its own hands. Thus, for readers opening or closing the book, the blurb trumpeting noisily on the book's front and back covers provided a set of reading instructions, as it were, in effect signifying that the publisher and designer were having their say in determining the impression of the reader's first and last—perhaps only—moments of experiencing the book. The blurb's provocative text and its audacious visual style made clear the publisher's position in relation to Wiebe and his story. In its cheeky display of (very non-Mennonite) authority, it claimed its role as cultural arbiter.

The twenty-eight words of the blurb jostle for space on a vividly red-and-black-on-white dust jacket of the first Canadian and American hardcover editions. The blurb—repeated with mirror precision on the back cover though with the colors reversed—elbows to all four edges, filling the space of the cover. For a "thoughtful reader" (to take one of Wiebe's own terms from another context), the jacket seems to be zanily at odds with the book that it covers or—perhaps it is not inappropriate to suggest—covers up. Its language implies that readers are in for an action story, one with "prejudice and bigotry erupting to destroy the people of a small Canadian community"—indeed, a small "Mennonite" community, as a peek inside the cover flap informs us.[7] The blurb seems less to acknowledge than to restlessly short-circuit the complex achievement of the book. Forcefully stated and daringly visualized, in its very presence it surely shaped—and, indeed, must have given cover to—the hostility directed toward Wiebe during the twelve months after the book's launch in October 1962.

Briefly, I want to propose an additional reading. The "look" of the blurb, I suggest, actually complicates how we read the saucily melodramatic statement on which it "draws." True, on the one hand, the look gives the blurb a casual irreverence, flip playfulness, or careless disregard for what thoughtful readers soon discover is an earnest and theologically freighted story lyrically informed by Wiebe's evocative treatment of the rhythms of rural life. However, on the other hand, the astonishing look of the blurb—its visual design—parodies and playfully deconstructs the strident clichés of its own wording, thus arguably freeing readers (and Wiebe) from any absolute demands of the statement's pushy and presumptuous jargon.

But either way the blurb content and blurb design taken together act rhetorically as a shock tactic that bespeaks M&S's breezy claim to mastery over a cover message marked as its own and over its decision to publish the untried "young theologian." The tactic signals to mainstream readers that the publisher jauntily approves the book for their quick consumption and entertainment. Indeed, with this daringly executed cover, M&S, I would argue, in a gesture of perhaps protesting too much, acts out both its ownership and its subtle disavowal of the book. As performance, the cover provides the publisher with a winking alibi that gives it permission to make the then-unknown and sober-minded Wiebe safe for its readers this time around. Jack McClelland himself—always privately concerned about his firm's taking on what seemed to him this unlikely project and at the start letting his trusted editor Claire Pratt know that M&S should "try and talk Wiebe into setting this aside" (letter, 26 Sept. 1960)—now proclaimed in the blurb that this was but a "first novel," with the implied promise of greater things ahead.

The cover's dramatic efficacy among and impact on readers were rooted not only in the wording but also in the design. M&S had recently begun to turn some of its covers (and, indeed, books)—including this one—over to the designer and illustrator Frank Newfeld (b. 1928). Newfeld used the Wiebe book cover—like others assigned to him—as a canvas for his own artistic, and sometimes iconoclastic, gesture and genius. Three years earlier, he had broken into the forefront of book design in Canada with his participation in novels such as Sheila Watson's *The Double Hook* (1959).[8] For Newfeld, both the Watson and the Wiebe projects occurred during what he later described as the "golden age" of book design in Canada (*Drawing* 313).[9]

Newfeld's inventive cover art for Wiebe's novel featured freehand, pen-and-ink calligraphy. The individually penned letters of the words, mostly in caps, include playful and allusive serifs—some appearing whimsically as soft double hooks, a few hinting at forked tongues or the double tails at the end of a whip. There are no punctuation marks, unless we count as a colon two stylized flowers that, we discover on opening the book, allude to the graphics in its "Summer" prelude. Newfeld's ironic awareness of the baldness, the declamatory stridency, of the language of the blurb, so at odds with the theological conversations in Wiebe's angst-ridden bildungsroman, emerges through the carnivalesque of his "drawn word" (Newfeld, *Drawing* 320), eleven lines bouncing frantically from top to bottom: "IN HIS FiRST NoVEL / RuDY WiEBE / A YoUNG THEOLoGIAN / WriTeS OF PREJUDICE / AND BIGoTRY ERuPTiNG / To DESTRoY THE PEOPLE / OF A SMALL CANADIAN / COMMUNITY: / PEACE / SHALL DESTROY / MANY."[10]

If this cocky signal of ownership and authority arose out of Jack McClelland's "old Toronto" (King xviii), it also bore the sly wit of a "new Toronto," for Newfeld was Czech born, his accent and manner making him readily discernible as "a newcomer to Canada" (Newfeld, *Drawing* 228).[11] "I wanted people to pick up the book," he recalls now of his exuberant cover, "even if they hadn't read any review!" (message, 24 May 2013).

During the summer of 1960, between mid-June and early August, some of Jack McClelland's editorial staff along with other assigned readers engaged in the first round of assessing Wiebe's manuscript. Their reports went directly to McClelland himself. Conway Turton, M&S's "dean of Canadian editors" (as Newfeld calls her [*Drawing* 324]), was particularly severe. She thought Wiebe's characters but "simple souls" left finally "bewildered"; she found his accounts of violence and tragedy "lurid" and the conclusion packed with "bathos." She could not envision readers "sufficiently serious-minded to bother about the beliefs, customs, and moral problems of the Mennonites." Another seasoned colleague, trained at the University of Toronto, Columbia University, and the Boston Museum of Fine Arts School, was Claire Pratt, whom McClelland's biographer calls a "dedicated and meticulous editor" (King 95). Pratt was more sympathetic to the novel's possibilities—and was subsequently put in charge of the project—but she was suspicious about Wiebe's capacity as an English speaker. A comic moment makes its mark when the reader encounters in the M&S archive Pratt's feeling that, should the manuscript be "completely rewritten in English," it might stand possibilities. Then someone's—possibly McClelland's—hand appears in the margin of her typed report: "have talked to him on phone—no accent."

Seven or eight of his colleagues provided McClelland with something of a split decision on the work, as he put it in his first letter to Wiebe (on 18 Aug. 1960), with "two of our senior editors . . . somewhat less than enthusiastic." However, these senior editors, he indicated, thought that the manuscript "could benefit from a careful revision." McClelland himself—then, according to his biographer, at the height of a period of "magnetic, dazzling leadership" at M&S and very involved in determining the fate of projects submitted there (King 95)—read the manuscript only in late August or September. While agreeing with Pratt that "the author has considerable talent" and was capable of "first-rate" description and some good characterization, he sided firmly with those who had doubts. "I think it's too dull and depressing at the start and too unconvincing at the end," he told Pratt. He even thought that the respected Salter—who earlier had brought Watson's *The Double Hook* to his attention and whose influence had spurred consideration of Wiebe's manuscript—was off the mark in suggesting that this work would sell: "The Mennonites certainly won't like it. I can't really imagine who will, at least, in anything close to its present form" (memo to Pratt, 26 Sept. 1960).

After further conversations with her boss that remain undisclosed—archives hide or ignore whatever they so choose—Pratt invited the McGill University–educated Joyce Marshall, a novelist, short-story writer, translator, and, most importantly for Pratt's purposes, well-established and highly regarded freelance literary editor (Everett xii–xv, 253–59), to give her a judgment on the novel. In an undated five-page report, Marshall submitted a thorough analysis of what she saw as the novel's strengths and weaknesses, concluding that the book could be interesting if the author could be persuaded to undertake "a great deal of revision of a fairly comprehensive sort." In a memo of 2 December 1960, Pratt suggested to McClelland that Marshall be invited "to guide" Wiebe. McClelland agreed.

The Marshall-Wiebe relationship was rich, complex, and far reaching, and I can but touch on it here. On 13 December, Marshall sent Wiebe six typed pages of queries and recommendations. Her impact was significant, affecting his articulation of character and theme as well as details of expression and style. But she (along with Pratt, with whom she stayed in close conversation) remained concerned about what M&S saw as his too-abrupt ending. And she worried about his lack of explicit attentiveness to issues of violence and non-violence. Furthermore, she looked in vain for a character offering a fixed and stable account of what she imagined might be the Mennonite culture's essential identity. Just who provided "the ultimate statement of Mennonite belief[?]" she asked Wiebe. Misunderstanding the culture of his prairie Mennonites, she looked for confirmation of "the particular plainness" that characterized Mennonites of whom she had some knowledge, the culturally quite different Old Order Mennonites of Ontario, with their "prayer caps and beards."

On 5 February 1961, Wiebe, expressing gratitude for her reading, provided an interim three-page reply. He resisted producing a single character representing any orthodoxy. He chose instead to address the desire for such clear definitions by having the schoolteacher, Razia, now ask "Who is a Mennonite?" and by having Thom respond "I doubt you'll get an answer in Wapiti—or anywhere" (*Peace* 178). Moreover, Wiebe now distinguished among kinds of Mennonites, having Joseph criticize those who had "fallen into the pitfalls" of "almost equat[ing] Christianity with a certain cut and colour of clothes, prayer caps and beards" (*Peace* 69).[12] Overall, Wiebe had a preference for the narrative gap and was not keen on long descriptions of his characters; he wanted to work with image and symbol and let the "thoughtful reader" do some work, as he mentioned to Marshall: "I don't wish to describe anyone in detail. I feel the reader should be able to see the character in his own mind from what that character says and does, not from names and descriptions I lay into his head."

Marshall responded on 8 February, noting that her worries about the abruptness of the conclusion concerned the lack of a solution to the "moral and ethical problems" that the book raises. She wondered why Wiebe had not adequately responded to her concern about the violence that simmers and erupts in the book. Wiebe wrote back on 11 February, offering a three-page analysis of the violence as well as a discussion of the ending with its intimation of possible new freedoms and responsibilities for Thom lying ahead (and where, later, to Wiebe's great pleasure and surprise, Newfeld would introduce a tiny sketch of a spring flower to replace Wiebe's original "The End"). Wiebe repeated: "I don't want to say these things in the book—the situation should say it for me."

On 14 February, Marshall assured Wiebe that she wanted him to carry on now, "untroubled" by her (or Pratt). On 14 March, Wiebe, returning the manuscript and declaring his work done, added, "At this time I feel this is all I can do with the novel."

In Toronto, Marshall gave her verdict to M&S, reporting that the novel was much improved but that some faults remained. Concluding that Wiebe was "too young" to transcend his material, she thought that he had taken it as far as he could and that the publisher might now "take a chance" on it (letter to Pratt, 23 Mar. 1961). In the second round of reading, this one from late March to early May 1961, the majority of the five or six readers, whatever their misgivings, in general now agreed that the press could attempt publication. But on 8 May, McClelland—reporting to senior administrative colleagues Hugh Kane and Mark Savage—weighed in. Acknowledging that the book was "quite well written," he remained worried about the commercial viability of a story "unlikely to commend itself to others than the non-believers in that [Mennonite] group." Fortunately, however, another matter was at stake for him: the nurturing of Canadian literature itself. With "this chap," McClelland believed that he had come across a "very young" Canadian voice with a promising future, and M&S could help that voice go public: "He is very serious about his writing and should produce more saleable works [than this one]. . . . We need more young writers and this chap is more likely to make good than most."[13] McClelland now claimed to "dislike the novel personally," but in a playful—and, it turned out, accurate—joke at his own expense, he took his doubts as a promising sign: "am certain it will be tough to sell, (which should mean it will sell very well indeed) I favour making it a publishing gesture for fall 1962." In a typed note from the 8 May meeting, there are instructions to inform Wiebe that "we don't anticipate commercial success but will publish because we think it should be published." Pratt put things more graciously to Wiebe on 31 May: "We feel this is a manuscript which should be published and are very pleased to be doing it."

Notwithstanding the press's decision to publish Wiebe's novel, McClelland himself remained worried that it could not possibly stand convincingly before the public. He lamented in his note to Kane and Savage that "[i]t has already been revised at our suggestion so no appreciable further improvement can be expected." His growing frustration with Wiebe and his deepening anxiety about sales found expression, I am suggesting, on the dust jacket of the book.

Cavalierly, and with some chutzpah, McClelland alone, it seems (though perhaps in conversation with Pratt)—clearly no disinterested third-party blurb writer would have had such nerve—devised a bald and spicy declaration for the cover: "In his first novel / RUDY WIEBE / a young theologian writes of the /

violence and hate that can destroy / a small Canadian community."[14] Pratt rushed McClelland's "tentative jacket blurb" (Pratt to McClelland, 29 Jan. 1962) to Wiebe for his approval (Pratt to Wiebe, 6 Feb. 1962). She urged his quick response to the "line" that M&S would "work . . . into" its dust jacket design, presumably unaware herself of the final look of that line. Meanwhile, McClelland passed that line along to Newfeld so that he could sketch a "rough." McClelland directly instructed him, as Newfeld recollects, to put "title, author, plus blurb on the *jacket front.*" It was, says Newfeld, "my first and only jacket with its own blurb on the front! Which made it a challenge" (messages, 23 May and 21 June 2013).

On 14 February 1962, Wiebe replied to Pratt with "some concern" about "[t]he sentence for the jacket." Remonstrating delicately, he pointed out that he was not a theologian and that to say so seemed pretentious, even if it might be "quite catching." He might have added that Mennonites had a history of anxiety about theologians of any kind and would have found use of the term quite foreign. He conceded that to say he was the "editor of a fairly small denominational paper" could not be stated "very fetchingly." Nonetheless, he was grudgingly prepared to consider letting "theologian" stand[15] in exchange for M&S's rethinking the words *violence* and *hate.* He repeated the kind of analysis that he had offered to Marshall: "There is violence there, but it is brought out only because of prejudice and tradition that has set like concrete in the minds of the Mennonites who oppose all change. I do not believe that there is any hate, however, at least not in the minds of those who call themselves Christians—and these are, after all, the ones about whom the story turns." Wishing "not to mislead the reader too much when he looks at the jacket," Wiebe—placing the term "a young theologian" between parentheses to suggest its deletion—proposed new wording: "In his first novel / RUDY WIEBE / (a young theologian) writes of the / prejudice and hardened tradition that can destroy / the people of a small Canadian community." He insisted that "it is important to show that not the community as such is the important item, but rather the faith and belief of the people in it." He conceded that "some of the adjectives could be dropped to make the whole matter a bit more solid," and he looked forward to Pratt's response.

Back in Toronto, McClelland glanced at Wiebe's suggestions and, in an undated handwritten note (perhaps 16 Feb. 1962) that seems to be sternly impatient in tone, informed Pratt that "[Wiebe's] copy defeats our purpose." Accepting Wiebe's word *prejudice,* he asked Pratt which "one strong word" could replace "hardened tradition." They came up with the word *bigotry.* In the meantime, McClelland reinstated the word *violence,* changing Wiebe's "that can destroy" to "that can erupt into violence and destroy." He retained "a young theologian."

On Friday, 16 February, Pratt rushed McClelland's modified sentence to Wiebe, firmly letting him know that his suggestions had not met M&S's—really McClelland's—purpose. She asked him to "wire" his response "collect, by Monday night." M&S, she said, was "in a desperate hurry for this": "'In his first novel / RUDY WIEBE / a young theologian, writes of the / prejudice and bigotry that can erupt / into violence and destroy the people / of a small Canadian community.' PEACE SHALL DESTROY MANY." On the Monday, Wiebe responded to Pratt with a brief sentence: "JACKET APPROVED AS YOUR LETTER FEBRUARY SIXTEENTH."

McClelland's wording for the blurb, as I pointed out earlier, is at odds with the lyrical temper, seasonal rhythms, and thematic reaches of the larger novel. And Wiebe, of course, had no opportunity to see the actual "look" of Newfeld's cover before the book was published (Wiebe to the author, 4 Aug. 2013).

At the fiftieth-anniversary celebration of *Peace Shall Destroy Many*'s appearance in print, Wiebe repeated that "It was truly an explosive cover" ("Hold" 6). Yet, when it appeared fifty years earlier, he did not have the language to comment on it as the work of a fellow artist—or counter-artist—whose name appears on the copyright page: "DESIGN: FRANK NEWFELD." When Wiebe saw the book, he wrote to McClelland on 27 October 1962: "I feel that you have done a very fine job in publishing the book." He was responding to the "kind letter" of 5 October in which a cordial McClelland expressed pleasure at having Wiebe's "very fine book on our list" and hoped that Wiebe would continue to publish with M&S.

Later, on reflection, Wiebe did recall his hesitation about the cover. He remarked more than once (typically with reference to his misgiving about "a young theologian") that "a first-time novelist has no power over cover copy, inside or out—that belongs to the promotion department's idea of what will sell the most books" ("Hold" 6).[16] But Wiebe has not, to my knowledge, deliberated on how the presence of Frank Newfeld (or, of course, McClelland, whom he could not have detected operating behind the scenes) as author of the blurb contributed to the "fantastic ruckus" (Wiebe, qtd. in Keith, *Epic* 25) mounted by his critics during 1962–63. Readers, however, can now identify the presence of "the English" in the quintessentially "Mennonite" *Peace Shall Destroy Many* project; they can even celebrate the blurb as a performance that deconstructively and provisionally loosens the book from its didactic moorings and multiplies its meanings and audiences, giving it an extra life alongside the one claimed and projected by Wiebe alone. Newfeld's vivid presence enables us to acknowledge as essential a critical paradigm that accounts for the non-Mennonite participants who add legitimation and success to the Mennonites' literary experiments. Given the role that *Peace Shall Destroy Many* has taken on as a "myth of origins" for Mennonite writers, it is a paradigm that points to the hybrid origins of Mennonite literary identity itself, to Mennonite literary culture as predicated on and validated by the participation and presence of "the English."

NOTES

1. In March 2012, presenting a paper in the lecture-and-reading series Mennonite/s Writing in Canada: The First 50 Years, I speculated—without the benefit of archival research—about the extent to which the cover of the first edition of *Peace Shall Destroy Many* might have affected reader reception among Mennonites in 1962–63. In 2002, in *Rudy Wiebe: A Tribute* (comp. Hildi Froese Tiessen), I indicated that, when I read *Peace Shall Destroy Many* in 1962 at age eighteen, three words particularly astonished and thrilled me: *McClelland and Stewart.* They signaled that it was possible for a Mennonite to find a literary voice within mainstream Canada. Concerning archives as problematic sources of reliable authority, see my essay "'I Want My Story Told': The Sheila Watson Archive, the Reader, and the Search for Voice." There I consider Wiebe's own exploration of the archive in his "Where Is the Voice Coming From?"

2. For eighteen months, Wiebe's central post in the Mennonite Brethren denomination in Canada had given him, as he describes it, "a 'presence' in every MB [Mennonite Brethren] household in Canada" ("Hold" 2)—a presence, he assumed, that held promise for the book's reception. On 28 September 1962, he wrote to Gretchen Perk, who worked for M&S's promotion department, that with the *Mennonite Brethren Herald* going into "every MB home in Canada . . . I am fairly well known. I believe that there should be good sales among these people."

3. I am using here a term commonly used by Mennonite immigrants to describe just about any non-Mennonite Canadian.

4. For example, in the January 1962 announcement that Wiebe ran in the first issue of the *Mennonite Brethren Herald,* he pointed with enthusiasm to his relationship with M&S: "**First Novel to be Published** / 'Peace Shall Destroy Many,' a novel about the Mennonites from Russia living in Western Canada, will be published . . . by McClelland and Stewart of Toronto. The author, Rudy Wiebe of Winnipeg, is the newly-appointed editor of the *Mennonite Brethren Herald.* It is his first novel and one of the first written by a member of the Mennonite Brethren Church to be published by a non-religious publishing house." In hindsight, these words, expressed with pride and pleasure, seem like the unintentional waving of a red flag.

5. For example, Wiebe went on to win the 1973 and 1994 Governor General's Award for Fiction for his novels *The Temptations of Big Bear* and *A Discovery of Strangers,* respectively.

6. Later, however, Wiebe introduced the idea of the Mennonite reader into his pre-publication correspondence with M&S. For example, on 11 November 1961, he wrote to

editor Claire Pratt about the forthcoming Mennonite World Conference (5–10 Aug. 1962) in Kitchener, Ontario: "Not too many novels have been published about the Mennonites recently, and I feel certain that if the book were out by that time, some good sales publicity could result. Mennonites are tremendously curious about themselves." McClelland expressed enthusiasm for having flyers available at the conference, with the book still not available from the printer in England. On 28 September 1962, Wiebe wrote to Gretchen Perk that people at the conference had been buying "everything that even smelled faintly of Mennonites."

7. The inside flaps—like the dark title of the novel and the ominous epigraph from the Old Testament book of Daniel—invite further analysis beyond my focus here.

8. Sheila Watson found Newfeld's cover design "work of a high order" (Watson to McClelland, 27 Mar. 1959). Years later, according to her biographer Fred Flahiff, she noted that Newfeld's contribution seemed like a "co-creation." She thought that "[s]he had been told something about her book by its cover" (199). In *Drawing on Type,* Newfeld expressed particular pleasure in his bold and experimental approach to Watson's book (326).

9. Newfeld was "[o]ne of Toronto's leading book designers" (Friskney 37), "the first notable postwar book designer in Toronto" (George Bowering, qtd. in Panofsky 224).

10. Where I have marked line breaks, the preceding word or sequence of words fills the entire line of the cover, from left to right; where I have used the colon, the original uses two tiny flowers. Newfeld's technique with Wiebe's book speaks to the title of his autobiography: *Drawing on Type.* Although unique to the cover of Wiebe's book, this technique uncannily anticipates elements of his cover for Dennis Lee's well-known 1974 book for children, *Alligator Pie.*

11. After training and working in England (and changing his name from Neufeld to Newfeld) and in Israel, Newfeld settled in Toronto in 1954, establishing his own design studio and developing a presence in the art-and-publishing world there. In 1958, he became M&S's art director, responsible for typography and design of books and related materials (Kane to Newfeld, 20 Oct. 1958). McClelland gave him free rein at the press, accepting his view that in the publishing industry there were occasions when what mattered "wasn't what the author wanted" but "what the book needed" (Newfeld, *Drawing* 317).

12. Stephanie Anne Larden has pinpointed these and many other changes, large and small, in her thesis "The History of the Editorial Process of Rudy Wiebe's *Peace Shall Destroy Many.*" Wiebe turned to a real-life version of the fictional Wapiti in his memoir, *Of This Earth: A Mennonite Boyhood in the Boreal Forest.* I examine this work, and its portrayal of Wiebe as a relaxed master of the historical telling of his own early life, in contrast to the tensions of the somewhat parallel historical world of *Peace Shall Destroy Many,* in "Memoir and the Re-Reading of Fiction: Rudy Wiebe's *Of This Earth* and *Peace Shall Destroy Many.*"

13. Sam Solecki, editor of McClelland's selected letters, suggests that Wiebe and M&S were a good fit as the 1960s got under way: "What was needed was a stable of M&S novelists, and that is precisely what McClelland gathered during the sixties, as Margaret Laurence, Leonard Cohen, Rudy Wiebe, Mordecai Richler, Brian Moore and Margaret Atwood enlivened the catalogues and the press releases" (41).

14. Here I am quoting Pratt's typed version, based on an earlier version in McClelland's hand. The line breaks follow those in Pratt's letter, though clearly they do not represent any precise intention by Pratt concerning format.

15. In an earlier rough draft, M&S—at least Pratt—toyed with saying "a young Mennonite theologian." In the end, the word "Mennonite" is not used on the outside cover, though both the community and Wiebe are described as Mennonite on the inside flap.

16. In 1987, on the twenty-fifth anniversary of the publication of *Peace Shall Destroy Many,* Wiebe said to a Winnipeg audience that "I had argued as much as any first novelist can about that cover" ("Skull" 15). And in 2001 he wrote, "No first novelist designs his own cover" ("Afterword" 294).

WORKS CITED

Announcement concerning the forthcoming publication of Rudy Wiebe's *Peace Shall Destroy Many. Mennonite Brethren Herald* 1.1 (1962): 3.

Everett, Jane, ed. *In Translation: The Gabrielle Roy–Joyce Marshall Correspondence.* Toronto: University of Toronto Press, 2005.

Flahiff, F.T. *Always Someone to Kill the Doves: A Life of Sheila Watson.* Edmonton: NeWest, 2005.

Friskney, Janet B. *New Canadian Library: The Ross-McClelland Years, 1952–1978.* Toronto: University of Toronto Press, 2007.

Giesbrecht, Herbert. "O Life, How Naked and How Hard When Known!" *A Voice in the Land: Essays by and About Rudy Wiebe.* Ed. W.J. Keith. Edmonton: NeWest Press, 1981. 50–63.

Kane, Hugh. Letter to Frank Newfeld. 20 Oct. 1958. M&S Archive, McMaster University.

Kasdorf, Julia Spicher. "Sunday Morning Confession." *Mennonite Quarterly Review* 87.1 (2013): 7–10.

Keith, W.J. *Epic Fictions: The Art of Rudy Wiebe.* Edmonton: University of Alberta Press, 1981.

King, James. *Jack, a Life with Writers: The Story of Jack McClelland.* Toronto: Knopf, 1999.

Kroeker, Wally. "The Printed Path to Unity." *For Everything a Season: Mennonite Brethren in North America, 1874–2002.* Ed. Paul Toews and Kevin Enns Rempel. Winnipeg: Kindred Productions, 2002. 81–83.

Larden, Stephanie Anne. "The History of the Editorial Process of Rudy Wiebe's *Peace Shall Destroy Many.*" MA thesis, University of Alberta, 1989.

Marshall, Joyce. Letters to Rudy Wiebe. 13 Dec. 1960; 8 Feb. 1961; 14 Feb. 1961. M&S Archive, McMaster University.

———. Report to Claire Pratt. 23 Mar. 1961. M&S Archive, McMaster University.

———. Report to Claire Pratt. N.d. (Nov. 1961?). M&S Archive, McMaster University.

McClelland, Jack. Memo to Claire Pratt. 26 Sept. 1960. M&S Archive, McMaster University.

———. Memo to Claire Pratt. N.d. [c. 16 Feb. 1962]. M&S Archive, McMaster University.

———. Memo to Hugh Kane and Mark Savage. 8 May 1961. M&S Archive, McMaster University.

———. Letters to Rudy Wiebe. 18 Aug. 1960; 5 Oct. 1962. M&S Archive, McMaster University.

Newfeld, Frank. *Drawing on Type.* Erin, ON: Porcupine's Quill, 2008.

———. Messages to the author. 23 May 2013; 24 May 2013; 21 June 2013. Email.

Panofsky, Ruth. *The Literary Legacy of the Macmillan Company of Canada: Making Books and Mapping Culture.* Toronto: University of Toronto Press, 2012.

Pratt, Claire. Letters to Rudy Wiebe. 8 Dec. 1960; 31 May 1961; 6 Feb. 1962; 16 Feb. 1962. M&S Archive, McMaster University.

———. Memos to Jack McClelland. 2 Dec. 1960; 29 Jan. 1962. M&S Archive, McMaster University.

———. Report to Jack McClelland. 2 Aug. 1960 (with undated marginal note). M&S Archive, McMaster University.

Salter, F.M. Letter to Jack McClelland. 30 May 1960. M&S Archive, McMaster University.

Solecki, Sam, ed. *Imagining Canadian Literature: The Selected Letters of Jack McClelland.* Toronto: Key Porter Books, 1998.

Tiessen, Hildi Froese, comp. *Rudy Wiebe: A Tribute.* Kitchener, ON: Sand Hills Books, 2002.

Tiessen, Paul. "'I Want My Story Told': The Sheila Watson Archive, the Reader, and the Search for Voice." *Basements and Attics, Closets and Cyberspace: Explorations in Canadian Women's Archives.* Ed. Linda Morra and Jessica Schagerl. Waterloo, ON: Wilfrid Laurier University Press, 2012. 263–80.

———. "Memoir and the Re-Reading of Fiction: Rudy Wiebe's *Of This Earth* and *Peace Shall Destroy Many.*" *Text Matters: A Journal of Literature, Theory, and Culture* 1 (2011): 201–15.

Turton, Conway. Report to Jack McClelland. 1 July 1960. M&S Archive, McMaster University.

Watson, Sheila. Letter to Jack McClelland. 27 Mar. 1959. M&S Archive, McMaster University.

Wiebe, Rudy. "Afterword." *Peace Shall Destroy Many.* Toronto: Vintage Canada, 2001. 291–96.

———. "Hold Your Peace." MS. 13 Oct. 2012. Collection of Rudy Wiebe, Edmonton.

———. Letter to Dear Sirs (M&S). 25 May 1960. M&S Archive, McMaster University.

———. Letter to Gretchen Perk. 28 Sept. 1962. M&S Archive, McMaster University.

———. Letter to Jack McClelland. 27 Oct. 1962. M&S Archive, McMaster University.

———. Letters to Claire Pratt. 11 Nov. 1961; 14. Feb. 1962. M&S Archive, McMaster University.

———. Letters to Joyce Marshall. 5 Feb. 1961; 11 Feb. 1961; 14 Mar. 1961. M&S Archive, McMaster University.

———. Message to the author. 4 Aug. 2013. Email.

———. *Peace Shall Destroy Many.* Toronto: McClelland and Stewart, 1962.

———. "The Skull in the Swamp." *Journal of Mennonite Studies* 5 (1987): 8–20.

———. Telegram to Claire Pratt. 19 Feb. 1962. M&S Archive, McMaster University.

5

After Ethnicity

Gender, Voice, and an Ethic of Care in the Work of Di Brandt and Julia Spicher Kasdorf

ANN HOSTETLER

In *Pocahontas's Daughters: Gender and Ethnicity in American Culture,* Mary V. Dearborn suggests that ethnic writing in America "allows us to see in a new light the ways in which difference or 'otherness' has always been an integral part of American culture" (4). Writing in the mid-1980s, when ethnic and women's writing entered the literary mainstream and inspired new critical approaches, Dearborn posits that both the ethnic writer and the woman writer in particular stand in for the other in cultural definitions of the self. Just as "woman" is implicitly both included and othered in the universal use of the term "man," the ethnic woman writer is both included and elided in definitions of ethnicity. However, because of her doubly othered status, the work of the ethnic woman writer can be an illuminating subject of inquiry for understanding the dynamics of an ethnic group as it represents itself to the larger culture.[1]

Over centuries of persecution, migration, and resettlement, Mennonites have evolved into an ethnic and religious diaspora with a specific set of shared beliefs, values, stories, and practices. Originating as a wing of the Radical Reformation in Europe, Mennonites scattered in several directions, some emigrating to the North American colonies before the American Revolution, others moving from Holland to Friesland and Prussia, and eventually Russia, before emigrating to the United States and Canada, and then Brazil and Paraguay, in several waves from the 1870s onward.[2] Mennonites refused to cooperate with a state church because of their Christian convictions that infant baptism and military service were unbiblical; this refusal, and their commitment to mutual accountability in living according to the Sermon on the Mount, have traditionally set them apart from the dominant culture and mainstream Christianity wherever they have settled. In recent generations, however, higher education and economic prosperity, along with the more widespread social acceptance of anti-war sentiments, especially during the American involvement in Vietnam, and the proliferation of ties with non-denominational evangelical Christianity, have caused a high degree of assimilation of many Mennonite groups.

Whereas women played a significant role in the formation of Mennonite (Anabaptist) groups during the Radical Reformation in Western Europe, until recently succeeding generations of Mennonites mirrored the patriarchal norms of the cultures that surrounded them. For instance, Mennonite preaching and theology became the exclusive provinces of men until the late twentieth century.[3] Thus, to be born female in such a group is, in a sense, to be triply othered.[4] As I have argued elsewhere, women writers have made major contributions to the recent development of Mennonite literature and literary studies in North America, perhaps partly because their marginal status within the religious hierarchy allowed them more freedom to explore avenues for literary production as their opportunities for higher education expanded.[5]

Di Brandt and Julia Spicher Kasdorf are major figures in Mennonite writing in Canada and the United States, respectively, who have distinguished themselves as poets, essayists, and scholars. Their award-winning first books, Brandt's *questions i asked my mother* (1987) and Kasdorf's *Sleeping Preacher* (1992), investigate the cultures and families of their Mennonite origins from a gendered perspective, negotiating the act of cultural crossing and individuation in the Mennonite context.[6] Their differences from each other as poets—formal, stylistic, geographic—as well as the distinct Mennonite experiences and geographies that shaped them demonstrate a variety of possibilities for the intersection of the terms "Mennonite," "woman," and "poet."[7] This chapter does not attempt to compare the works of these two writers in terms of literary accomplishment; rather, it inquires into parallels between the roughly contemporaneous careers of these two writers in order to better understand the development of ethnic women's writing in the twenty-first century and Mennonite women's writing in particular. Is it still true, as Dearborn suggested, that the ethnic woman writer is always valued primarily in terms of her ethnic identity, or is it now possible for Pocahontas to come into her own—to speak from a transcultural, gendered subject position for a broader audience? What does she (do they) write about after a first path-breaking book in which a crafted literary voice differentiates itself from its inscribed otherness within the received culture? Does the later work reflect a departure from, or a re-engagement with, the ethnic culture of origin?

Without reducing their work to a list of gendered and sociological categories, I wish to show that the unfolding of Brandt's and Kasdorf's work shares a similar trajectory. This trajectory begins by writing from the embodied self and an awareness of the natural world and moves on to explore stages of female embodiment (sexuality, mothering, vulnerability, nurture, care), drawing on values from the subculture even as it addresses broader issues in the world. By investigating this trajectory, I hope to address the larger question of how the ethnic woman writer can claim and develop her voice in relationship with the broader literary community while retaining, or transforming, her relationship with her ethnic origins.

Brandt's and Kasdorf's first, award-winning books of poetry were, in a sense, "ethnographic announcements," as Kasdorf articulates in her chapter in this volume. Both books create a female Mennonite persona engaged in dialogue with her parental, ancestral culture. As Robert Zacharias notes, in the case of Brandt, entering the literary world with such a gesture means that the ethnic or cultural identity of the writer will always factor into how her work is understood in the discourse of Canadian Mennonite literature, whether or not she considers herself a Mennonite (42). The same can be said of Kasdorf in the context of American Mennonite writing. Yet the work of Brandt and Kasdorf is widely reviewed and discussed in literary circles that exist apart from and beyond that of Mennonite literature as well. Grounded in the exploration of personal voice and the articulation of female subjectivity in relationship to their communities of origin, the first books of Kasdorf and Brandt thus share much common ground with other widely appreciated contemporary ethnic women writers. Their subsequent collections of poetry show a deepened commitment to exploring feminist themes such as embodiment, gender socialization, and voice, though they do not completely abandon ethnic references. The third phase of their writing emerges from the exploration of othering as woman and ethnic subject to embrace themes of environmental, economic, and social justice, articulating an ethic of care. This focus on restorative relationships and cultural healing is rooted in their earlier work but also draws on deeply inscribed pacifist values from their Mennonite heritage, reclaimed and refined in a contemporary idiom and expressed as a desire to engage the world with compassion. This is what I call an "ethic of care": a compassionate witness of oppression, an ecological awareness of the human impact on the planet, and a commitment to share resources and live responsibly with others in the world.

Engaging with the broader communities of poets, writers, and critical theorists, Brandt and Kasdorf have taken on prestigious positions in universities of national rank. At the same time, their work has continued to negotiate a relationship with Mennonite readers and critics—in part because the broader literary community has deemed it worthy of attention. This has prompted Mennonite readers in particular to integrate Mennonite literary production into their broader experiences as readers and to engage in the critique, revision, and reclamation of received Mennonite narratives and histories from a literary point of view. Women writers from Mennonite contexts might be triply othered, but their significant contributions in the literary sphere offer counter-narratives and critiques that can renew and revise the ways that people within and without the subgroup encounter and experience it.

Both Brandt and Kasdorf have benefited from the critical and literary climate in Canada and the United States during their active careers (the 1980s and beyond), a climate that has been receptive not only to women's writing but also to theories by women scholars and critics. Both authors have also participated in shaping this critical discourse. After their first books of poetry were published, Brandt and Kasdorf earned PhDs and took teaching positions in higher education. In addition to authoring multiple books of poetry, both have written collections of essays and scholarly monographs and edited significant anthologies in fields outside Mennonite writing. Brandt, for instance, has engaged in the Canadian feminist literary community in a significant way, co-editing, with Barbara Godard, *Wider Boundaries of Daring: The Modernist Impulse in Canadian Women's Poetry,* while Kasdorf has engaged in the New York literary scene, co-editing, with Michael Tyrell, *Broken Land: Poems of Brooklyn.* By creating intellectual homes for themselves in literary and academic communities outside the Mennonite community, they have garnered support for their daring intellectual and creative work that challenges received narratives from their Mennonite communities.

Brandt's book of lyric essays, *So this is the world & here I am in it* (2007), for example, combines her criticism of Canadian literature with essays that radically revise stories that Mennonites tell themselves about their history, language, relationship with the land, and faith. Her earlier essay collection, *Dancing Naked: Narrative Strategies for Writing Across Centuries* (1995), explored issues of gender and voice in relation to Mennonite identity. In the United States, Kasdorf has framed the conversation about Mennonite voice and writing through her collection of essays, *The Body and the Book: Writing from a Mennonite Life* (2001). Her biography of Big Valley, Pennsylvania, writer Joseph W. Yoder demonstrates her commitment to the historically grounded study of the effects of place, environment, and religious values on shaping the writer's voice. Her recent essay "Sunday Morning Confession"—written in response to the 2012 Mennonite/s Writing conference at Eastern Mennonite University—suggests strategic revisions to the developmental narrative of Mennonite literature in English. Her current project on the effects of fracking for natural gas in western Pennsylvania explores this commitment to understanding the reciprocal relationship of place and voice from a contemporary environmental and ethical perspective. Thus, throughout their careers as scholars and poets, both Brandt and Kasdorf have critiqued and reclaimed values from their Anabaptist communities of origin even as their work addresses broader cultural issues—such as labor, class, and environmental degradation—for multiple audiences.

Forms of Resistance: Establishing Voice, Framing Arguments

In their first books, Brandt and Kasdorf establish their voices in the contemporary lyric mode, drawing on personal experience to articulate their positions as artists in relation to their cultures of origin. "If female ethnicity is . . . a shifting concept on a sliding scale," asserts Dearborn, "it becomes meaningful when the ethnic woman, in writing, fixes her place on the continuum, when, that is, she enters culture" (17). As they create voices and establish styles in these first books, Brandt and Kasdorf also authorize themselves as ethnic writers. Brandt's foreword poem to *questions i asked my mother,* for example, embraces the separation from her community that Brandt foresees will come from her commitment to publish her poetry:

> learning to speak *in public* to write love poems
> for all the world to read meant betraying once &
> for all the good Mennonite daughter I tried so
> unsuccessfully to become

But presciently, the poem ends by suggesting that writing will also bring her "home":

> translating remembering claiming my past
> living my inheritance on this black earth among
> strangers prodigally making love in a foreign
> country writing coming home

In her earlier work, the price of speaking is betrayal, but in her later work Brandt uses her voice to revisit and reclaim her Mennonite past, lament her loss of Plautdietsch, and reinscribe her relationship with the land by revising the Mennonite origin story in her book of essays *So this is the world & here I am in it.* In "Hymns for Detroit: Trans(e)lations of Traditional German Mennonite Hymns," a poetic sequence published in her most recent collection of poems, *Walking to Mojácar* (2010), Brandt revisits favorite hymns with both a critical and a reparative approach.[8] But before such rapprochement could occur, Brandt had to establish the terms on which she would address the narratives received from her family and community of origin. This was the bold and fearless expression of her voice, claiming its power to speak its truths, as experienced in her female body and psyche. "For Brandt, writing and transforming the world are the same act," writes Lorraine Weir in her review of *Dancing Naked* in *Canadian Literature:* "To dance naked, to write the naked self is the ultimate challenge to Mennonite custom and dogma, a challenge which Brandt takes up and records with power and vulnerability." Brandt's recent writing uses the work of writing the "naked self" as a prelude to revising communal narratives in order to reclaim the values that Brandt wishes to salvage and preserve.

Kasdorf's first book, *Sleeping Preacher,* brings together the urban narrator in a cosmopolitan setting with figures and images from her rural Amish and Mennonite heritage, exploring the spaces between. The volume begins with "Green Market, New York," in which the poet encounters an Amish woman at a market stand in Union Square in Manhattan. The poem is written in Kasdorf's signature style, characterized by a clean lyric, the ghost of form, keenly observed details, and metaphors that naturally arise from description.[9] After the two women in the poem recognize their ancestral connection, the poet plays her role of city slicker while the saleswoman displays homespun skepticism: "I choose a pie while she eyes my short hair / then looks square on my face. She knows / I know better than to pay six dollars for this" (3). But the tone shifts from playful to serious when the narrator answers "no" to the Amish woman's question about whether she likes the city, insisting to readers that she does not lie and revealing what she does not say to the Amish woman:

> I don't like New York, but sometimes these streets
> hold me as hard as we're held by rich earth.
> I have not forgotten that Bible verse:
> Whoever puts his hand to the plow and looks back
> is not fit for the kingdom of God. (3)

Thus, Kasdorf announces her commitment to the work of writing and making poetry. Labor, and writing as a form of work, are themes that resurface in her later poems, particularly in her third book, *Poetry in America,* her essay "Work and Hope" in *The Body and the Book,* and her current project on fracking,[10] which builds on her poetic exploration of earth, labor, and place. *Plowing* is also the root word for *verse,* as Kasdorf demonstrates in "Boustrophedon," a sestina written for the artist Warren Rohrer that appears in *Eve's Striptease.* Kasdorf's innovation is her integration of Mennonite ethnography and the lyric poem.[11]

Brandt is an experimental poet, a form breaker, fitting for a poet from an iconoclastic tradition. Her refusal of punctuation, stanzas, and capitalization in *questions i asked my mother,* and her use of spaces on the page to guide the breath and pace of the reader, are hallmarks of her early style. The effect of "breathing with" the poet, and relying on her pauses and syntax to guide one through the logic of the poem, create a sense of intimacy. Although this intimacy invites the reader to conflate the poet's voice with the author's voice, it is crucial to keep in mind when reading both Brandt and Kasdorf that the first-person speaker of a lyric poem is a persona that modulates its distance from the reader and preserves the right to poetic license, as suggested in Brandt's epigraph to *questions i asked my mother:* "Some of this is autobiographical / & some is not." In her early work, the lyric I (or, in her case, the i) plunges the reader into the midst of an argument or a painful—even transgressive—scene, as in "but what do you think," the third poem in *questions i asked my mother,* an argument with the poet's father about the interpretation of scripture:

> but what do you think my father says this verse means if it's not
> about the end of the world look that's obviously a misreading i say
> the verb grammatically speaking doesn't have an object in this
> instance so it can't possibly be made to that's exactly what i mean
> he says waving the book in mid air if my father ever shouted he
> would be shouting now you don't really care about the meaning all
> you ever think about is grammar & fancy words I never even heard of (4)

Even as the poet takes on paternal authority with her school-learned grammar and logic, she refuses standard punctuation and instead runs the two speakers together in a formal entanglement.[12] Thus, the poem enacts the enmeshment and entanglement that it describes, an intimate argument without a solution except the tears of the mother—she is "crying as usual" by the end of the poem—that attempt, unsuccessfully, to dissolve it.

Rather than argue openly with the tradition, Kasdorf's early lyrics present information and offer critique by inference. In contrast to Brandt's argument with the father figure, Kasdorf reveals the socialization of a young girl trained to protect others and deflect attention from herself in "The Interesting Thing," in which she introduces the embodied themes of violation, vulnerability, and how a girl internalizes her "secondary" status. In contrast to Brandt's intimate, breathless style, this poem uses a voice of deliberate detachment, no less intense for its restraint:

> The interesting thing is not that a boy
> would cut off the head of a doll with a toy
> saw. The interesting thing is that the parents
> would blame the girl . . . (*Sleeping Preacher* 30)

The analytical, almost clinical, third-person reportorial style reveals a socialization that forces a child into accepting a false accusation, protecting the brother who tied her up and keeping a neighbor's molestation to herself. Rather than rush the reader into the poem, Kasdorf asks the reader to "notice" what happens and to observe a series of outrages as "interesting things." It is as though the reader becomes an ethnographer, taking notes on a cultural phenomenon. Poet and critic Jeff Gundy suggests that Kasdorf's second book, *Eve's Striptease,* can be viewed as an unfolding of the silences introduced in this poem (213).

Thus, in their first books, Brandt and Kasdorf establish themselves as lyric poets in relationship to the cultural and religious community that has formed them as gendered subjects. Although each poet develops a distinctive tone and style within a different national literary context, their work shares key concerns: the claiming of an individual voice in relation to the particular Mennonite subculture in which the poet was raised, the rebellion implicit in daring to tell family or "insider" stories to an "outside" audience, and the articulation of a specifically female subject position, especially in relation to the ways in which community beliefs have been inscribed or internalized into gendered, bodily experience.

Whereas the scholarly, critical responses to *questions i asked my mother* and *Sleeping Preacher* were overwhelmingly positive, some Mennonite readers responded to Brandt's and Kasdorf's work with criticism and sometimes hostility. In "Bringing Home the Work," Kasdorf recounts her mother's corrections of details in Kasdorf's poems and concerns that Kasdorf told community or family stories in inaccurate ways. The publication of *questions i asked my mother* created a rift between Brandt and her family and community, only recently bridged when she returned to Reinland during the 2009 Mennonite/s Writing conference to read a poem from the collection in the community center at a "faspa" hosted by her home community for a group of Mennonite writers and literary scholars.

Speaking of Gender

Brandt's and Kasdorf's second books are explicitly feminist in focus, relying less on an ethnic construction of voice and identity and more on the perspective of gender that cuts across the boundaries of ethnicity. Brandt's *Agnes in the Sky* (1990) and Kasdorf's *Eve's Striptease* (1998) probe manifestations of love and desire in both their life-affirming and their destructive forms. Each poet, in her distinctive style, intensifies the exploration of boundaries between self and other—between received teachings about living in community and the hard-won voice of an individuated self—as she addresses situations of abuse, both physical and sexual. The teachings of Christian non-resistance in Mennonite culture are ironically revealed to be complicit in silencing women and girls in a culture in which women especially are encouraged to "love their enemies."

In "Non-Resistance, or Love Mennonite Style," from *Agnes in the Sky,* Brandt recounts the ways in which teachings of Mennonite pacifism are internalized by a female child subjected to patriarchal authority and trained in submission:

> turn the other cheek when your brother
> hits you & your best friend tells fibs
> about you & the teacher punishes you
> unfairly . . .
> . . . where
> it gets tricky is when your grandfather
> tickles you too hard . . .
> . . . & the
> only way you will be saved is by
> submitting quietly in your grandfather's
> house your flesh smouldering in the
> darkened room as you love your enemy
> deeply unwillingly & full of shame (38–39)

Brandt exposes the results of schooling a girl in the doctrine of non-resistance in toxic combination with the values of obedience, respect for authority, and submission, all in the breathless style of her early work. She also complicates it by registering the child's own desires aroused in this inappropriate situation. Readers are drawn pell-mell into the child's logic through the second person and a flow of phrases without punctuation that leaves the reader breathless. Brandt's style does not allow the reader to pause and question, for instance, whether the doctrine of "turning the other cheek" logically applies to molestation. In lieu of punctuation, Brandt uses extra spaces, serving, like gulps of air in a child's sobbing, as places to breathe while holding onto the syntax that might break without warning or continue onto the next line.

Both Brandt and Kasdorf, as I will show, use juxtaposition and the arrangement of the poems to create an array of approaches to love, intimacy, and transgression. *Agnes in the Sky* explores and juxtaposes multiple forms of love and healing, not only in its second section, "so many different kinds of love," but also throughout the collection. For instance, the poem "why my father beat us (when we were little)" exposes the practice of corporal punishment in her family and community[13] and how those who experienced it internalized the schema of "the Punisher" and passed it on to subsequent generations:

> . . . he was too big for us Daddy
> too big even for you remembering
> the sting of leather on your own
> little back . . . (54)

It is followed by "my father's hands" (55), in which the poet praises hands that "could fix / anything even our feet our sore ankles / rubbing them at the end of the day." The final poems lament the limits of language, sing praises to the prairie, mourn the degradation of the earth, and celebrate "the alphabet / of desire," invoking a variety of themes taken up in Brandt's later work. Brandt wrote two other volumes of poetry in the 1990s: *Mother/Not Mother* (1992) and *Jerusalem, beloved* (1995). In the words of critic Tanis MacDonald, the former volume "turns toward addressing the historical trauma of political forms of fear and divisiveness as the origin of family violence, extrapolated to the large structures of racism and sexism" (ix). The latter volume emerges logically out of Brandt's shift from personal, embodied experience to explorations of social and historical conflict.[14]

In *Eve's Striptease,* Kasdorf explores the development of a girl into a woman through a variety of experiences of love and abuse. Gundy notes that "*Eve's Striptease* is a book about desire in many forms, both within and without, about gestures of resistance and joyful joining with others as well as pain and submission" (213). His summary gestures toward Kasdorf's multifaceted approach to this subject, exploring stories of victim and perpetrator in the light of an almost relentless self-examination. The collection begins with poems that portray a female speaker as a desiring subject ("First Gestures") who takes pleasure in her own body ("The Sun Lover"), even as she learns about sexual sins in the setting of church discipline ("Sinning"). The four poems that follow explore memories of abuse. The first three—"Flu," "Ghost," and "A Pass"—explore the poet's childhood relationship with an older (non-Mennonite) neighbor who molested her repeatedly. In "A Pass," the poet grapples with the problem of forgiveness:

> *Forgive us our trespasses*
> *as we forgive*, I softly recite
>
> among strangers, remembering
> the hand of an older man
>
> gliding up my thin dress.
> I twist free of him,
>
> keep speaking as if he is just
> a rich family friend chatting,
>
> and I am still safe
> in the shape of my skin. (14)

As the speaker of the poem invokes a formal prayer of forgiveness, she probes the complex ways that the habit of covering over the violation has become encoded in her psyche. The poem ends with the suggestion that the speaker can release the burden of this memory when she acknowledges her own complexity as a desiring subject:

> At last, the lusts of *those*
>
> *who trespass against us* bear
> some resemblance to our own:
>
> shame and rage, heavy as coins
> sewn in the lining of an exile's coat. (15)

The closing image of immigrants drowning because they refused to "shed their heavy garments" (15) implies that compassion for self and other—an acknowledgment of common humanity of victim and perpetrator—is ultimately life giving, an empowering act of release and restitution. "There is no pure use for history," the poet asserts in "Bulbs," as she recalls the history of a friend accused of impropriety and refuses "to slap his famished hand" (17). These poems that explore boundary transgressions are followed by a sequence that brings the striptease of confession into a relationship with broader themes of identity formation, theological narratives, and forgiveness: "Onion, Fruit of Grace," "The Knowledge of Good and Evil," and the title poem, "Eve's Striptease," in which the poet invokes a complex image of "all the desires / a body can hold, how they grow stronger / and wilder with age, tugging in every direction" (22). Drawing on Simone de Beauvoir's reading of immanence and transcendence as rooted in gender, critic Beth Martin Birky notes that in *Eve's Striptease* Kasdorf "portrays a female poet's creative coming of age without relinquishing either the desires her body holds or the knowledge of her body's vulnerability. . . . The poems themselves are the striptease act, the gesture, the performance that reveals that the ideal can never be attained" (611). In these poems, Kasdorf rejects a binary approach and chooses instead one of layered complexity that acknowledges the humanity of speaker and subject.

Both Brandt and Kasdorf expand on individual experience and illuminate it as culturally symbolic,[15] enacting the feminist credo that "the personal is the political." By locating their writing in the condition of embodiment, in particular in the body of the other who has been violated by one with greater power, Brandt and Kasdorf open their poems beyond the boundaries of ideology and tradition to empathic engagement with the reader. Brandt writes extensively about culturally sanctioned and silenced hierarchies and abuses in her book of essays *Dancing Naked;* Kasdorf explores the ways in which Mennonite narratives infused her own response to, and interpretation of, abuse by a non-Mennonite neighbor in *The Body and the Book.* By creating a female voice and feminist critique through which to articulate their experiences as members of the Mennonite body, these writers move beyond ethnicity in their frame of reference but continue their dialogue with Mennonite teachings on nonviolence by challenging and testing them from a feminist perspective, with a view to refining and developing them.

Reclaiming a Usable Past

Both Brandt and Kasdorf "thresh" received values in their poems, attempting to preserve the kernel within the chaff—to borrow an agrarian metaphor invoked by Kasdorf in her poem "Mennonites"—as they revise and incorporate them into their own work. The difference in their stylistic and formal approaches is exemplified in their approach to Mennonite hymns. In particular, we can see this by juxtaposing Brandt's "trans(e)lations" of German Mennonite hymns in *Walking to Mojácar* with Kasdorf's "Rachel on the Threshing Floor," a poetic sequence in *Poetry in America.* Brandt's "trans(e)lations," a term coined by the multilingual poet Erin Mouré, bear little formal resemblance, in terms of either phrase or cadence, to the original hymns that appear in High German beside the poems. Rather, they demonstrate the ways in which hymns are "triggers" for individual associations, even though they might carry over some resonance with the originals.[16]

Kasdorf's elegiac sequence, on the other hand, stays closer to its documentary sources. The entire second section of this four-part poem is taken from Rachel's diaries. The first and third sections rely heavily on anecdote. The final section, "Floating on the *Lobsang,*" invokes a song of praise sung at every Amish church service except for funerals. Kasdorf uses the mechanism of a recording, a distancing technology, to bring her closer to the memory of the grandmother whom she never knew, killed in a tragic buggy accident, through the tones of this hymn:

> . . . Against all tradition,
> I play a recording of that hymn
>
> of praise, as if its long tones
> could shoulder me home, float
>
> me to her. . . .
>
> No one can carry that heavy chant
> alone; there is no place to pause
>
> between the notes to take a breath . . . (71)

The poet's confession that she plays a recording of the *Lobsang* "against all tradition" to insert that tradition into a new context shows both her departure from the traditions and her impulse to preserve them in a way that is meaningful to her complex, multifaceted, adult self. Not only is use of the tape recorder "against" the tradition, but so is the juxtaposition of the *Lobsang* with a memory of the funeral. Yet the elegy is also, in some respects, an act of praise for the one who has passed away. The poet adapts this capacious literary structure as a place to join her longing for home, and a past way of life, to her current values. Thus, this third book of poems ends on a note of longing that sounds throughout a work that Kasdorf created, by choice, at a distance from the community that she re-creates imaginatively. Although it did not find its place in a poetry collection until 2012, this sequence was originally written for and performed at Quietly Landed, as a musical performance piece, in 1995.[17] In a similar loop back into her earlier work, Brandt returned to the "Prairie Songs" of *Agnes in the Sky* in choosing a title for *So this is the world & here I am in it.*

Brandt decries the "separation of Anabaptist and Mennonite faith principles from folk customs and farming practices" as she offers an alternative story of Mennonite origins in her ambitious essay "*Je jelieda, je vechieda:* Canadian Mennonite (Alter)identifications" (*So* 118). She seeks to repair the damage of such alienation from the land and within herself by articulating an ethic of care that she found latent in the more reciprocal practices of everyday life preserved in the oral traditions of Reinland, Manitoba, and other such villages, a heritage that the young Brandt herself outright rejected in her search for a language that would transport her from the village and into the world. The lines of "Dog Days in Maribor"—"Now that it's much, much too late, / now you care" (*Now You Care* 38)—are spoken first by her mother when Brandt shared her regret at not maintaining her knowledge of the *muttersprache* (*So* 106). For Brandt, recovering an ethic of care is also a recovery of the maternal narrative, a way of restoring the feminine of the Mennonite community into dialogue from its position of alterity.

Toward an Ethic of Care

In their later work, both Brandt and Kasdorf shift from examining formative experiences to an engagement with the world that they inhabit. In Brandt's work, this shift is clear in her fourth book, *Jerusalem, beloved* (1995). Written after a two-week trip to Gaza with a friend who works with American Friends Service on behalf of Palestinians, these poems employ the lens of personal witness to reveal a city in crisis, a city beloved in the biblical imagination shaped in Brandt's church-going years. Eight years later her next book of poetry, *Now You Care* (2003), marked a distinctive turn in her style, incorporating stanzaic forms along with postmodern techniques of collage and pastiche, splicing fragments from T.S. Eliot and Baudelaire into poems about environmental degradation, violence, and repair. Her sequence "le Détroit," for example, references the industrial corridor of Windsor and Detroit, a landscape that Brandt inhabited for over a decade as a professor at the University of Windsor. As a whole, the book features a wide range of experiments, from scientific prose poems to short-line lyrics, invoking the multilingual context of the conversations that must take place on multiple levels if we are to save the planet.[18] Her most recent book of essays, *So this is the world & here I am in it,* further develops the themes of reclamation and repair as Brandt returns to Manitoba and voices a lament for the prairie, now broken up into fields on formerly Aboriginal land. However, the title of this book is also the first line of the opening poem of *Agnes in the Sky,* suggesting that her concern with the environment, and her evocation of the land as both mother and sacred space, had its beginning much earlier in her work.[19] After first claiming voice and power through her education and the publication of her earlier books, Brandt is in a strong position to reclaim and lament her relationship with the maternal oral tradition, which she rejected at first but now views as a fragile thread to an ancient heritage eroded by the modern world. In *Walking to Mojácar,* her sixth full-length book of poetry, she extends the environmental theme, with poems that emphasize place and relationship with the land, this time employing translations in multiple languages, demonstrating the ways in which the intersection of languages creates culture and community, enabling multiple perspectives.

The shift toward a broader field of engagement in Kasdorf's work is revealed in the poems of her third collection, *Poetry in America,* written during the decade in which America experienced 9/11, the war in Iraq, economic crisis, and, in central Pennsylvania, devastating new mining technology. Kasdorf's political statements merge with her own experience of motherhood ("The Baby Screaming in the Back Seat"; "Mother and Toddler in Wartime"), as her compassion for others extends to students ("Bat Boy, Break a Leg") and to the wives and mothers of servicemen in Iraq and Afghanistan ("Cardio-Kickboxing in a Town of 6,000"). The cover of the book reproduces a poster of a woman digging with a shovel, which recalls the mysterious "digger" who decorated the title page of the first American edition of the *Martyrs Mirror,* previously explored in Kasdorf's essay "Work and Hope" (*Body*). In describing *Poetry in America,* the University of Pittsburgh Press website notes that it "offers lyric and narrative poems that function like works of social realism for our times."[20] Through the collection's focus on the realities of American life, Kasdorf retains the strong commitment to the lyric and lyric narrative poems of her earlier work. In the spirit of the poet who puts her hand to the plow in "Green Market," the collection features characters who are laborers, veterans, students, teachers. For Kasdorf, poetry writing, too, is a kind of labor: the sale of books at a reading can buy a new radiator hose in a small town where mechanics take only cash, as in "English 213: Introduction to Poetry Writing."[21] In *Poetry in America,* her focus on laboring people in particular places is supported by a preoccupation with earth, in poems that portray the poet lying on the earth, observing graveyards, refusing a ride in favor of walking, and experiencing a birth "as common as dirt" (26). This is not just a veiled reference to the particular soil of her Amish ancestors but also an evocation of the mountainous lands of central Pennsylvania, where she lives and works, now fractured by fracking for natural gas—the theme of her current work in progress.

As they articulate an ethic of care in their work, both Brandt and Kasdorf create a loop of connection to the past as they move forward. Reclaiming the New Testament commandment to love the other as the self, they transform the doctrine of non-resistance into compassion. The individual bid for freedom of voice in their early work initiates a commitment to build on the peacemaking ethic of their cultural tradition in such a way as to broaden it, accounting for a wider spectrum of relationships damaged in a hierarchical world.

Conclusion

Both Julia Spicher Kasdorf and Di Brandt have claimed spaces in multiple discourses during a period of late twentieth-century and early twenty-first-century literature open to the voices of women and minorities. Both have cited Jewish and First Nations writers and critics as inspirations for their hybrid approach to a dialogic ethnic identity. Their accomplishments rest, in part, on their full embrace of the artist's lived experience filtered through a gendered body, shaped by culture, and consciously developed by gleaning the past for values that shape a larger vision of art and community. Their oeuvre shows how artists challenge the master narrative of a cultural or religious life to create complex and fresh engagements with ideas hardened into traditions. As Franz Kafka has said, "A book must be the axe for the frozen sea within us."

The cultural work of Brandt's and Kasdorf's poems is one of mourning, purging, and re-creation. Each author forges a distinctive voice to salvage an ethic of care from the Mennonite tradition into which she was born and to engage in a continuing dialogue of critique and renewal. Like Diane Enns, a philosopher from a Mennonite background, they see, from their distinctive cultural perspectives, the potential in their heritage not only for damage and despair but also for an ethic of renewal and repair. Enns writes,

> The paradox of my inheritance has become clear: the very experiences that might lead a community to moralism and exclusivity, perhaps even hypocrisy and racism, are those that enable a revaluation of our notions

> of community and ethics. In other words, individuals and communities who have experienced hardship and violence have a choice: they can attempt to secure themselves from the random and unexpected events of the future by fortifying their borders, hardening an identity against another, and nurturing a melancholic attachment to past victimhood that is in danger of sabotaging any kind of political survival; or they can engage in what is no doubt a painful, seemingly impossible struggle to accept a fundamental vulnerability to violence and injury and risk the trust and openness necessary for ethical and political practices that do not in turn victimize others. (189)

In addressing both the wounds and the rich particularities of their early Mennonite experiences, the damaging assumptions of patriarchal Christianity and its potential for restorative relationships, and the scars of abuse as well as the power of articulating themselves as beings of autonomy and desire, both Brandt and Kasdorf risk a similar openness and vulnerability. The trajectory of their work forges a vision of community through language—an ethic of care—that challenges us to love ourselves and the particulars of our earthly lives, to reimagine our relationships with each other, and to care for the world that we inhabit.

NOTES

1. This focus on the intersection of gender and ethnicity in Dearborn's work, published the year before Brandt's *questions i asked my mother,* suggests the critical moment—at least from the perspective of American studies—in which both Kasdorf and Brandt were writing.

2. For a nuanced discussion of Mennonite ethnicity in Canada, see Zacharias 11, 37–43.

3. Today the ordination of women among Mennonites is widespread among mainstream groups but not permitted in some of the more conservative groups.

4. Dearborn's argument is based, in part, on her reading of Simone de Beauvoir's definition of woman as "other" in relation to man as the "Subject . . . the Absolute" (qtd. in Dearborn 5). It builds on de Beauvoir's definition to form a definition of ethnicity in a gendered context: "Only in relation to other groups can a group be defined as ethnic. Ethnicity has always been defined as otherness; the other is always ethnic. . . . [W]hite males exist as a dominant group only insofar as there are other entities whom they can perceive as ethnic and female, or colonizable" (17).

5. See Hostetler, "Three."

6. Brandt and Kasdorf are not the only strong Mennonite women poets writing in their respective countries today, but they exemplify women poets who have written themselves beyond ethnicity through the trajectory of careers both in the academy and in their respective national scenes. In fact, poetry by women with Mennonite heritage began to emerge in a significant way during the late 1980s. Jean Janzen, Sarah Klassen, and Audrey Poetker have

all published multiple volumes of poetry and won awards and recognition for their work (Hostetler, "Three").

7. Brandt and Kasdorf come from two different strands in the history of Mennonites of European origin: Brandt (nee Janzen) is descended from the Dutch-Prussian-Russian strand of Mennonites that immigrated to Canada in the 1870s, Kasdorf (nee Spicher) from the Pennsylvania Amish who immigrated to America from Bern, Switzerland, in the mid-1700s. The different immigration histories of these groups, and the communities that they produced, have contributed to these poets' particular perceptions of their Mennonite heritage.

8. See Redekop, who characterizes Brandt's "Hymns for Detroit" as inviting readers "into a transposition of the old hymns and a political commitment to cherish the environment" (256). She quotes from a letter that Brandt wrote to her: "[Brandt's] aim . . . was to 'stay true to the rhetorical and formal strategies of these hymns.' The experience of writing the poems put her into a state of 'awakening and lament for what we've lost.' Although she set out to write them as an exercise in irony, it became a 'reparative' act—an effort to 'pull the lost strategies back into the present'" (256).

9. For a detailed discussion of ornament and plain speech in Kasdorf's poems, see Meyer-Lee.

10. Message to the author, 17 Sept. 2013, email.

11. Kasdorf is the first American poet from Mennonite origins to publish an entire collection—*Sleeping Preacher*—organized around the portrayal of an American Amish-Mennonite community and its stories. The collection won the Agnes Lynch Starrett Prize from the University of Pittsburgh Press, and four of the poems from the collection were published in the *New Yorker.*

12. For a detailed discussion of this poem in relation to Brandt's recent work, see Hostetler, "Valediction."

13. Such a practice is not registered in Kasdorf's work, suggesting that corporal punishment of young children might have been a practice in Brandt's family or local community but not generalizable to Mennonites as a larger group.

14. Brandt, in "Black Ball," writes about her trip to Jerusalem and Occupied Palestine in relation to her own memories as a survivor of abuse and ancestral memories of persecution.

15. The connection between pacifist ideology and female oppression in Mennonite culture has been present in Mennonite literature since it was articulated in Rudy Wiebe's first novel, *Peace Shall Destroy Many* (1962), in the figure of Elizabeth Block, forced by her father to work like a man, denied her only romantic and sexual attachment, then cursed and disowned when she miscarries and dies.

16. For more on Brandt's "trans(e)lations," see Redekop.

17. This, the first conference on Anabaptist women, took place at Millersville University in Millersville, Pennsylvania, in 1995.

18. At this time, Brandt moved to Brandon University, where she held a Canada Research Chair in ecopoetics. She also inaugurated the Ogamas literary festival with the local Aboriginal community.

19. For an extensive discussion of ecopoetics as a vehicle for Brandt's intellectual reconciliation with her Mennonite community of origin, see Hostetler, "Valediction."

20. See the note on the text on the University of Pittsburgh Press's website, at http://www.upress.pitt.edu/BookDetails.aspx?bookId=36256.

21. See Hostetler, review.

WORKS CITED

Birky, Beth Martin. "'Sloughing Off Ribs': Revealing the Second Sex in Julia Kasdorf's Poetry." *Mennonite Quarterly Review* 7.4 (2003): 589–611.

Brandt, Di. *Agnes in the Sky.* Winnipeg: Turnstone Press, 1990.

———. "The Black Ball We Carry Around Inside Us." *Siolence: Poets on Women, Violence, and Silence.* Ed. Susan McMaster. Kingston: Quarry Women's Books, 1998. 52–54.

———. *Dancing Naked: Narrative Strategies for Writing Across Centuries.* Stratford, ON: Mercury, 1996.

———. *Jerusalem, beloved.* Winnipeg: Turnstone, 1995.

———. *Mother/Not Mother.* Stratford, ON: The Mercury Press, 1992.

———. *Now You Care.* Toronto: Coach House, 2003.

———. *questions i asked my mother.* Winnipeg: Turnstone Press, 1987.

———. *So this is the world & here I am in it.* Edmonton: NeWest Press, 2007.

———. *Walking to Mojácar.* Winnipeg: Turnstone Press, 2010.

Brandt, Di, and Barbara Godard, eds. *Wider Boundaries of Daring: The Modernist Impulse in Canadian Women's Poetry.* Waterloo, ON: Wilfrid Laurier University Press, 2009.

Dearborn, Mary V. *Pocahontas's Daughters: Gender and Ethnicity in American Culture.* New York: Oxford University Press, 1986.

Enns, Diane. "For the Love of Paradox: Mennonite Morality and Philosophy." *Religious Upbringing and the Costs of Freedom.* Ed. Peter Caws and Stefani Jones. University Park: Pennsylvania State University Press, 2010. 176–91.

Kafka, Franz. "Letter to Oskar Pollak, January 27, 1904." *Letters to Friends, Family, and Editors.* Trans. Richard Winston and Clara Winston. New York: Schocken Books, 1977.

Gundy, Jeff. "Enigmas of Embodiment." *Walker in the Fog: On Mennonite Writing.* Telford: Cascadia, 2005. 204–24.

Hostetler, Ann. Rev. of *Poetry in America,* by Julia Spicher Kasdorf. *Mennonite Quarterly Review* 88.1 (2014): 150–52.

———. "Three Women Poets and the Beginning of Mennonite Poetry in the U.S.: Anna Ruth Ediger Baehr, Jane Rohrer, Jean Janzen." *Mennonite Quarterly Review* 77.4 (2003): 521–46.

———. "A Valediction Forbidding Excommunication: Ecopoetics and the Reparative Journey Home in Recent Work by Di Brandt." *Journal of Mennonite Studies* 28 (2010): 69–86.

Kasdorf, Julia Spicher. *The Body and the Book: Writing from a Mennonite Life.* 2001. University Park: Pennsylvania State University Press, 2009.

———. *Eve's Striptease.* Pittsburgh: University of Pittsburgh Press, 1998.

———. *Poetry in America.* Pittsburgh: University of Pittsburgh Press, 2011.

———. *Sleeping Preacher.* Pittsburgh: University of Pittsburgh Press, 1992.

———. "Sunday Morning Confession." *Mennonite Quarterly Review* 87.1 (2013): 7–10.

Kasdorf, Julia Spicher, and Michael Tyrell, eds. *Broken Land: Poems of Brooklyn.* New York: New York University Press, 2007.

MacDonald, Tanis, ed. *Speaking of Power: The Poetry of Di Brandt.* Waterloo, ON: Wilfrid Laurier University Press, 2004.

Meyer-Lee, Robert. "A Defense of Ornament: The Supplement of Literary Language and Julia Kasdorf's 'Catholics' and 'Mennonites.'" *Mennonite Quarterly Review* 82.1 (2008): 43–63.

Redekop, Magdalene. "Haunted by Hymns: The Fate of Melody in 'Mennonite' Poetry." *Sound in the Lands: Mennonite Music Across Borders.* Ed. Maureen Epp et al. Kitchener, ON: Pandora Press, 2011. 243–70.

Weir, Lorraine. "Witnessing Brandt & Tostevin." Rev. of *Dancing Naked: Narrative Strategies for Writing Across Centuries,* by Di Brandt, and *Subject to Criticism,* by Lola Lemire Tostevin. *Canadian Literature* 8 Dec. 2011. Web. 26 Aug. 2013.

Wiebe, Rudy. *Peace Shall Destroy Many.* Toronto: McClelland and Stewart, 1962.

Zacharias, Robert. *Rewriting the Break Event: Mennonites and Migration in Canadian Literature.* Winnipeg: University of Manitoba Press, 2013.

6

The Mennonite Thing

Identity for a Post-Identity Age

ROBERT ZACHARIAS

There is a well-known joke in Mennonite circles that begins with a question that is already a punchline of its own: "Why don't Mennonites have sex standing up?" The humor of the answer—"Because it might lead to dancing"—lies in the suggestion that, in the absurdly uptight world of the Mennonites, rules and regulations have become more important than the religious principles that they once reflected. An essay in the recent "Sex" special issue of *Rhubarb* magazine identifies this as "likely the first joke any Mennonite child understands about our shared heritage" (Redekop 64), while Jeff Gundy has christened it the "ur-Mennonite joke" (*Walker* 193). Still, it is worth noting that the joke refers to no particular group or denomination of Mennonites, nor does it seek to engage with their actual lived realities, possibilities, or difficulties.[1] Instead, it simply invokes a generalized and abstracted notion of a conservative Mennonite identity, of which it offers less a pointed critique than a playful affirmation. The implied original rule (No dancing, for it might lead to sex!) may be inverted (No sex, for it might lead to dancing!), but the result in behavior is the same (No dancing! No sex!). The rule itself might be held up to ridicule, but the animating principles of modesty, abstinence, and so on are left untouched, much like the bodies in question.

Drawing on Slavoj Žižek's work on the inversion of ideology and the fetishistic structure of the "Ethnic Thing," I want to suggest that the structure of the above joke—or, more specifically, the function of Mennonite identity within it—reflects the role that Mennonite identity currently plays for much of the larger field of Mennonite literary studies. In this chapter, I focus on a prominent strand of writing that routes its engagement with the most conventional aspects of Mennonite identity through a variety of distancing gestures (irony, self-consciousness, and so on), strategically mobilizing notions of cultural authenticity and cohesive group identity in such a way that it is not directly readable as autoethnography. In such texts, I want to argue, an essentialized and decontextualized Mennonite identity—what I am calling "the Mennonite Thing"—is self-consciously invoked, exposed, and explored, a process through which it is reanimated as identity for a post-identity age.

Contemporary scholarship has widely accepted that identities are best understood to be hybrid, shifting, constructed, and contingent, less as reified "things" in themselves than as positions or locations that can be temporarily occupied and perhaps strategically mobilized.[2] At the same time, identity-based area studies have proven to be remarkably resilient, continuing to emphasize race, ethnicity, gender, and sexuality as primary avenues for engaging literary texts. I see nothing particularly surprising about this enduring critical focus on identity, however, as recognizing the constructed multiplicity of our identities, along with the clear need to continue grappling with the questions of individual belonging and collective meaning that remain powerful forces in contemporary life, seems to make the discussion of identity more compelling rather than less. In the context of Mennonite writing, I am sympathetic to the (admittedly tautological) concern that the enduring focus on identity might have limited our appreciation of the aesthetic accomplishments of Mennonite authors; however, if it is true that Mennonite literary criticism has been tied a bit too tightly to sociological concerns about identity, it is also true that much of what circulates as contemporary Mennonite literature continues to directly invoke and explicitly explore Mennonite identity as one of its central concerns. Given that the larger cultural and commercial contexts of multicultural literature remain deeply invested in highly conventional identity claims—with recent "Mennonite texts" such as Rhoda Janzen's *Mennonite in a Little Black Dress* or Darcie Friesen Hossack's *Mennonites Don't Dance* circulating as implicitly authentic engagements with a traditional Mennonite identity—perhaps what is needed now is less a new focus than a new perspective.

One way to understand how identity functions in such a context is to turn to a passage of Žižek's *Sublime Object of Ideology*, entitled (appropriately enough) "The Ideological Quilt." Žižek suggests that identity is constructed and maintained as a "structured network of meaning" through ideology, as the "multitude of 'floating signifiers,' of proto-ideological elements, is structured into a unified field through the intervention of a certain 'nodal point'" (95–96). If "Mennonite" serves as the ideological "nodal point" holding together a discourse of Mennonite/s writing, however, there is no reason to begin searching for the particular group or definition of Mennonites to which it corresponds. "The element which holds together a given community cannot be reduced to the point of symbolic identification," Žižek writes elsewhere. "[T]he bond linking together its members always implies a shared relationship toward a Thing" (*Tarrying* 201). For Žižek, the various elements that one might point to as giving structure to a community—its shared history, rituals, theology, kinship ties, and so on—will always be insufficient to explain its constitutive element. "The Thing is not directly a collection of these features," he writes; "there is 'something more' in it, something that *is present* in these features, that *appears* through them" (201).

In *First as Tragedy, Then as Farce,* Žižek builds a similar argument regarding the role of ideology more generally. Despite the widespread argument that ideology can no longer function in the context of today's cynical population, Žižek insists that it is the very belief in the absence of ideology that demonstrates just how deeply imbedded we continue to be within it. Ideology continues to function, he suggests, but it does so today through the appearance of its rejection. He goes on to offer a number of brief but telling illustrations of this process at work, including two that are of particular interest to my discussion here. In the first, he notes the mockery of pseudo-oriental spiritualism in the popular film *Kung Fu Panda* but argues that despite "constantly being undermined by a vulgar-cynical sense of humour . . . this continuous self-mockery in no way impedes on the efficiency of the oriental spiritualism—the film ultimately takes the butt of its endless jokes seriously" (50–51). In the second, he recounts an anecdote about the Dutch physicist Niels Bohr in which a scientist visiting his house expressed dismay at finding a horseshoe nailed above the door. "[T]he fellow scientist visiting him exclaimed that he did not share the superstitious belief regarding horseshoes keeping evil spirits out of the house," Žižek writes, "to which Bohr snapped back: 'I don't believe in it either. I have it there because I was told that it works even when one doesn't believe in it'" (51). For Žižek, such stories exemplify the cynical logic at play in contemporary ideology, in which "nobody takes democracy or justice seriously, we are all aware of their corrupted nature, but we participate in them, we display our belief in them, because we assume that they work even if we do not believe in them" (51).

The Mennonite Thing, as I am formulating it here, is simply the conceit of an essential, static, and authentic Mennonite identity expressed through (but not reducible to) stereotypical markers of Mennonite culture, language, and faith. Conventional markers of the Mennonite Thing often become associated with Mennonites for historical reasons, of course, but, through the exoticizing logic that reifies and commodifies them into easily consumable tokens of cultural difference, the most recognizable aspects of a broadly understood "Mennonite culture," such as quilts, *Borscht*, head coverings, *Zwiebach*, and so on, become overdetermined signifiers of an essentialized Mennoniteness that exists only as an abstract ideal. For a recent example, consider the original cover of Janzen's bestselling *Mennonite in a Little Black Dress,* which displayed a prayer cap the likes of which are nowhere to be found in the Mennonite Brethren tradition explored in the memoir. Whatever one might think of Janzen's representation of Mennonite identity *within* the book, it is clear that the designers of the original cover were much less interested in historical accuracy than in connecting the text with the idea of Mennoniteness itself—that is, with the Mennonite Thing.

My description of the conceit of reified ethnicity as a "Thing" is meant to gesture to Žižek's work, of course, but in sketching the Mennonite Thing I am also picking up on a term already in circulation. Take, for example, the comments of David Arnason, an editor at Turnstone Press. Turnstone has no connection to Mennonites beyond being located in Winnipeg, but it played an integral role in the emergence of Mennonite writing during the 1980s and 1990s. In an essay first presented at the inaugural Mennonite/s Writing conference, Arnason tried to distinguish between writing by and about Mennonites and some other, vaguely defined aspect of Mennonite literary identity from which he attempted to distance himself. "We have no interest whatsoever in Mennonite history or anything particularly Mennonite," he insisted. "We are interested in good fiction, good poetry, and it just happens that a lot of Mennonites are writing good fiction and good poetry. But again I want to make it absolutely clear that we have very little interest in 'the Mennonite thing'" (213). This may well be true, but it is equally true that the broader fascination with the Mennonite Thing was enabling Turnstone at the time. Elsewhere, I put it this way: "The socio-political contexts that encouraged a generation of Mennonite authors to write out of their experiences as 'ethnic Canadians' are the same contexts in which it became culturally compelling and economically viable for a small press to begin publishing book after book of and often about a rural, separatist, deeply conservative Christian community, and to be able to reasonably expect a 'mainstream literary market' to respond enthusiastically" (43). Although Arnason uses the term derogatively, it more commonly circulates as an affectionate shorthand, as in John Barber's *Globe and Mail* review of *Irma Voth,* succinctly entitled "Miriam Toews: It's a Mennonite Thing," or as in the Mennonite Artist Project, a New York–based web initiative launched in 2009 that now connects some 500 Mennonite artists in its stated effort to "find other people who make art and get the Mennonite thing."

To be sure, there is nothing particularly new in the use of stereotypical elements of culture in Mennonite writing. In fact, as Julia Spicher Kasdorf notes in her introduction to a recent reissue of one of the earliest such texts, Joseph W. Yoder felt compelled to write his novel *Rosanna of the Amish* (1940)—a surprise hit that has sold more than 500,000 copies over the past seventy-five years—specifically to "strategically" confront and undermine "the stereotypes" that characterized the representation of Mennonites and Amish in the "local color" literature of the day (14). "All the episodes in ROSANNA OF THE AMISH are based on fact," Yoder wrote in his preface to the novel, announcing that he was "prompted and inspired" to write the book in response to the work of "several writers with seemingly vivid imaginations and apparently little regard for facts" (25).

Although circulation of the Mennonite Thing in literature is not new, then, what does seem to be different today is that many authors now are willing to engage with elements of it as a primary mode of identity rather than strictly as the falsification of a "true" identity in need of defense (or, as the case might be, as a stable identity in need of critique). Yoder responded to what he saw as the naked commodification of Amish identity in literature by attempting to present it more accurately. If authors of Mennonite descent today are no more likely than Yoder to celebrate the commodification of Anabaptist identity, they are much more likely to respond with a metafictional awareness of the impossibility of ever truly "fixing" the tradition in any meaningful way.[3] Today, when the very aspects of Mennonite identity that would make it recognizable in literature are the ones most heavily overdetermined, a common response has been to engage this identity indirectly, through some form of critical distancing, so that the Mennonite Thing is simultaneously invoked and disavowed.

In this chapter, I am most interested in works that seem to engage with Mennonite identity as Thing self-consciously, but, as I hope will become clear, this need not be the case. In fact, this is one reason why I turned to Žižek's work to help me explore the function of identity in these texts rather than, say, Gayatri Chakravorty Spivak's work on strategic essentialism, or Rey Chow's work on coercive mimicry: Mennonite/s writing's engagement with its own essentialized identity seems to be neither as politically motivated nor as tactically deployed as the former, nor is it as subjugated or as racially determined as the latter. Although the role of identity in Mennonite/s writing is not strictly ideological in Žižek's sense either, I want to suggest that in key ways it is strikingly similar in its function. Where Žižek is concerned with ideology in its most political sense, here I mean ideology simply as an ordering framework structuring thought and experience through an overarching principle or concern, similar to Kasdorf's use of the term as the politicized "name [for] the set of ideas that shape expectations, actions, and goals, and that get reproduced within the group as normative" ("Mightier" 46). "At the point of contact with the dominant world view," Kasdorf continues, "ideological difference becomes evident and signifies—even clarifies—identity: 'just what we do' escalates into 'what it means to be us'" (46). Žižek relies heavily on Lacan, of course, but one need not fully adopt a Lacanian understanding of subjectivity to acknowledge the ways that desire and identity are closely intertwined in literary studies, or the ways that ideological difference is ripe for reification.

It is now fifteen years since Ann Hostetler and Hildi Froese Tiessen each drew on Stuart Hall to caution critics against the dangers of essentialized notions of Mennonite identity,[4] and it has long been common practice for critics of Mennonite writing to avoid defining the field's parameters in anything but the broadest of terms. More than one prominent author of Mennonite descent has publicly denied being a "Mennonite author," and critics have been warning of the field's potential collapse since before it was established.[5] Is it not possible that, lacking a clear, coherent, and static understanding of the "Mennonite" in "Mennonite literary studies," the wider field is sustained in important ways simply through a shared commitment to its existence, aided by a collective willingness to actively defer the definition of its central concern? And if the sustaining feature of identity in Mennonite/s writing is not some reified set of practices or beliefs but our shared investment in its endurance, the question of whether or not a text's representation of Mennonite identity (as opposed to Mennonite history or even specific Mennonite communities) is "true" or "accurate" is not only secondary to understanding the role of identity in the field, it also fails to recognize that this indeterminacy is a central aspect of its function. In a critical context in which the identity in the field's disciplinary signature is deeply unstable, and in which this instability is overcome largely by a shared willingness to forge on without a stable referent, it does little good to respond to Mennonite literary texts by railing against the loss or misrepresentation of a true, essential identity, one characterized by a history and a vision with clear origins and parameters, which we must protect at all costs, and so on. To make this argument in the context of much of contemporary Mennonite/s writing, it seems, is to push against an open door.

Perhaps the best example of how contemporary Mennonite literature strategically engages with identity as Thing is one that is also deeply self-conscious about the process at play. In 1986, Jeff Gundy—whose poetry, unlike his nonfiction, rarely directly addresses his Mennonite background—wrote a brief essay for *Mennonite Life* entitled "Being Mennonite and Writing Mennonite." "[F]or someone like me, whose immediate background is largely without the colorful, obvious markers of Mennonite identity, it is not all that easy to decide how to go about making my work distinctly Mennonite," he writes. "Do I dredge up any scraps of 'heritage' I can, like the dim memory of the great-aunt asking 'Sprichen sie Dietsch?'" (11). Several years later, Gundy returned to this topic with a prescriptive parody, "How to Write the New Mennonite Poem." Under the guise of instruction, the poem critiques the instrumentalization of Mennonite identity in contemporary poetry, but its critique is complicated by the fact that the poem closely follows its own advice. It makes sure to "Get the word 'Mennonite' in at least / twice, once in the title," for example, and it deploys each of the markers of Mennonite identity that it suggests are problematically tokenized. "Choose two from old Bibles, humbly beautiful quilts, / Fraktur, and the *Martyrs Mirror* in Dutch," it begins, going on to encourage authors to include "zwiebach / vareniki, borscht, and the farm, / which if possible should be lost now" (86).

If the poem critiques the use of what Gundy earlier called the "colorful, obvious markers of Mennonite identity" in poetry, it does so precisely by raising each of them in turn, capitalizing on their exoticism even as it exposes and disavows this process. Shirley Showalter and Julia Spicher Kasdorf, poets themselves, both point to this poem as critiquing the dilemmas facing the contemporary Mennonite author. Showalter sees the poem as Gundy's "gentle prod to himself as well as to other poets," noting the particular challenge facing authors who engage Mennonite identity in their writing today. "The problem of being a Mennonite writer is that you cannot be one completely un-self-consciously anymore, and too much self-consciousness has ruined many a writer," Showalter observes, pointing to the poem as evidence that "[p]erhaps awareness of the paradox itself is the only answer to this dilemma." Kasdorf, meanwhile, suggests that the poem "pokes fun at the overly self-conscious 'new Mennonite' poet who has internalized society's desire for cultural stereotypes and who clutters his poems with signs of authenticity" (*Body* 54). But if the poem does address an aspiring poet—"You, of course, are a backslidden, / overlearned, doubtridden, egodriven / quasibeliever," it reads (86–87)—its primary reference remains something called "the new Mennonite poem." It is this slight distance, from *poem about identity* to *poem about identity in poetry,* that enables Gundy's work to capitalize on the very process of exoticizing what it critiques, so that the ostensible object of the poem's concern (i.e., a discredited, reified form of traditional Mennonite cultural identity) can continue its function as the work's animating force. What is more, by embedding this account of Mennonite writing in a poem, rather than an essay, Gundy not only identifies but also demonstrates how the critique of essentialized identity does nothing to prevent its ongoing function in literary texts.

Gundy has published five books of poetry, in addition to several hundred poems in various journals, and "How to Write the New Mennonite Poem" is one of the few to explicitly address Mennonite identity. Gundy himself has called the poem an "exception" to his larger body of work (*Greatest* 8), and concedes that he wrote it "mainly as a sort of joke" (*Walker* 122) and "partly out of frustration at being turned down by a Mennonite magazine because [his] poems lacked particular cultural markers" (*Greatest* 8). In spite of this—or, as I am arguing here, at least partly because of it—it quickly became one of his most discussed and reproduced poems. After first being published in the inaugural issue of *Mennonot* in 1993, it was promptly reprinted in the *Mennonite Weekly Review.* Gundy himself selected it as the only one of his own poems to include in his 1997 review of American Mennonite poetry for the *Mennonite Quarterly Review,* an essay later republished in his award-winning collection *Walker in the Fog: On Mennonite Writing.*[6] He included the poem again in his 2003 chapbook, *Greatest Hits: 1986–2003.* Kasdorf, meanwhile, reproduced "How to Write the New Mennonite Poem" in full in her own collection of essays, *The Body and the Book: Writing from a Mennonite Life,* while Ann Hostetler selected it as one of six poems by Gundy for inclusion in her anthology, *A Cappella: Mennonite Voices in Poetry.* The poem's enduring popularity is surely due, in no small part, to its reproduction of the most clichéd representations of Mennonite cultural authenticity. But if it succeeds because of its ambivalent adherence to the logic that it critiques, this stands as further testament to the precision of its argument: readers want that Mennonite Thing. And in this, I would argue, the logic of Gundy's poem is far from unique. In fact, I would risk suggesting that it is but the clearest example of a leading paradigm in the field.

Gundy's poem reads in direct conversation with a number of other poems explicitly engaging Mennonite identity, including Kasdorf's much-anthologized poem "Mennonites."[7] In one sense, Kasdorf's poem, first published in her acclaimed debut collection, *Sleeping Preacher,* is a fitting object for Gundy's critique. Not only does it bear many of the identity markers parodied by Gundy—and there is little question that it has circulated, at least in part, because of the capital that it gains within the multicultural exoticization of ethnicity—Kasdorf herself notes that, when the poem was anthologized in Stuart Hirschberg's multicultural reader *The Many Worlds of Literature,* it came complete with what she calls a "wildly embellished" biographical blurb about her own Mennonite past, one that effectively "wrapped [her] in a quilt" ("Preacher's" 57). At the same time, however, her poem is far from a naive replication of an essentialized cultural identity. In fact, the poem's enigmatic first line, "We keep our quilts in closets and do not dance," raises the specter of the Mennonite Thing through its disavowal, opening with an archetypal Mennonite object only to immediately close the door on it. In his concise reading of the poem, Gundy points to its description of Mennonites as rushing to "clean up [God's] disasters," its positioning of Nazi soldiers as "heroes" for helping Mennonite refugees, and its closing image of the Mennonite singing voices "lift[ing], as chaff lifts toward God," as evidence of an "understated but radical irony" that raises "primary markers of Mennonite identity" only to have them threaten to "dissolve, to be inadequate against the gathering sense of lack of worth or identity" (*Walker* 99).

In fact, because of the rural, pastoral, and "simple" connotations of the Mennonite Thing, subtle markers of irony or ambivalence often risk being misrecognized by those who come to such texts seeking authenticity. According to Kasdorf, not only has her poem been widely misread as straightforward autoethnography, but there have also been some for whom the poem's ambivalent ending is so out of keeping with their expectations that they have simply assumed she does not understand the meaning of "chaff" ("Preacher's" 69). Similarly, readers' responses to the poem's central question, posited midway through the piece, will largely depend on how they have read the poem's engagement with Mennonite identity. "This is why we cannot leave the beliefs," the narrator declares, after recounting the persecutions of earlier generations of Mennonites, "or what else would we be?" (129). This question seems to have been taken as rhetorical by many readers,[8] but I chose it as the epigraph for this volume on the assumption that it presents, quite seriously, a radical invitation for us to reconsider the foundational narratives and markers of our collective identity. Gundy's interrogation of a clichéd Mennonite identity in "How to Write the New Mennonite Poem" is obviously much more explicit, but Kasdorf's "Mennonites," too, seems to offer its markers of Mennonite identity self-consciously, invoking a "traditional" Mennonite identity as part of a larger effort to interrogate her readers' expectations for it.

For a seemingly more earnest critique of what is at stake in Kasdorf's representation of Mennonite identity, it is worth turning briefly to David Wright's poem "A New Mennonite Replies to Julia Kasdorf."[9] Although Wright's poem engages most obviously with Kasdorf's work, it also seems to play off of Gundy's piece, turning the "New" of Gundy's title from a literary narrative (a new Mennonite poem) into a conversion narrative (a newly converted Mennonite). Wright's poem suggests that appeals to the conventional markers of a traditional Mennonite cultural identity implicitly exclude members of Mennonite churches who were not born into the Swiss or Russian communities. "As best

I can tell, most of our quilts here were inherited," Wright's poem begins. "Not much borscht, / few shoofly pies at potlucks—instead it's / hummus, free range chicken, carob brownies." The poem speaks of the "Many new and remade and restless / and not-quite Mennonites" who "cannot play / the name game," and who "park ourselves in pews / next to women and men who know better / what real Mennonites really are." If Gundy's poem takes up identity via representational issues within Mennonite writing, Wright's poem can be understood as extending this concern to Mennonite identity in and of itself. In fact, the ironic repetition of "real"—"what real Mennonites really are"—questions the function of the Mennonite Thing not in literature but in the pews of the church itself.

Wright's poem makes an important argument about the exclusivity of a certain form of Mennonite identity, and engages with these markers of cultural authenticity in order to disturb their normativity and blend them into an expanded vision for the community. It places a productive pressure not only on the easily fetishized objects of a conventional Mennonite identity (quilts, *Borscht*, and so on) but also on the divisiveness of a certain form of Mennonite theology, one that leads church members to "seem amused," "grieved," or "simply angry" at the prospect of an expanded vision that would include touchstones from other cultures or denominations. However, it would be a mistake to read the poem as nakedly didactic. Take, for example, the confession, midway through the poem, that the narrator "need[s] the book / on 606." On the surface, such a confession emphasizes that the narrator feels himself or herself to be outside the conventions that govern the Mennonite church. But by leaving the reference to "606" unexplained, Wright deploys it as a shibboleth of sorts, exercising something like the type of insider knowledge against which much of the poem rails, and quietly reinscribing the narrator within the boundaries of the community.[10] As in its closing image of a Mennonite woman in a "heavy head covering" eating at China Buffet (coupled with a sly reference to ethnicity and passing), the poem quietly signals its awareness that the line between insiders and outsiders is less firm than it might appear. What is more, the largely earnest theological critique is destabilized, at least in part, by how closely Wright's poem follows the prescription offered by Gundy's parody: it, too, is sure to "Get the word 'Mennonite' in at least twice, once in the title," as Gundy recommends, and it, too, references quilts, *Borscht*, and shoofly pies, as well as a character from the *Martyrs Mirror*. There is even a Mennonite mother (though, unlike per Gundy's recommendation regarding grandmothers, she is alive and does not appear to have suffered). Much like Gundy's and Kasdorf's poems, then, it seems that the success of Wright's poem depends, in part, on the very Thing that it sets out to interrogate.

Quite apart from the legitimate question of how readers position themselves in relation to texts like the above poems, it seems important to keep in mind that what is being invoked and engaged in each of these pieces is not a specific ethnoreligious community at all. That is, the question of whether or not a reified and exclusionary Mennonite identity like the ones constructed by these poems truly exists—and it clearly does not, for all three poems showcase an amalgamation of Swiss and Russian Mennonite history and identity markers—is largely irrelevant to the function of Mennonite identity within them. Is not the argument of Gundy's poem, lodged at work such as Kasdorf's "Mennonites" and Wright's "A New Mennonite Replies to Julia Kasdorf," precisely that the Mennonite identity being invoked and circulating in such works is simply the *idea* of an authentic conservative Mennonite identity, one expressed through (though not reducible to) stereotypical markers of Mennonite dress, language, and belief? And yet, even as these poems carefully distance themselves from an essentialized, decontextualized Mennonite identity, they also constitute fine illustrations of how that identity continues to function in contemporary Mennonite/s writing, each having become an important "Mennonite poem" in its own right. Hostetler not only included all three of these poems in her anthology of Mennonite poetry, for example, but also positioned each as the first poem for each author. And little wonder: paraphrasing Žižek, we can see how each of these poems takes the butt of its own joke seriously, showing how identity continues to function even when we do not "believe" in it.

It should be amply clear, I hope, that in suggesting that these poems do not demonstrate an unqualified belief in the Mennonite Thing I am speaking solely about the literary representations of a reified, static Mennonite identity. Nonetheless, to the extent that Mennonite writing actively participates in the wider construction and negotiation of Mennonite identity, we might also ask what role the Thing plays beyond the field of Mennonite/s writing. Here I am much less willing to follow Žižek through to his politicized conclusions about ideology, but the questions prompted by his work are nevertheless worth asking. What role has the abstract idea of a distinct, reified Mennonite identity—one that might be founded on but is often extrapolated far beyond the lived experiences of Mennonite communities—come to play in the structure of these communities, institutions, and churches? To what extent has the threat of the disappearance of the Mennonite Thing, or what Di Brandt, writing in this volume, calls "the myth of the vanishing Mennonites," become indispensable to the shoring up of the community's borders? Is it even possible that, rather than a communal heritage and theological tradition under threat, much of what endures and circulates today as distinctly Mennonite in North America is best understood as the product, rather than the object, of such a myth? If so, how might this process have limited, rather than protected, the community? Perhaps, following Žižek, we ought to consider whether the distance taking that I have been tracking in the literature is a form of "inherent transgression," in which "the very emergence of a certain 'value' which serves as the point of ideological identification relies on its transgression, on some mode of taking a distance towards it" ("Inherent" 3).

Once we recognize how the Mennonite Thing functions in contemporary Mennonite writing, we can find examples of it strewn across the field. We can see it throughout much of Kirsten Eve Beachy's recent edited collection *Tongue Screws and Testimonies,* for example, in which it seems that many of the Mennonite writers and artists who took up Beachy's call to engage the *Martyrs Mirror,* a sixteenth-century martyrology that is an iconic text in the Mennonite tradition, do so in order to carefully distance themselves from it. We can see it in Alayna Munce's *When I Was Young and in My Prime,* with its young urban protagonist struggling to repurpose the most traditional elements of her family's heritage as part of her attempt to negotiate the shifting contours of a transgenerational, collective Mennonite identity.[11] We see it in highly self-conscious works like Stephen Beachy's *Boneyard* and Nathan Dueck's *He'll,* each of which distances itself from its own account of Amish and Mennonite characters by presenting itself as a "found manuscript." And we can certainly see it in much of Miriam Toews's work, in which, despite her clear critiques of readily identifiable communities, she also seems eager to expose the simulacrum of identity as Thing. In *A Complicated Kindness,* for example, teenagers work in a heritage village standing at the edge of East Village, Mennonites dressing up as "Mennonites" to meet the expectations of the tourists who arrive to gawk. In *Irma Voth,* a Mexican Mennonite colony is literally turned into a film set, yet the eccentric filmmaker makes it clear that he is uninterested in the Mennonites themselves. "I don't care about the Mennonites as a group," he insists. "I'm interested in the fact that nobody would understand their language and that they were uniform. There's no distinction, one from the other, and so they are props, essentially, for pure emotion" (243). Here the Lacanian logic of the Mennonite Thing reaches it peak: while "real" Mennonites self-consciously perform their Mennoniteness, the signification of Mennonite identity is completely emptied, signaling nothing but the idea of otherness itself.

Although I am suggesting that literature addressing identity as Thing is particularly prevalent today, a couple of quick final examples should make it clear that self-conscious literary engagements with Mennonite identity are not entirely new. In 1974, for example, Elmer Suderman published "Directions for

Celebrating the Centennial of the Coming of the Low German Mennonites from the Steppes of Russia to the American Prairies," a prescriptive poem that eerily anticipates Gundy's "How to Write the New Mennonite Poem" by nearly twenty years. "It is best to be a Birthright Mennonite and have / grandparents who came from the Molotschna in / the 1870s," it begins, admonishing readers to "Avoid / laughter unless you can laugh in Low German." It closes with a warning that folds back on itself with precisely the type of self-conscious declaration through disavowal that I am discussing here:

> Above all, and you must remember this, so pay
> very careful attention: Don't write poems about
> being a Mennonite. No poems. A poem, remember,
> is a lie, is a lie. No poem, please, not even a
> prose poem.

A decade later, in the 1983 poem "Roots," David Waltner-Toews playfully describes Rudy Wiebe, already a well-known Mennonite Canadian author, as digging through a potato field. Although Wiebe is unable to find his "roots"—the genealogical urge in Russian Mennonite culture being the poem's primary trope—he does stumble on an unidentifiable bone that gets up and walks to Winnipeg and back before ending up in his mother's potato soup. Like his popular Tante Tina poems, in which Waltner-Toews takes on the heavily accented voice and persona of a conservative Mennonite woman, and which he occasionally performs in drag, "Roots" raises the most conventional markers of Mennonite ethnic identity—from *Rollkuchen* and *Borscht* to stories of the Russian colonies—strategically, his ironic tone establishing a distance from the material even as he engages it sympathetically. And, much like Gundy's poem, Waltner-Toews's poem self-consciously capitalizes on the very form of identity that it is ostensibly interrogating. Nowhere is this clearer than in the poem's italicized first line, which, in declaring the poem to be "*not about Rudy Wiebe, but for him*" (75), neatly encapsulates the inversion of identity that I have been wrestling with in this chapter. Just as it is possible to write an entire poem about "Rudy Wiebe" and declare that it is not about Rudy Wiebe, Mennonite identity is able to function throughout contemporary Mennonite literature, much of which continues to be about "Mennonites" even where it has stopped being about Mennonites.

I am conscious of having moved too quickly here, even as I need to come to a close, so let me offer a few clarifications. My point in this brief survey is not simply that *any* discussion of Mennonites in literature can be read as participating in and perpetuating the field's long-standing focus on Mennonite identity, though that is certainly true. And I do not mean to suggest that there is any clear distinction to be drawn between an ideological identity as Thing and some implicitly "real" or "authentic" identity that can fully and accurately manifest the contemporary Mennonite experience. Such a desire for the "real" is what produces the conceit of identity as Thing in the first place. What is more, I do not mean to suggest that engaging identity as Thing precludes a serious engagement with its political, cultural, or theological concerns. More broadly but also more simply, I am suggesting that a partial disavowal has become a primary means through which a widely discredited form of reified or essentialized Mennonite identity—which I have named the Mennonite Thing—not only continues to function in the field but remains one of its central animating forces.

Importantly, the engagement with identity as Thing can be located in the nonfiction tradition as well. This is obviously the case, for example, in books such as Emerson L. Lesher's *The Muppie Manual: The Mennonite Urban Professional's Handbook for Humility and Success*, and J. Craig Haas and Steve Nolt's *The Mennonite Starter Kit: A Handy Guide for the New Mennonites (Everything They Forgot to Tell You in Church Membership Class!).* Both of these how-to-be-a-Mennonite texts, the latter of which includes a pseudo-academic article entitled "Identifying an Identifiable Identity" (27), gently mock Mennonite frivols and clichés in order to restore the notion of Mennonite identity. A less obvious case, perhaps, is my decision to open this chapter with a discussion of the "ur-Mennonite" sex joke. Is there not a sense in which my discussion of the joke also functions as a form of disavowal? As if the act of analysis somehow diminishes the fact that I began my critique of the Mennonite Thing by animating it as forcefully as possible? I would argue that many critical works operate in this manner, deeply indebted to identitarian logic even where they claim to set it aside. Perhaps it is true, as Maurice Mierau writes in a slightly different argument about Mennonite writing, that "the quintessential Mennonite position" is to be "detached and obsessively attached at the same time" (78).

In *Dancing Naked: Narrative Strategies for Writing Across Centuries,* Di Brandt describes the Mennonite writer of the early 1990s as undertaking an emotional and spiritual striptease, "taking off the clothes of the official story, layer by layer, stripping away the codes we have lived by to get to the stories underneath of our real, aching bodies in the world" (36). Gesturing toward the joke with which I began this chapter, she writes, "What the new Mennonite poets are doing is *yup,* confessing, taking their clothes off in public all right, but they're doing it standing up, and yes, the old joke was right, if you do it that way, it turns in to a kind of dancing" (36). Today, Mennonite poets continue to take their clothes off in this sense of an ontological striptease, but many seem increasingly self-conscious about it, as if they are now well aware of the particular audience that gathers when Mennonites get naked. Today, when authors and critics of Mennonite descent choose to engage Mennonite identity in their writing, many begin by anticipating their interpellation into an exoticizing discourse of cultural authenticity, a process they set out to counter through a series of distancing gestures that leaves them at least a little clothed. In simultaneously satisfying and disturbing their readers' expectations for the Mennonite Thing, writers such as Gundy, Kasdorf, and Wright, like Suderman and Waltner-Toews before them, manage to engage the conventions of Mennonite identity without fully occupying its predetermined position. Far from lodging simple critiques at an outdated model of Mennonite identity, however, such works are quickly becoming its constitutive mode, operating as identity for a post-identity age.

NOTES

1. In fact, the joke is not even specific to Mennonites: a quick Internet search turns up versions of the joke poking fun at the moral conservatism of Baptists, Muslims, and others.

2. Here I am thinking primarily of the critique of identity initiated in the 1990s in the context of postcolonial and poststructural theory, including influential work by Stuart Hall, Homi Bhabha, and Gayatri Chakravorty Spivak, extended more recently by critics such as Judith Butler, Rey Chow, and Slavoj Žižek. Although their work obviously differs in important ways, each of these scholars has helped to advance a radical critique of identity as the transparent foundation of the liberal autonomous subject.

3. I am gesturing here to the two meanings of "fixing tradition"—both in terms of restoring it and in terms of reducing it to a static entity—at play in the title of Kasdorf's *Fixing Tradition: Joseph W. Yoder, Amish American.*

4. See Hostetler, "Unofficial Voice," and Tiessen.

5. Perhaps the first essay in the surprisingly persistent tradition of critics worrying about the fate of the field was written by J.H. Janzen and published in a 1948 issue of *Mennonite Life.* After surveying what he saw as the once promising but then dying field of Mennonite Canadian writing, Janzen was near despair. "I feel," he wrote, "as if I am writing epitaphs on tombstones" (28).

6. See "Beyond Dr. Johnson's Dog: American Mennonite Poetry and Poets" (*Walker* 97–132).

7. Hostetler suggests that Gundy wrote "How to Write the New Mennonite Poem" in direct response to Kasdorf's "Mennonites" (*A Cappella* xviii).

8. Gundy, who points to this question as the sign of a certain frustration with Mennonite identity, is a notable exception (*Walker* 99).

9. Important note for the uninitiated: not all Mennonite poems have such stubbornly descriptive titles.

10. In *Tongue Screws and Testimonies: Poems, Stories, and Essays Inspired by the Martyrs Mirror,* Beachy disarms this gesture, adding an editorial note explaining that "606" refers to the

hymnal pagination for the doxology, a favorite song among many Mennonite congregations (271).

11. See Zacharias, "'Learning Sauerkraut.'"

WORKS CITED

Arnason, David. "A History of Turnstone Press." *Acts of Concealment: Mennonite/s Writing in Canada.* Ed. Hildi Froese Tiessen and Peter Hinchcliffe. Waterloo, ON: University of Waterloo Press, 1992. 212–22.

Barber, John. "Miriam Toews: It's a Mennonite Thing." Rev. of *Irma Voth,* by Miriam Toews. *Globe and Mail* 8 Apr. 2011. Web. 6 May 2013.

Beachy, Kirsten Eve, ed. *Tongue Screws and Testimonies: Poems, Stories, and Essays Inspired by the Martyrs Mirror.* Waterloo, ON: Herald Press, 2010.

Beachy, Stephen. *boneyard.* Portland: Verse Chorus, 2011.

Brandt, Di. *Dancing Naked: Narrative Strategies for Writing Across Centuries.* Stratford, ON: Mercury, 1996.

Dueck, Nathan. *He'll.* St John's: Pedlar Press, 2014.

Gundy, Jeff. "Being Mennonite and Writing Mennonite." *Mennonite Life* 40.4 (1986): 11.

———. *Greatest Hits: 1986–2003.* Columbus: Pudding House, 2003.

———. "How to Write the New Mennonite Poem." 1993. Hostetler, ed. 86–87.

———. *Walker in the Fog: On Mennonite Writing.* Telford: Cascadia, 2005.

Haas, Craig, and Steve Nolt. *The Mennonite Starter Kit: A Handy Guide for the New Mennonites (Everything They Forgot to Tell You in Church Membership Class!).* Intercourse, PA: Good Books, 1993.

Hossack, Darcie Friesen. *Mennonites Don't Dance.* Saskatoon: Thistledown, 2010.

Hostetler, Ann, ed. *A Cappella: Mennonite Voices in Poetry.* Iowa City: University of Iowa Press, 2003.

———. "The Unofficial Voice: The Poetics of Cultural Identity and Contemporary U.S. Mennonite Poetry." *Mennonite Muses: Mennonite/s Writing in the U.S.* Ed. John D. Roth and Ervin Beck. Goshen, IN: Mennonite Historical Society, 1998. 31–48.

Janzen, J.H. "The Literature of the Russo-Canadian Mennonites." *Mennonite Life* 1–3 (1946–48): 22–25, 28.

Janzen, Rhoda. *Mennonite in a Little Black Dress.* New York: Henry Holt, 2009.

Kasdorf, Julia Spicher. *The Body and the Book: Writing from a Mennonite Life.* 2001. University Park: Pennsylvania State University Press, 2009.

———. *Fixing Tradition: Joseph W. Yoder, Amish American.* Telford: Pandora, 2003.

———. "Introduction." *Rosanna of the Amish,* by Joseph W. Yoder. The Restored Text. Ed. Joshua R. Brown and Julia Spicher Kasdorf. Scottdale: Herald Press, 2008. 11–23.

———. "Mennonites." Hostetler, ed. 129.

———. "Mightier than the Sword: *Martyrs Mirror* in the New World." *Conrad Grebel Review* 31.1 (2013): 44–70.

Lesher, Emerson L. *The Muppie Manual: The Mennonite Urban Professional's Handbook for Humility and Success.* Intercourse, PA: Good Books, 1985.

Mierau, Maurice. "Why Rudy Wiebe Is Not the Last Mennonite Writer." *Conrad Grebel Review* 22.2 (2004): 69–82.

Mennonite Artist Project. Web. 7 May 2013. http://mennoniteartistproject.ning.com.

Munce, Alayna. *When I Was Young and in My Prime.* Roberts Creek, BC: Nightwood Editions, 2005.

Redekop, Corey. "The Sexual Menno: Or, Wouldst Thou Accompany Me to the Barn Raising?" *Rhubarb* 32 (2013): 64.

Showalter, Shirley. "*Mennonite in a Little Black Dress:* An Old Mennonite Review." 21 Nov. 2009. Web. 7 May 2013. http://www.shirleyshowalter.com.

Suderman, Elmer F. "Directions for Celebrating the Centennial of the Coming of the Low German Mennonites from the Steppes of Russia to the American Prairies." *What Can We Do Here?* St. Peter, MN: Daguerreotype Publishers, 1974. 2.

Tiessen, Hildi Froese. "Beyond the Binary: Reinscribing Cultural Identity in the Literature of Mennonites." *Mennonite Quarterly Review* 72.4 (1998): 491–501.

Toews, Miriam. *A Complicated Kindness.* Toronto: Knopf, 2004.

———. *Irma Voth.* Toronto: Knopf, 2011.

Waltner-Toews, David. "Roots." *Good Housekeeping.* Winnipeg: Turnstone Press, 1983. 75–77.

Wright, David. "A New Mennonite Replies to Julia Kasdorf." *Mennonite* 25 May 1999: 5.

Yoder, Joseph W. *Rosanna of the Amish.* 1940. Ed. Joshua R. Brown and Julia Spicher Kasdorf. Scottdale: Herald Press, 2008.

Zacharias, Robert. "'Learning Sauerkraut': Ethnic Food, Cultural Memory, and Traces of Mennonite Identity in Alayna Munce's *When I Was Young and in My Prime.*" *Canadian Literature and Cultural Memory.* Ed. Cynthia Sugars and Eleanor Ty. Don Mills, ON: Oxford University Press, 2014. 103–17.

———. *Rewriting the Break Event: Mennonites and Migration in Canadian Literature.* Winnipeg: University of Manitoba Press, 2013.

Žižek, Slavoj. *First as Tragedy, Then as Farce.* New York: Verso, 2009.

———. "The Inherent Transgression." *Cultural Values* 2.1 (1998): 1–17.

———. *The Sublime Object of Ideology.* London: Verso, 1989.

———. *Tarrying with the Negative: Kant, Hegel, and the Critique of Ideology.* 1993. Durham: Duke University Press, 2003.

PART TWO EXPANDING IDENTITY

7

In Praise of Hybridity

Reflections from Southwestern Manitoba

DI BRANDT

Who are we? This is a question we ask ourselves a lot on the Canadian prairies, where I live, especially when we write. Are we, for example, prairie writers, defined by this big wide flat land we live in and love? Are we more broadly Canadians, or western Canadians, or more generally North Americans? Are we all Métis, as some people have argued, all of us the product of a creative (and sometimes fraught) marriage between indigenous and immigrant settler cultures, beholden to the legacy of the spirited card-carrying official Métis, the mixed-blood French and English Indians, the acknowledged "founders of Manitoba"? When we try to locate ourselves in history and culture, should it be the history and culture of our own tribe, our own blood people, whoever they are, wherever they came from? Or should it be the history and culture of the nation we find ourselves part of now? Or, more largely, the history and culture of "Western" civilization as such? Or should it be, rather, the history of this continent and the culture of the people who have lived here for so many centuries and who showed us how to live here (which would require us to look squarely at the mixed refugee-colonialist dynamics that brought us here and still influence us to some extent)?

Some say it's time to update Northrop Frye's famous question for immigrant peoples in North America from "Where is here?" to "Who is here?" and "What is here?" Some say the history and culture we study and write about should be the history and culture of the people whose books we read. Some say we should more generally identify ourselves within (or against) or at least in relation to the institutions we are part of and the economic affiliations and social engagements we participate in. And when we name and celebrate "family" now, is it the people who gave birth to us and raised us? Or is it the people who taught and mentored us to become who we now are, living and dead? Or is it the people we mostly hang out with, our sustaining communities in the present? And when we write, are we directed by ethnic, or political, or spiritual affiliations? Are we mostly invested in racial and biological and cultural inheritance or by who and where and what we are now and where we imagine we're going? Is our writing mostly inflected by sexual affiliation and gender and style and class? Or is it more influenced by location, by locale, by geography, the genius loci of place? Or are we, rather, chameleonic cosmopolitans who look to the whole world, including our own dreams and fantasies and aspirations, random associations, for inspiration and engagement, strange gods whispering in our ears, in the widest way possible?

Surely it is all of the above at one time and another! I am currently writing a book of poems inspired by Laozi's *Dao De Jing,* a gift from a visiting Chinese scholar and friend. Reading up on the history of Daoism, I was delighted to discover how many of the concepts and practices were familiar to me: I'm a Daoist, and I didn't even know it! How exciting! Partly, I imagine, through Eastern-influenced Beat mystics Allen Ginsberg and Alan Watts and Ram Dass, so influential to youth culture in North America in the '60s and '70s when I was growing up, but also partly by intuition and through ancient intercultural connections picked up from First Nations and Chinese friends and teachers of tai chi. I've travelled a lot in my literary career and have discovered the most wonderful kindred spirits in the most foreign places—Barcelona, northern Scotland, Kyoto, Ramallah in Palestine, to name a few. And the most magical sense of connection to certain foreign places as well, something more mysterious and intangible but very real. The way the light shone through the broad leaves of the linden trees, with their mysterious delicious hidden flowery scent, onto the elegant granite sidewalks of east Berlin. The rustling leaves of the stately eucalyptus trees overlooking the silvery shimmering *vegas* outside Mojácar, Spain. The little blue mountains cradling the lively city of Medellín, Colombia, with poetry gods still living in them, overseeing the grand poetry festival that happens there every year. Who knew! The 1,001 golden Buddhas standing so serenely in their places in the Sanjūsangen-dō Buddhist temple in Kyoto, offering supernatural solace and support to supplicants and visitors. Sometimes the magical sense of connection happens by previous association, sometimes by surprise—it is surely the same for most travelers, including the other writers and scholars represented in this volume.

We've had extraordinarily privileged lives in North America this past half century, the whole world of knowledge and cultural practices at our fingertips, traveling where we liked, thinking and talking about and to whom we liked, reading whichever books our personal interests and desires led us to, and choosing whichever strands of inheritance and affiliation called out to us, to either promote or let go. We can also say it the other way around. Cultural hybridity is not something most people have had a choice about in North America. It is the postmodern condition thrust upon us, here more so than anywhere. Whether we've experienced it as a melting pot or a mosaic, whether we've embraced the new globalizing economic and media and traveling arrangements eagerly or reluctantly, whether we've rejoiced in the coming together of all the world's nations in our towns and cities, or whether we've mostly lamented our displacements from more stable differentiated traditional affiliations, we have been forced to practice fluid multiculti hybrid po/mo relations in our professional and personal lives and to come up with new, provisional understandings of who "we" are in relation to the "other," in relation to the rest of the world.

We've also had to come to understand our own othernesses in the face of so many other othernesses around us and discover that they add up to a recognition of surprising sameness. We were sent into exile from our homelands? So were millions of others. We suffered large-scale traumas in our past? So did most of the peoples of the world. We worked hard to hold on to a local sense of communal and spiritual practices and some semblance of family and tradition, despite volatile geographically and economically displaced and rapidly changing lives? So did everyone. It was all a terrible loss, a tragic falling away of the cultural treasures of our inheritance, but it was also—let's admit it—a wonderful setting free, a wonderful adventure, a trip into never-before-imagined possibilities of what it means to be human. In the Mennonite context under discussion here, the changes were frankly lifesaving for those in the culture who didn't fit the standard norms, independent-minded women, for example, the disabled, gay people, and others. Though I remember numerous gay and ambiguously transgendered people in our traditional Manitoba Mennonite villages—we didn't call them that then, we called them, more euphemistically, "Aunt So and So and her *friend*," or "that *man woman* in such and such village and her friend," and so on. There was a lot of eccentricity of various sorts tolerated in the villages, much more than is allowed in our communities now. More eccentricity than is permitted in the postmodern, too, where hermaphroditism tends to be surgically and prosthetically corrected to fit stereotypical gender images and gayness is strongly coded in social terms, as opposed to, for example, the more intuitively and fluidly understood phenomenon of "two spiritedness" in shamanic cultures, which enacts an overt celebration of biologically/spiritually inflected border crossers in multiple dimensions.[1]

Certainly it's time to revisit questions of gender inclusiveness in the Mennonite context generally, and particularly in Manitoba, now, where Mennonites are being tarred with a broad brush in the media on the issue of gay-straight alliances in the schools and accused of "bullying" minor groups and individuals in the community in cruel and intolerable ways. This cuts to the heart of a certain dynamic of exclusivity and intolerance, indeed active scapegoating, of difference that has characterized Mennonite communal identity, particularly in its institutionalized church-based versions, for a long time. As I write this, another story prominent in the Canadian news involves a traditionalist southwestern Manitoba Mennonite village whose children were taken away, en masse, due to allegations of widespread child beating. Numerous parents have been charged with repeated violence against young children. And the whole world has heard by now of the horrific incidents of pervasive sexual abuse in the Mennonite community of Bolivia. Should we hide and go back into cultural "martyr" mode and/or simply pretend that these things aren't happening, as many of the churches and church schools seem tempted to do? Or should we look these issues squarely in the face and do the hard work of revising our approaches to identity making in order to reply to these charges with integrity and courage?[2]

It seems the more modernity has encroached upon traditionally minded Mennonite culture in North America the narrower the definition of "belonging" has become, with sometimes pretty bizarre measurements of who is "in" and who is not. Shunning is, also, still pervasively practiced among Mennonites, both as a formal church discipline and less formally in a range of scapegoating and ostracizing practices that have scarred families and communities beyond measure—usually for progressive or feminist cultural expressions, rarely for actual misdemeanors, such as domestic abuse or violence, which tend to be overlooked and hushed up. What if we went the other way? What if, instead of spending so much (often vicious) energy on policing our borders and controlling each other's creative expressions, we accepted the carnivalesque multiculti hybridizing, and especially liberatory, influences of modernization and the postmodern on our imaginary and social practices, especially those that have already, pervasively, happened, which we deny at the expense of a very large portion of the reality of our actual lives? What if we actively embraced the trade of influences and lineages and goods that sustains all cultures and celebrated them more overtly and joyfully, and gratefully, alongside the unique internal differences that distinguish us from others? (And then spent more time trying to clean up our internal domestic and community abuse issues instead of hushing them up and then fearing outside censure?)

It's ironic and amusing, if also obvious and irrefutable, to think of the postmodern mainstream as having a subversive carnivalesque and liberatory effect on the Mennonite status quo in our time, when historically it would have been indigenous-minded peasants who staged the slyly subversive carnival against the institutionalized mainstream. The carnival tradition was allowed by the authorities of medieval Europe as a way for economically beleaguered peasants to "let off steam" by behaving with irreverence and social license for a designated week of the year. But these elaborately staged rituals also fed rebellious democratizing energies, as cultural theorists Mikhail Bakhtin and especially Natalie Zemon Davis have shown, and in this way fed directly into the Protestant and Radical Reformations (see also Howard). Not all Mennonites are of peasant origin, of course, nor are Mennonites the only group claiming the inheritance of the radically minded Anabaptists: the great revolutionary European thinkers of the early twentieth century, Lenin, Barth, Heidegger, Spengler, and so on, all turned to the Anabaptist movement for inspiration and direction (Steiner), as do innovative contemporary cultural philosophers such as Julia Kristeva and Carolyn Merchant.[3] Indeed, the civil rights and feminist movements of the twentieth century had a lot in common with the medieval European carnival and early modern Anabaptist movements, and it is ironic, therefore, that the Mennonite status quo has often—though not always—found itself on the other side of the institutional power divide, in these analogous and perhaps directly related contemporary liberation movements. It seems that institutional Mennonitism has recuperated to a considerable extent the hierarchy of repressive authority we were trying to escape from in our founding moment as a religious and cultural community, while the contemporary mainstream has gone in the opposite direction, to creatively accommodate cultural and gender differences within the multiculti multitrack consciousness of the postmodern. Certainly Miriam Toews's acclaimed novels corroborate this view. The project of this volume itself is a testament to the hybrid nature of contemporary Mennonite literary scholarship, despite its gestures of homage to more traditional models of Mennonite identity.

Would embracing our own hybridity and acknowledging the liberatory effect of the postmodern on Mennonite culture make us vanish instantly as a Mennonite people, as many people fear? Ah! The myth of the vanishing Mennonites rears its head regularly whenever Mennonites feel threatened by change! I have heard it used to warn young people against the use of lipstick, against professional education, especially for women, against movie attendance, against reading a particular book, against whatever arbitrary thing the speaker, usually a male authority figure, considers a threat to his privileged status as lawmaker and enforcer, particularly over youth. I have heard it used to warn Mennonite readers against pretty well every literary publication by Mennonite writers in the past several decades. In his chapter in this volume, Paul Tiessen recalls an instance of it in his insightful recalling of the original volatile reception of Rudy Wiebe's *Peace Shall Destroy Many* in 1962. It would be a laughable thing if it weren't still so often and arbitrarily evoked as a normative gesture in our communities, suggesting, among other things, a sort of regressive level of survivalist thinking among our people. This is so even in contemporary North America, where we have been widely welcomed as citizens, with negotiated rights to conscientious objection in the case of war, general prosperity, and worldwide cultural opportunities.

Or would a more honest and grateful celebration of our cultural hybridities allow us to shake off some of the insecure identifications of our past and rise up into the greater fullness of our being? In fact, we were always a thoroughly hybrid people, from the beginning of the Mennonite movement in the sixteenth century in northern Europe, where we congregated as part tribal kinship network, part international peasant land rights coalition, part cosmopolitan urban intellectual church reform movement, part utopian commune, part Christian, part indigenous multicultural pagan from different parts of Europe, part Converso Jew (Brandt, "*Je jelieda*"). Thereafter, we traveled from one country to another, picking up numerous further hybridities, including food, clothing, and farming practices, while retaining our own languages and customs to a remarkable degree. Our strength and robustness in retaining ancient languages and customs and beliefs despite widespread political opposition and our internal differences over several centuries have been impressive. Our appreciation of our original and evolving hybridities through centuries of cleverly bricolaging nomadism, not so much. Why not take lessons from our First Nations and Jewish neighbors and friends, who seem to be able to negotiate cultural survival at the community level much more gracefully than we do, without the same levels of reprisal for those members interested in greater honesty and graciousness in these matters?[4] Why not, indeed, listen more closely to the words of our creative writers, who have been engaged in the project of greater honesty and integrity in the matter of Mennonite identification in the multicultural postmodern context this past half century?

Someone should write a history of Mennonite cuisine, so strongly inflected by the cultures and countries we considered ourselves to be barely tolerated refugees in—Poland, Ukraine, Russia, Germany, in the Canadian Mennonite instance. My friend Natalia Lebedinskaia, recently arrived in Brandon from Moscow via Montreal, is teaching me to distinguish between their different inflections: Manitoba Mennonites make *Warenijke* in the delicate Russian fashion, she notes happily, filled with ricotta cheese or fruit, and spell it that way too, quite different from the more robust potato-and-cheese-filled Polish or Ukrainian *Pierogi* common on the Canadian prairies. *Summa Borscht,* the conventional holiday soup so loved in our villages, is a subtly flavored sour milk and potato soup made with sorrel, again in the Russian fashion, very different from the hearty beet-and-cabbage-based Polish and Ukrainian *Borscht* (which we like to cook on other, less important, occasions too). The various countries that hosted us as refugees over the centuries can't have been all that hostile if we learned nearly all our recipes from them!

In fact, there is an exciting currently developing oeuvre of scholarship on the subject of Mennonite food practices. Social historian Norma Jost Voth has cataloged some of the influences on Mennonite cuisine from neighboring peoples in her study *Mennonite Foods and Folkways from South Russia* (1990). *Zweiback,* she observes, harkens back to the Netherlands, our home country until the sixteenth-century persecutions forced us into prolonged exile and migration. *Pluma Moos* and *Plautz* were adopted from Poland; *Sauerkraut* stems from Germany; *Halopsei* comes from Ukraine. Marlene Epp has written widely and perceptively about the cultural and historical implications of Mennonite food practices, identifying our foodways as maps of our migration history, among other things.[5] I'm interested in tackling the question of cultural influence from the other side here: as instances of hospitality from our hosting countries, and positive hybridity, and cultural trade with our neighbors, throughout our history as a migrant people from the sixteenth century to the present.

It's fascinating to think about how much intercultural exchange went into the making of our thoroughly hybrid cuisine. The potatoes in *Summa Borscht* and in so many of our popular dishes, for example, were introduced in Europe from South America around the eighteenth century and thus connect us and our family customs and celebrations intimately, albeit in a roundabout way, with the indigenous customs and heritage of First Nations people in the Americas. Anthropologist Jack Weatherford observes that almost all of the material goods we associate with traditional European culture were vastly influenced by contact with First Nations people from the sixteenth century onward. Along with potatoes came tomatoes, linen, cotton, squash, and silver, also from Central and South America, where they had been cultivated with respect, innovation, and intelligence by indigenous peoples over many centuries. These goods vastly improved and extended European lives, and eventually came to epitomize what we now call modernity.

What if we acknowledged the huge contribution of First Nations cultures of the Americas to our modern well-being? Why not invite First Nations elders and artists to participate as honored guests in our various cultural gatherings, as we did recently at the WORSCHT en RHUBUABA Manitoba Mennonite Creative Arts Festival at Brandon University (in March 2013), an event, incidentally, more enthusiastically and sympathetically received by the local multiculti southwestern Manitoba community, including First Nations people, and by the creative arts communities of Brandon and Winnipeg, than by Manitoba Mennonites. Have we, in the churches and church-based schools, become our own "hostile" context by clinging too closely to our outdated separatist past? And if we really still think of ourselves as exiles from originary homelands, why don't we make more efforts to visit those lost homelands in the present, when such travel is relatively easy? Where is our homeland now?

The same is true of pretty well everything! What if we said *thank you* a little more often to the various countries and people who have shown us neighborly hospitality in their lands during our many years of emigration and travel from then to the present? Hockey came from the Cree. The concept of leisure fashion, as Paula Gunn Allen points out, came from the First Nations, who found European fashion customs bizarre and unwieldy and unnecessarily cumbersome, as they were. Many of the founding principles of modern democracy, as inscribed in the American Constitution and other such founding documents, came from the Treaty of the Iroquois League, which united five Indian nations, the Mohawk, Onondaga, Seneca, Oneida, and Cayuga (Weatherford). Every liberation movement of Europe and North America, argues Allen, including the French Revolution and the civil rights and feminist movements of the 1960s and 1970s, derived from the First Nations concept of the vision quest, finding your "dream," your utopian plan of action, in a supervised religious experience.

Did the Anabaptist movement, with its radical belief in the "priesthood of all believers" and its insistence on the freedom of each person to choose his or her religious affiliation and faith expression in adulthood, the admired heritage of our people in the sixteenth century, also derive from contact with First Nations people? Or was there a prior indigenous culture in Europe with similar principles of personal and sexual freedom, egalitarianism in matters of governance, and the importance of personal visionary experience in the development of religious belief and action? Who were our ancestors before they became martyrs and DPs ("deported peoples") during the early modern Spanish-based Inquisition across continental Europe? Did we have local independent cultural practices before then, our own literature, our own music, theatre, and design customs? Were we pagans, were we Catholics? Did we practice May Day fertility rites and worship the Sun, and/or Moon, and/or Earth? Did we participate in special religious orders such as the Waldensians or the Beguines, or the Brothers and Sisters of the Common Life, who held all their worldly goods in common (Ward 186)? Were we the instigators of the exuberant transgressive medieval carnival? Were we devotees of the Matron Cult, which, according to extensive archaeological evidence, stretched from ancient to recent times across all of Europe, including the United Kingdom, eventually morphing into the veneration of Mother and Child in Christmas pageants and art (Hodge; Schoell)? How come we know so little about the medieval and ancient aspects of our people's history?

Where did our Mennonite creative arts traditions, our robust Plautdietsch and German practices of singing, and theater, come from? Who taught them to us, or were they homegrown? How did the current pervasive disapproval of the creative arts (other than choral music) in our Manitoba Mennonite churches and home communities, so different from our self-sufficient widely expressive traditions, come about? Where did our current insularity against even closely related groups who share our Anabaptist heritage come from? Why are we not in greater cultural dialogue, as a community, with, say, the Amish, the Hutterites, the Brethren, and the Moravians, or other groups that have been affiliated with or influenced by our ways, such as the kibbutz movement in Israel and the communitarian movement in Japan?

Or, for that matter, with anyone, or everyone? A question I am asked frequently in Brandon, where I live, is, why do the Mennonites stick together so much? Why are they not interested in being part of the town and participating in its activities and getting to know other people? Why not, for example, initiate a dialogue with the Catholics, our old "enemies," in the spirit of radical forgiveness and creative change? Now that would be belief in action! I tried to organize a party in Brandon a few years ago, in celebration of the official end of our Mennonite minority/martyr story, after I heard about the official apology of the World Lutheran Churches to the World Mennonite Churches in Germany in 2010 (Liske). I couldn't find any Mennonites in Brandon able to understand the concept, let alone want to be part of such a celebration, it so deeply undercut their attachment to that particular version of our history and identity—though I found several Lutherans delighted by the idea! Why not participate as a community in the active ecumenical dialogue of different religious groups, as well as the carnivalesque celebration of different cultural customs and traditions in various festivals and fairs, which make North America such an interesting and colorful place to live?

Why do we not include H.D. (Hilda Doolittle) among our writerly identifications, the extraordinary modernist woman poet who brought such a powerful visionary element to contemporary English poetry, deriving directly from the mystical strand of our heritage, through Jakob Boehme and Hans Denk and the Moravians? The great German thinkers of the late nineteenth century and early twentieth century, Karl Barth, Ernst Bloch, Oswald Spengler, and Franz Rosenzweig, and later Martin Heidegger, were all influenced by the Anabaptist movement and its radical democratic thinking (Steiner). Far from expelling us and our visions from their lands, the mainstream thinkers of Europe remember our ancestors, retrospectively, with great admiration. If you go there now, you can find a friendly and engaged reception among German, Austrian, Swiss, Dutch, and Belgian intellectuals, our long-lost relatives, an uplifting and enlightening experience, which some of the contributors to this collection volume have happily experienced first hand.

If my thesis is correct, that Anabaptist thinking and affiliation were strongly influenced by the Conversos of Rotterdam and Amsterdam, the freethinking port cities of the sixteenth century, where a number of the Jews expelled from Spain ended up in superficially Christianized guise (Brandt, "*Je jelieda*"), then we can also claim direct kinship with innovative European Jewish thinkers such as Karl Marx and Sigmund Freud, and contemporary Jewish American thinkers such as Joel Kovel and Richard Heinberg (both of whom look to the Anabaptists, the Hutterites, and the Amish, respectively, as exemplary economic models for the present), as well as Canadian poet-intellectuals Miriam Waddington and, yes, Leonard Cohen.

Speaking of Jakob Boehme, whither has gone that whole mystical and visionary tradition of our heritage? Whither has gone unmediated mythopoetic inspiration, whispering straight into your heart in the middle of the night no matter how lowly or marginal your social station, directly from God? Spirituality, these days, seems to have become yet again a closely guarded notion in our Mennonite churches and church-based schools, available only to the weekly institutionalized, and only by way of approval from the pulpit, which itself is reduced to a secondary analytical reading of primary texts, never to contemporary revelation. Isn't this precisely what the Anabaptist reformation was against? In any case, it wasn't so in the old villages, even in my childhood in the 1950s, where God still spoke frequently and directly to the oddest people, both women and men, and even children, in voices and visions and a range of spectacles, where magic and mystery and wild diversity in the old sense abounded.

When did that all that stop? Was it when our churches changed languages from archaic German to modern English (in the mid-1960s)? Was it part of the loss of mystery and romance that many North American churches associate with Vatican II, which happened around the same time, as my friend and neighbor Reta Chapman suggests? What about Rembrandt and Erasmus, those grand Dutch artist-intellectuals, whose works courageously supported the "free thinking" and "inner light" aspects of the Anabaptist movement, why don't we remember and celebrate them more? What about the English visionary poet and painter William Blake, who was so powerfully influenced by Boehme: is he not also our spiritual cousin? As he says in *All Religions Are One,* "The Religions of all Nations are derived from each Nations different reception of the Poetic Genius, which is every where call'd the Spirit of Prophecy" (1). How did we come to have so much narrower a focus in our churches and schools and communities in terms of identifications and practices than our exuberantly visionary ancestors had?

What about the distinguished European women mystics and writers of the Middle Ages, who likely contributed in a direct way to the development of Anabaptism in the fifteenth and sixteenth centuries, women such as the German ninth-century poet Dhuoda, the first known European woman writer; Hrotsvit of Gandersheim, the first known dramatist of Christianity, the first Saxon poet, and the first woman historian of Germany; Hildegard von Bingen, the famous twelfth-century German scientist, mystic, poet, dramatist, composer, and cultural leader; the thirteenth-century Dutch poet Hadewijch of Antwerp, who influenced the establishment of a women's movement in Holland; and the influential Mechthild of Magdeburg, who wrote a famous prose treatise on Christianity, *Flowing Light of the Godhead,* in Plautdietsch in the thirteenth century (Jantzen, *Power;* Wilson)?

It is interesting to note that these women writers were cultural and spiritual leaders in their own right, as were the Anabaptist women leaders we know of from the sixteenth century. How was it that our communities did such an about-face on the role of women later on, quite against the Anabaptist belief in the priesthood of all believers, and against our traditionalist feminine-inflected practices of matrilocality and extended family systems, and political nonviolence? And why aren't we all reading Grace Jantzen, of Saskatchewan and later of Manchester, England, who made such a brilliant international name for herself as a philosopher of nonviolence in the last few decades—everywhere, that is, except in her home Mennonite community in Canada? Jantzen, incidentally, champions the same medieval women mystics as exemplary for a more egalitarian and courageous and visionary contemporary approach to spiritual practices (*Becoming; Power*).

One of the questions I'm moving toward here is why the new Mennonite literary writing of the past half century, beginning with Rudy Wiebe's 1962 novel *Peace Shall Destroy Many* and continuing to the present with Miriam Toews's internationally celebrated fictions, has been received with such diffidence (at best) and hostility (at worst) by most Mennonites in North America, excepting the specialized cultural circles represented in this volume. How is it that our people for the most part have treated their brightest, most gifted, and even most celebrated spirits—those thinkers and artists willing to talk about the cultural questions at the heart of the culture in sparkly and creative ways—extraordinarily badly? (It happened to me too in so many ways: where is the peace and justice witness of the Mennonites when it comes to issues of "truth and reconciliation" within our own communities, where it matters most, after all, existentially and ethically speaking?)

We have always had strong homegrown creative arts traditions in our towns and villages, from poetry composition and recitation to local playwriting and theater to folk dancing and mumming, and above all, music, ranging from Plautdietsch folksongs to traditional German hymns and chorales, to Russian and English songs.[6] In Reinland, the traditionalist Manitoba peasant village I grew up in, children were taught to recite poems and sing songs and perform piano and violin pieces for *Oma* on ceremonial occasions, such as Christmas and Easter and her birthday, from the tender age of two to young adulthood. That made for a highly competitive performance at my maternal grandmother's house, all the aunts and uncles gathered around, watching eagerly and giving ratings for excellence. (It is no surprise that so many of the grandchildren and great-grandchildren in Grandma Aganetha's large family became professional musicians and painters and writers after that rigorous early training, presided over by her precise and generous queenly appreciation!)

My paternal uncles, who were mostly farmers or house builders and barely literate, nevertheless carried on a robust homemade poetry practice throughout the summer farming season. One of them would write a parodic verse about a brother in carpenter's pencil on the machine shed wall, perhaps to the tune of *O du lieber Augustin.* It would remain there for anyone to see until the named brother came in and immediately retaliated with a witty reprisal in a second stanza. And so it would go all summer long. Around harvest time, all the uncles would gather in the shed and laugh their heads off about the poetic word jostling and ribbing and retaliations that had carried on all summer. (I'd love to see one of those rambling off-color humorous long poems now!) At birthday parties and weddings in the villages, someone would inevitably get up and perform a parodic song or poem about the featured guests, written in Plautdietsch or in the "buggered-up language" of our people (to use the expression made famous by Armin Wiebe), a witty patois of English and Plautdietsch we children (and sometimes adults) often spoke with gusto and risqué enjoyment, despite strict injunctions by parents and teachers against doing so for the sake of preserving the originating languages.

The mystery of Mennonite resistance to the contemporary creative arts deepens if you consider the impressive incidence of (reputedly) Mennonite names in the professional creative arts in North America at this time, in addition to the writers under discussion here, from Johnny Denver, Phyllis Diller, Dyan Cannon, Daryl Hannah, Matt Groening, David Foster Wallace, and Pamela Anderson in the United States to Fred Penner, Tracy Dahl, Ben Heppner, John Hess, Vern Thiessen, Wanda Koop, Aganetha Dyck, Randolph Peters, and Alan Kroeker in Canada, among many others. All this cultural excellence didn't just spring out of nowhere! There must have been strong local interest in and support of these artists and their art forms—in people's homes if not in the churches. Perhaps it is the women of the culture, denied public expression from the pulpit but extensively involved in the beautification of our lives through sewing, embroidery, baking, and the numerous intimate social tasks of raising children, who have been our true creative arts patrons, or rather matrons, keeping the desire and talent for beauty and creative expression alive for our people through the centuries, despite poverty and the negative attitudes of the church. Is there a gender bias implicit in the critical reception of creative writers in the culture in this sense, that all writers are being denigrated for their creative expressiveness and desire for beauty the way women traditionally have been?

To come back to location, the question of *here* with which this chapter began, let me end this meditation with a few regionally based observations on *who is here* and *what is here,* in literary terms, in my corner of the world. I was astonished and delighted, a few years ago, to realize that southwestern Manitoba, where I live, was the birthplace of the modern Canadian novel, not just in one instance, but in several! Frances Beynon of Hartney published the first modern Canadian novel, *Aleta Day,* in 1919. Frederick Philip Grove of Rapid City and Martha Ostenso of Brandon published the second and third modern Canadian novels in 1925, *Settlers of the Marsh* and *Wild Geese,* respectively. Grove previously taught school in Haskett, a Mennonite village in southern Manitoba, and married a Catherine Wiens there, who became very influential in his literary success. Paul Hiebert, who wrote a parodic literary critical account of the "Sweet Songstress of Saskatchewan" and her ditties in the popular classic *Sarah Binks* (1947), grew up in Pilot Mound, not far from Brandon, and taught chemistry at the University of Manitoba for many years before retiring to Carman, Manitoba. A.E. Vogt, the so-called father of modern science fiction in North America, grew up near the Mennonite town of Altona, Manitoba. This makes Mennonites, ironically enough, intimately connected with the birth of modern writing in several genres in Canada, and even North America! Though we must surely credit the best-selling suffragist novelist Nellie

McClung and long before her, the well-sung and -storied landscape of the Métis and First Nations peoples of this region for making the birth of modern fiction possible here, at the heart of the continent. In any case, we have been far from *die Stille im Lande* we sometimes make ourselves out to be!

I was lucky to meet Paul Hiebert in person, in the Carman museum, as an impressionable high school student wandering off from a family gathering in the Carman park many years ago. He was a sparkly bright-eyed old man in his eighties, and a fascinating storyteller. He recognized my intellectual and literary interests in an instant and promptly invited me to his cottage, The Burrs, for tea, showering me with gifts and letters thereafter, and occasionally taking me for lunch during my college years in Winnipeg. The great modernist poet Dorothy Livesay, who grew up in Winnipeg and whose daughter married a traditional Mennonite farmer in Ontario, was another actively adoptive literary mentor for me, among many such fortuitous adoptions by a range of writers and scholars and fans across Canada and elsewhere, who have sustained me greatly in my life and career against the hostilities of my home communities. I'm sure every Manitoba Mennonite writer has similar stories of intercultural sustenance to tell: let's not ignore these generous gestures of support to us and our people, let's say thank you and give something of value back to them instead.

I recently heard a Mennonite pastor in Brandon preach a sermon called "God Wants Us to Suffer," laboring to uphold our ebbing marginalized martyr identity for the Mennonite churches with their faltering attendance and enthusiasm even though we have enjoyed unusual privileges since our arrival in this country and are mostly well assimilated to modernity. This is precisely the wrong direction to go in, in my view, as is the still widely held idea that churches are the keepers of the "sacred" and that artists (and other adventurers and visionaries) are dabblers in the "secular." I'm with Grace Jantzen on this point: "Ever since the 'sacred canopy' of the medieval world was shattered," she writes in *Becoming Divine: Toward a Feminist Philosophy of Religion,* "secularism and religion have often defined themselves over against one another; yet they are deeply implicated in each other." Both need to be radically rethought as "mutually imbricated in some of the most objectionable aspects of the project of modernity," in order to move from what Jantzen calls the philosophy of "necrophilia" to a more feminine and earth-respecting poetics of "natality" (8). A spirituality centered in natality, as she envisions it, is "'not concerned with death, coercion, or preventing people from harming one another, but with birth which . . . dignifies uniqueness, human plurality, joy, appearance, new beginning, hope, creativity and unpredictability'" (Bhikhu Parekh, qtd. 144).

It's hard to give up a narrow minority martyr identity if it has been held onto for a very long time. It was valuable to us in the past, perhaps, in helping us to think through the social and psychic foundations of violence and non-violence experientially, in our chosen project of trying to learn how to live for and in peace. But it's definitely stale-dated now as a PTSD effect of that long-vanished time. If we keep invoking it past its psychic usefulness, it risks becoming an inverted argument for the very violence we are trying to avoid by investing in dynamics that will ensure its repetition, rather than moving beyond them into greater health and joy.[7] It's also hard to give up a tightly controlled authoritarian system, for our community is habituated to protecting its social insecurities from creative scrutiny by controlling what is said and by whom within the group. But alas, such a practice brings with it a thoroughly bifurcated vision of the world, shored up at the terrible expense of its most vulnerable and its most gifted, visionary members, who bear the burden at a deep spiritual/imaginative level, of the truths expelled from public view by the official stories.

Why not, rather, move toward appreciating more truthfully, generously, gratefully, inclusively, interactively who we were well before the sad moment of our historical displacement into suffering and, above all, who we are now, and *where* and *what* we are now, not in a narrow fictional sense but in astonishing actuality—as I believe the project of this volume is trying to do—in relation to our many friends and our grace-filled lives, on this bountiful earth, in this magical cosmos, infused with the most astonishing processes of deconstruction and creative renewal. Such inclusiveness will help us to think more clearly, at this critical, liminal, and sacred time, when many of the premises and promises that fueled modernity are coming apart, about what kind of future we wish to imagine, to birth, into being, among its myriad extraordinary possibilities.

NOTES

1. See Allen; Boym; Elias; Foucault; Hogue; and Kelly-Gadol on the disciplining/silencing of the body and homogenization of cultural norms that accompanied the rise and development of modernity.

2. Joan Friedman-Rudovsky, the brilliant and sensitive reporter who broke to the American media recently the story of the pervasive drugging and raping of women among the Bolivian Mennonites by their own village men, spent a lot of time in the community, interviewing both women and men, trying to understand how such a thing could happen. In a recent interview, she analyzed the systemic factors contributing to these horrific incidents: "A lack of checks and balances, warped use of forgiveness, lack of sexual and reproductive health education, and a religion that tells them that their time on earth is meant for suffering so when something bad happens, you just accept it rather than raising a fuss, particularly

if you are a woman." She further reflected that "whenever you have a group that sees itself outside the limits of the rest of society and that values the reputation or integrity of the group over the safety and protection of the individual, that community is more likely to be prone to sexual abuse" ("How"). These are familiar dynamics throughout the international Mennonite world, and I hope that leaders and community members take note and choose to embark on radical self-scrutiny and creative revision in the horrifying aftermath of this terrible story, taking clues from Friedman-Rudovsky's insightful portrayal of what happened and is, we understand, still happening, despite legal action taken in 2011. See also Friedman-Rudovsky, "Ghost-Rapes."

3. Although neither Kristeva nor Merchant uses the term "Anabaptist" specifically, both refer to the historical movements that sought to re-create premodern values that synchronize with Anabaptism. See Kristeva, especially 36–63; and Merchant, especially 42–68; see also Brandt, "*Je jelieda.*"

4. The *Globe and Mail* featured an insightful article by Doug Saunders recently on the alterity of many peoples to the modern global definition of statehood. The 1648 Peace of Westphalia, observes Saunders, "created a set of institutions that reshaped the world: national self-determination, exclusive sovereignty of governments over agreed-upon territory, fixed borders and the citizenship rights of people living within those borders. But this new invention failed to take into account groups of people who had lived in the same territory, often longer than the Europeans, but did not necessarily see themselves as members of the Westphalian nation." Saunders is interested in the self-definition of indigenous nations, but many of his comments apply to other self-defining groups, such as the Mennonites. Are we a nation within a nation? If so, what kind of nation? Our principles of self-government as "a people" were perhaps much better understood and more ethically practiced in earlier times, when we were forced to rely on ourselves much more thoroughly in all matters, and are in need of radical scrutiny and revision now.

5. See her entries in the Works Cited.

6. Lesley Glendinning has written an MA thesis on the oeuvre of Plautdietsch drama as practiced in Manitoba Mennonite culture; see Glendinning for a summary of that work.

7. I find the project of the recent literary anthology *Tongue Screws and Testimonies: Poems, Stories, and Essays Inspired by the Martyrs Mirror* (see Beachy) problematic in precisely this way, in trying to put the "new" Mennonite writing back into the "old wineskins" of our past martyr history—though it is an important document in illustrating the Mennonite temptation to invest imaginative and erotic, even pornographic, energies in the traumas of our past, reminiscent of Catholic crucifixion and saint veneration but without the same ritual mediation or theological understanding.

WORKS CITED

Allen, Paula Gunn. "Who Is Your Mother? The Red Roots of White Feminism." *The Sacred Hoop: Recovering the Feminine in American Indian Traditions.* 1986. Boston: Beacon Press, 1992. 209–21.

Bakhtin, Mikhail M. *The Dialogic Imagination: Four Essays.* Ed. Michael Holquist. Trans. Caryl Emerson and Michael Holquist. Austin: University of Texas Press, 1981.

Beachy, Kirsten Eve, ed. *Tongue Screws and Testimonies: Poems, Stories, and Essays Inspired by the Martyrs Mirror.* Scottdale: Herald Press, 2010.

Blake, William. "All Religions Are One." 1788, 1795. *The Complete Poetry and Prose of William Blake.* Ed. David V. Erdman. Berkeley: University of California Press, 2008.

Boym, Svetlana. *The Future of Nostalgia.* New York: Basic Books, 2001.

Brandt, Di. "*Je jelieda, je vechieda:* Canadian Mennonite (Alter)Identifications." *So this is the world & here I am in it.* Edmonton: NeWest Press, 2007. 105–32.

———. *SHE: Poems Inspired by Laozi's* Dao De Jing. Ink drawings by Lin Xu. Brandon, MB: Radish Press, 2011.

Davis, Natalie Zemon. *Society and Culture in Early Modern France: Eight Essays.* Stanford: Stanford University Press, 1975.

Elias, Norbert. *The Civilizing Process: Sociogenetic and Psychogenetic Investigations.* Rev. ed. Oxford: Blackwell, 2000.

Epp, Marlene. "Memories of Sauerkraut and Zwieback: Foodways in the Mennonite Diaspora." *Rhubarb* 26 (2010): 33–40.

———. "More than 'Just' Recipes: Mennonite Cookbooks in Mid-Twentieth Century North America." *Edible Histories, Cultural Politics: Towards a Canadian Food History.* Ed. Franca Iacovetta, Valerie J. Korinek, and Marlene Epp. Toronto: University of Toronto Press, 2012. 173–88.

———. "The Semiotics of Zwieback: Feast and Famine in the Narratives of Mennonite Refugee Women." *Sisters or Strangers? Immigrant, Ethnic, and Racialized Women in Canadian History.* Ed. Marlene Epp, Franca Iacovetta, and Frances Swyripa. Toronto: University of Toronto Press, 2004. 314–40.

Foucault, Michel. *The History of Sexuality, Vol. 1: An Introduction.* Trans. Robert Hurley. New York: Vintage Books, 1990.

Friedman-Rudovsky, Joan. "The Ghost-Rapes of Bolivia: The Perpetrators Were Caught but the Crimes Continue." *Vice Magazine* Aug. 2013. Web. 22 Aug. 2013.

———. "'How Do You Heal?': A Journalist Revisits a Colony Traumatized by Rape." Interview by Jina Moore. Ochberg Society for Trauma Journalism 15 Aug. 2013. Web. 22 Aug. 2013.

Glendinning, Lesley. ". . . *Oba de Sproak es uns sehe wijchtijch*" [". . . But the Language Is Very Important to Us"]. *Rhubarb* 33 (2013): 9–13.

Heinberg, Richard. *The Party's Over: Oil, War, and the Fate of Industrial Societies.* Gabriola Island, BC: New Society Publishing, 2005.

Hodge, Winifred. "Matrons and Disir: The Heathen Tribal Mothers." Frigagsweb.org 28 Mar. 1998. Web. 12 Mar. 2014.

Hogue, W. Lawrence. *Postmodern American Literature and Its Other.* Urbana: University of Illinois Press, 2008.

Howard, Sharon. "Carnival and Carnivalesque." *Early Modern Notes* 31 Aug. 2004. Web. 4 June 2014.

Jantzen, Grace. *Becoming Divine: Toward a Feminist Philosophy of Religion.* Bloomington: Indiana University Press, 1999.

———. *Power, Gender, and Christian Mysticism.* Cambridge, UK: Cambridge University Press, 1995.

Kelly-Gadol, Joan. "Did Women Have a Renaissance?" *Becoming Visible: Women in European History.* Ed. Renate Bridenthal and Claudia Koonz. Boston: Houghton Mifflin, 1977. 137–64.

Kovel, Joel. *The Enemy of Nature: The End of Capitalism or the End of the World?* New York: Fernwood Publishing, 2002.

Kristeva, Julia. *Desire in Language: A Semiotic Approach to Literature and Art.* Ed. Leon S. Roudiez. Trans. Thomas Gora, Alice Jardine, and Leon S. Roudiez. New York: Columbia University Press, 1980.

Liske, Colin. "Lutherans Apologize to Mennonites." Faithvictoria.wordpress.com 9 Aug. 2010. Web. 1 Aug. 2013.

Merchant, Carolyn. *The Death of Nature: Women, Ecology, and the Scientific Revolution.* New York: HarperCollins, 1980.

Saunders, Doug. "What Kind of Nation Is a First Nation? We Need to Decide." *Globe and Mail* 12 Jan. 2013: F9.

Schoell, Hans Christoph. *Die Drei Ewigen: Eine Untersuchung über Germanische Bauernglauben.* Jena, Germany: Eugen Diederichs Verlag, 1936.

Steiner, George. *Martin Heidegger.* Chicago: University of Chicago Press, 1989.

Voth, Norma Jost. *Mennonite Foods and Folkways from South Russia.* 2 vols. Intercourse, PA: Good Books, 1990, 1994.

Ward, Jennifer. *Women in Medieval Europe 1200–1500.* London: Longman, 2002.

Weatherford, Jack. "The Indian Founding Fathers." *Indian Givers: How the Indians of the Americas Transformed the World.* New York: Random House, 1988. 133–50.

Wilson, Katharina M., ed. *Medieval Women Writers.* Athens: University of Georgia Press, 1988.

8

Queering Mennonite Literature

DANIEL SHANK CRUZ

In Jan Guenther Braun's 2008 novel *Somewhere Else,* the protagonist Jess laments that "the words 'queer Mennonite' are an oxymoron" (137). Although *Somewhere Else* offers a model of how these two seemingly opposed identities can coexist, and though such modeling is present in other recent examples of Mennonite literature, such as Stephen Beachy's 2011 novel *boneyard* and Casey Plett's 2012 short story "Other Women,"[1] little has been done in the realm of Mennonite literary criticism[2] to explore the tension between these two identities. This lack is dangerous because, as the history of literary criticism on various minority literatures shows, focusing on a single aspect of a person's identity is ultimately an oppressive dead end both for academic theory and for lived practice. One might be a Mennonite—itself a term that glosses over numerous variations—but one is also female, or Canadian, or Latino, or middle class, or, yes, queer, and it is necessary to examine these intersections. Literary critics must therefore wrestle with questions such as how these hybrid identities manifest themselves in Mennonite literature. How should we as critics write about these identities? And, perhaps more basically, why should we care?

One immediate answer to the last question is that, if Mennonite literary criticism is going to have something to say to the field of literary studies in general, it must figure out how to make the social activist messages found in much of Mennonite literature accessible to those readers who otherwise have no connection to the Mennonite community.[3] The work of Mennonite writers is often radical compared with mainstream societal standards, not just traditional Mennonite values. It is important to recognize that Mennonite literature critiques not only the Mennonite community (when it does so at all) but also society in general, often using Mennonite subject matter to do so. For instance,

"Other Women" is about Sophie's struggle against North American society's transphobia, shared by her Mennonite community as a learned behavior from its broader context. If, however, the Mennonite elements were removed from the story, its primary political import would remain the same.

It is time for critics to acknowledge this wider focus and to examine what Mennonite literature says to an extended audience. Hildi Froese Tiessen writes about the struggle of "Mennonite writers" to be seen as writers who happen to be Mennonite instead of vice versa (14); likewise, those of us critics who are Mennonite have the opportunity to approach Mennonite literature as scholars who happen to be Mennonite rather than the other way around.[4] It is time for Mennonite literary criticism to be in the world *and* of it in order to help non-Mennonite readers and critics see why Mennonite literature is worth reading.

In light of this necessity, this chapter examines the intersection of queer and Mennonite elements in recent Mennonite literature as an example of how Mennonite literary criticism can dialogue with other areas within literary criticism and theory.[5] The clear critical tool for investigating queer Mennonite literature is queer theory. The hybrid queer-Mennonite identities of the protagonists in these texts offer rich ground for literary critics without any kind of Mennonite affiliation to explore. Queer Mennonite texts offer a particular vision of queerness that acknowledges the importance of some kind of moral journey, an element that can seem marginalized in queer discourse.

Mennonite critics, too, should pay attention to the radical products of this hybridity. Just as there is a long tradition of Mennonite novelists and poets writing as activists,[6] we as critics should highlight these activist elements, and this is especially the case with the recent trend of queer Mennonite literature. Braun posits in an essay about naming herself as a queer Mennonite that she writes "in an effort to begin the building of queer Mennonite academic history" ("From" 70). It is essential for literary critics to participate in this task.

Before investigating some of the queer aspects of Braun's, Plett's, and Beachy's texts, I make a personal digression about the position from which I write, in part as a reminder of the complexity inherent in the notion of "identity." I am a middle-class male in his thirties born to a Swiss-German Mennonite mother and a Puerto Rican father. I am bisexual, though I prefer the term "queer" because of its openness. I want my two ethnicities and my queerness to be conversant with one another, and the space created by queer theory is one place where this dialogue can happen. For me (and perhaps for the protagonists of queer Mennonite literature), the phrase "after identity" signifies a desire to pursue, to go *after,* a healthy understanding of selfhood rather than a desire to be beyond identity as a concept, because that naming of our queer identities is an essential act of resistance in our homophobic society.

I am specifically interested in the works at hand because I am drawn to their activist nature and because of my strong reactions to them. As I first read each of these texts, I found myself experiencing more and more stress, which manifested itself in heart palpitations and feelings of nausea. For example, even though it is not especially well written, *Somewhere Else* moved me to the point where, on several occasions, I had to stop reading because my visceral reaction was so intense that I worried I would have a heart attack if I kept going.

Despite voraciously reading all of my life, I never had these physical reactions to literature before. My feelings were a vivid reminder that personal experience is always connected to broader collective realities, and that it is necessary for us as critics to explore how individual experiences with literature relate to the larger issue of working for social justice. The authors of recent queer Mennonite literature are forced into the role of writer-as-transgressor because of society's continuing homophobia. Braun wrote to me in an email that after *Somewhere Else* was published she felt "guilt for transgressing (writing about Mennonite queers), guilt for taking up space." This admission that the oppression felt under homophobia does not go away even when one can use one's voice to claim discursive "space" is a heart-wrenching reminder of how far North American society still has to go in order to become queer friendly.

As critics, we can help to ease this oppression by highlighting queer stories. I write this chapter to pay homage to writers such as Braun, Plett, and Beachy for their willingness to speak out against oppression with the hope that my readers will be inspired to read these texts for themselves and to take action to ensure that their communities—whether Mennonite or not—become more welcoming to these voices. I am sincere in my advocacy of queer theory as a potential force for positive social change, especially when it is combined with radical Anabaptism. But it is also necessary to respond to real-world oppression, which is not nuanced, on a clear, basic level: homophobia, biphobia, and transphobia are wrong. Therefore, in responding to these oppressions, in part by calling on other critics to also take up the cause, this chapter is intentionally polemic. This rhetorical strategy is meant to provoke rather than be rigidly prescriptive, just as queer theory's strength lies in the coexistence of its revolutionary openness and its firm stance against intolerance.

One reason that viewing Mennonite literature through the lens of queer theory can be advantageous is that the term "queer" is so flexible. It can refer to sexuality, but it can also refer to a generally transgressive outlook. Thomas

Piontek contends that "queer" is "a questioning stance" (2); this emphasis on interrogation of the normative is also evident in Mennonite literature. Neither tradition is satisfied with the status quo. The "queer" in queer theory is malleable, just as individual identity is malleable, and thus offers space for a seemingly antithetical term such as "Mennonite" to coexist with it. At its broadest, being queer is simply being against hegemonic discourses, and it is therefore an inherently political position.[7] Mennonite literature is often political in that it critiques the authoritarian discourse present both in the Mennonite community and in society as a whole, so it can be illuminated by queer theoretical concepts. As Braun writes, "'queer' . . . reflects the most broad and inclusive way of discussing 'other'" ("From" 71). The Mennonite tradition claims to embrace those whom society makes other, and interacting with queer theory is one way to learn how to perform this welcoming better. Although historically Mennonites themselves have been culturally other and the early Anabaptist tradition epitomized queer transgressiveness,[8] this position has largely been lost in North America, and the official Mennonite community[9] now participates in the marginalization of lesbian, gay, bisexual, and trans (LGBT) persons. Engaging with queer theory is one way for Mennonites to return to their liberating roots.

The protagonists in recent Mennonite literature recognize the openness inherent in being queer. Although, as the quotation that opens this chapter shows, Jess struggles to reconcile her queer and Mennonite identities, her act of naming herself as queer in this struggle is important. It gives her an initial sense of selfhood that acknowledges her desires while giving her space to continue to discover and construct her self in a way that works for her because it is not prescriptive. Living as queer and placing the Mennonite element of herself to the side for much of *Somewhere Else* allows Jess to learn how to accept her attraction to women. It is only once she takes this step that she can then return to a healthier, more compatible version of her Mennonite identity.

Similarly, in Plett's "Other Women," though Sophie names herself as trans, embracing her womanhood, she is open to sexual experiences with different genders even though she claims to prefer women (99). In fact, she refuses to answer when her cousin asks whether she dates women or men, and the story culminates in a night when she is intimate with both a woman and a man (106, 115–21). Sophie is interested more in whether her partners listen to her desires and respect her transitioning body than in their gender; the act—how it is performed—is more important than the person with whom it is performed. She rejects Megan in favor of Mark because he does a better job of letting Sophie explore her desires. It is significant that his sexual orientation also remains unnamed (99, 105). Mark is attracted to Sophie as a person, not specifically as a man or woman. Sophie's lack of knowledge about his sexual preferences allows her to relax around him and ultimately accept his advances. The openness present in these interactions is invigorating rather than threatening. Although the amorphousness of openness might be scary, which is why boundaries can be comforting and are often defended vigorously, the lack of limits can also allow for revolutionary change. Seeing one's romantic partner as a person rather than as a man or woman begins to erode the gender binary central to homophobia and patriarchy.

Although *boneyard*'s protagonist, Jake, embraces a queer kind of openness by never using a label for his sexuality in his search for truth and simply describing the acts that he engages in instead, the novel's postmodern form also affirms this openness. Common postmodern fiction tropes such as extensive footnotes and the use of various fonts and visual images abound. The book is supposedly a series of short stories written by Jake, an Amish man who wrote them before joining the church, and edited from a partially burnt manuscript by Beachy for public consumption (9, 13). But Beachy's version of Jake's narrative is constantly questioned in footnotes ostensibly inserted by his Verse Chorus Press editor, Judith Owsley Brown (e.g., 38–39). That her initials spell out Job (i.e., the biblical character) points to how torturous she finds her relationship with Beachy because of his perceived unreliability and the resulting unreliability of his/Jake's text. *boneyard*'s playful, perplexing structure posits that it does not matter where the story originates, only that it forces readers to sift through it in search of truth. This idea radically destabilizes the very base of the field of Mennonite literature (i.e., that there is something unique about writing from authors with Mennonite origins), even as the novel itself is a part of that field, causing us to question our assumptions about this critical endeavor. *boneyard* is such a multifoliate text that viewing it only through a Mennonite lens leads to a woefully inadequate understanding of the book, as does simply viewing it through a queer lens. A combination of the two is necessary.

Although the radical openness of queer subjectivity means that it inevitably comes into conflict with communities bound by strict rules and conventions, queer theory's view of "community" is useful for examining the tension that characters in queer Mennonite literature feel between the worldly milieus that they participate in and their home communities. The traditional definition of this concept assumes sameness among group members. This is how Mennonites have officially understood community through their use of confessions of faith as a requirement for church membership. In the past, some Mennonite groups employed the practice of shunning individuals who acted transgressively, and in the present even the two most liberal North American Mennonite denominations, Mennonite Church USA and Mennonite Church Canada, discipline congregations that embrace sexually active LGBT persons. The protagonists in Plett's, Braun's, and Beachy's works experience this exclusion informally. They know that the church offers no room for their queer selves, so they leave it before they are officially rejected. In contrast to this restrictive form of community, Nikki Sullivan writes that queer theorists redefine community as a space of "fracturing" that allows room for "productive differences," instead of enforcing conformity, and "enables . . . diversity and the radical unknowability" that this variety brings (148). Instead of a group based on a shared identity, queer community is based on a desire to learn from one another via the multiplicity of individual experiences. Numerous pieces of Mennonite literature describe the breakdown or oppressiveness of community as a result of an insistence that all members adhere to a single standard,[10] but the queer notion of community as a place that is contentious, allowing dialogue despite disagreement, offers a healthy alternative model.[11] The slipperiness of the term "queer" allows the boundaries of its community to be permeable rather than enforcing an inside/outside dichotomy. This is the kind of community present in Braun's and Plett's works in the healthiest scenarios, which take place outside Mennonitism.

In Braun's *Somewhere Else,* Jess finds her first welcoming community in literature, in texts written, significantly, by both Mennonite and secular authors. She draws strength from the activist nature of previous Mennonite literature such as Di Brandt's *questions i asked my mother,* which gives Jess the words to stand up to her father even as he tries to forbid her from reading such radical material. Her reading helps her to realize that she must leave her home in order to survive (13–15, 18). Once she is away from the Mennonite community, Jess reads lesbian stories such as Sarah Waters's *Tipping the Velvet* and feminist texts such as Margaret Atwood's *The Edible Woman* (73, 87). Both are coming-of-age narratives that reflect Jess back to herself as she continues to construct her queer identity. She struggles throughout the novel to find other people who care about her in a healthy way, but she is never completely alone because of her reading. Jess recognizes that the importance of community in Mennonite thought is a good thing, and she knows that she cannot survive alone, so she searches for a group who will accept her. Paradoxically, being taught the Mennonite ideal of community helps Jess to realize that her home community is flawed and that she must seek a better one. She needs a place where openness is practiced, not just preached, and finds it in the secular university world. Jess's healthy experiences with community during her time of exile allow her to return home at the end of the novel in order to rebuild community with her family alongside her female lover, Shea.

In Plett's "Other Women," Sophie returns to her home in Winnipeg from Portland in an attempt to figure out where she fits because she has found that transphobia is the same on both sides of the border. Her search for a welcoming community, however, is thwarted throughout most of the story. For instance, though her mother tries to be understanding of her transition, asking whether Sophie is safe from transphobic violence in the United States, she also worries that the trans community is a "cult" (100, 108). This comment is offensive in part because it implies that being trans is a choice, even though Sophie explains throughout the story that she has always felt like a woman. Her family members are unable to see that, though she can choose just how she would like to perform her femininity, she has always known that her self is better expressed through this gender. Similar to her mother's reluctance to accept Sophie's identity, members of Sophie's family refuse to come to Christmas dinner simply because she is there (110). They prefer to sacrifice their experience of community rather than open the community to those who are at all different from them. As such, their transphobia is detrimental to themselves as well as Sophie. We see the negative aspect of the traditional Mennonite concept of community here, as her family participates in an informal shunning of her. In fact, this shunning is even worse than the formal kind because it is chosen voluntarily by her family instead of being forced on them by church leadership.

The place where Sophie should find an unconditionally loving and accepting community, church, is likewise an unwelcoming space. Although Mennonites have a long history of being persecuted exiles themselves, and thus should be especially cognizant of Jesus's mandate to embrace those at the margins of society, the congregation in "Other Women" refuses to do so. Even worse, it conveys its lack of welcome to Sophie via her family. Her mother asks her not to sit with the family during the Christmas service because her transition might be too controversial for the congregation to handle and put the family in a bad light. Sophie complies by using her hair to hide her face so that the older congregants do not recognize her and waiting out in the car after the service for the rest of the family to finish greeting their friends (103–05). Sophie is constantly asked to accommodate others even though she interacts with those who should welcome her. The scene's critique of Mennonite transphobia is symbolized by her physical location: she is outside in the cold because there is no space for her within the community's warmth. The church neglects Jesus's command to welcome the stranger because of its fear of difference. It betrays its central teaching in order to protect its boundaries.

In contrast, Mark accepts Sophie throughout the story even though they have just met, and this shows hope for her to find a safe, nurturing community.

He tells her that he does not care about her being trans but is simply attracted to her (120). The inconclusiveness of the story's ending as they are in the middle of sex offers the possibility that Sophie has finally found an accepting community, even if it is only with one other person. Much like *Somewhere Else,* "Other Women" affirms the importance of community while arguing that one should not remain in a community that denies one's full selfhood. All three of these works advocate a preference for exile over self-negation, a process that offers the protagonists the difficult but necessary opportunity to emerge as fully realized individuals who can then return to the community and share what they have learned, transforming it for the good.

As a result of their time in exile, Jess, Sophie, and Jake learn to respond positively to their bodies' desires. These responses dovetail with another key aspect of queer theory's openness: its resistance to the traditional Western degradation of the body through its affirmation of a wide range of bodily experiences. Piontek explains that queer theory prefers to examine specific "practices" rather than identity-based categories such as sexual orientation (6), thereby liberating bodies from oppressive theoretical categories. One of these categorizations in the Mennonite tradition is the view of bodies as sinful. For instance, *A Call to Affirmation, Confession, and Covenant Regarding Human Sexuality,* the document that officially names same-sex acts as "sin" for Mennonite Church Canada and Mennonite Church USA, states, "No one can boast of perfection in th[e] area" of sexuality. In other words, it is impossible to experience sexual desire without sinning. Contrary to this tyrannical view, queer theory offers an alternative to the mind/body split in its insistence on the goodness of bodies as well as its insistence that communities ought to make space for a range of individual choices.

Douglas Reimer's 2002 assertion that Mennonite writers are guilty of "typically avoid[ing] representing the pleasuring body" by refusing to describe sex when it occurs in their work or excluding it altogether is a fair comment on earlier works (181), but Beachy, Braun, and Plett offer unabashed correctives to this problem in their work via vivid, detailed sex scenes.[12] In Beachy's *boneyard,* for example, Jake describes a number of sexual encounters—both real and imagined—with men (e.g., 35, 290). His admission that he "thought sex was the answer to something" (179) implies that he is still searching for the peace that he could not find in the Amish community, but it is significant that he sees the potential for his physical desires to liberate him. Jake has sex throughout the book because he enjoys it, and this is justification enough. *boneyard* thus celebrates sexuality instead of surrounding it with the usual Mennonite/Amish barriers of shame and guilt.

For much of Braun's *Somewhere Else,* there is a shyness in Jess's narration of her sex life, but there is one scene with her first lover, Freya, in which Jess is unabashed about claiming the beauty of women's bodies. Jess wakes Freya one morning by giving her cunnilingus, and she describes becoming enchanted by the "perfume" of Freya's vagina, admitting that even years later the memory of the smell causes her to "stop breathing" and lose her train of thought (91). The scene is important because it embodies the antithesis of the Mennonite taboo against bodily pleasure that Jess has been taught, both in the gender of her partner and in the specific act, which has no purpose other than sexual gratification. It also writes against the broader societal discomfort with vaginal scent. Jess does not feel squeamish about going down on Freya but does it for her own enjoyment as well as her partner's, finding enjoyment in the act's raw physicality.

Plett's "Other Women" similarly emphasizes the importance of bodily pleasure via its ending, with the last fifth of the story dedicated to two sex scenes. In the first, Sophie and her longtime best friend Megan are turned on by each other and engage in satisfying foreplay, but Megan gets frustrated when Sophie cannot get an erection because she is on estrogen. Megan then fellates Sophie, who resists and ultimately refuses to have sex with Megan because it reminds her too much of her old male self (115–17). Instead of listening to how Sophie feels and working together to find a nontraditional way for the two of them to pleasure one another, which would symbolize a better version of the drug-addled sex that they had before Sophie's transition (93), Megan quits. The passage shows how deeply ingrained her transphobia is even though she has tried to eradicate it. She can only focus on Sophie's penis instead of her entire person. The end of the story, however, provides a healthier experience when Sophie has sex with Mark. He repeatedly tells her how beautiful she is and listens to what she says feels pleasurable (120–21). As noted above, this scene offers a hopeful vision for the acceptance of trans persons. Sex can create a space in which the construction of gender is stripped away, leaving two bodies focusing on their acts instead of their societal labels, whether secular or religious.

Queer theory is also useful for examining the oppressive use of power and authority within a community. This issue is immediately thrown to the forefront in "Other Women" as Sophie describes her decision to adopt her new name even though her mother, her extended family, and some of her friends would prefer to silence her trans identity by using her old name, Leon. Sophie refuses to give up her voice, but it is a constant fight. The process of always needing to be on guard against those who wish to use her former name, and the act of correcting people when they do, takes a toll. This is a task that she must undertake alone because no one is willing to do it for her. She just wants acceptance, to be able to blend in instead of constantly being treated as other. Instead, her mother is only able to use overly polite phrases such as "your new lifestyle" to describe her child's gender (100), and this partial acknowledgment is just as frustrating as no acknowledgment at all because it still treats Sophie as though she is somehow abnormal. Her grandmother also attempts to silence her new identity, refusing to talk with Sophie about her transition and attempting to hide behind religious authority by slipping a Bible verse into Sophie's boots (108). Plett's story shows, via this episode, that new language to explain individuals' relationships with collective norms is needed in both the Mennonite community and society as a whole. The story implies that the healthy aspects of Mennonite community have fallen away in favor of a view of community as an entity that exists primarily to enforce an us/them divide. Building community becomes an exercise in power rather than in welcoming mutual aid.

Queer theory presents a solution to this misuse of power by offering a new model for investigating the language of authority (whether religious or otherwise), and thus for both finding ways to subvert it and finding ways to wield it in a healthier manner, via its explorations of BDSM (bondage, discipline, Domination/submission, sadism, and masochism). Tristan Taormino writes that power relations are everywhere in the real world, but they often go unacknowledged because it is uncomfortable to discuss them, so BDSM is valuable because it makes them explicit ("S" 11). In helping its participants think about power, BDSM can lead to an interrogation of the systemic violence present in society.

BDSM is one element of queer sexuality that does not necessarily fit into the LGBT spectrum because it emphasizes specific acts rather than the gender of one's partner and thereby epitomizes queer theory's distrust of categorizable identities. Pat[rick] Califia argues that BDSM "roles are not related to gender or sexual orientation or race or class" and that these "roles and dialogue become a parody of authority, a challenge to it" (166).[13] The openness of BDSM is similar to that found in Sophie's choices of sexual partners and Jake's decision to simply name his sexual acts without placing a specific sexual label onto himself. BDSM can thus lead participants into a liberating state of mind that illuminates one's conception of the world, not just of sexuality. Anyone can act as a Dominant and anyone can act as a submissive in a BDSM scene, regardless of their position within the power structures of society. Likewise, for many BDSM practitioners, the experience of dominating/being dominated and the headspace where one is transported via these acts are central to a scene rather than the characteristics of one's partner. David Halperin highlights another revolutionary aspect of BDSM, contending that it focuses on the entire body instead of just the genitals (qtd. in Sullivan 156). This holistic emphasis offers a healthy alternative to the traditional mind/body binary (a favorite of Mennonite namesake Menno Simons), reminding us that our sexuality should be fully integrated into our lives rather than kept to the side as shameful acts. The protagonists in queer Mennonite literature experience hatred for their bodies at times, but come to a healthy acceptance of themselves by the end of the story. Jess is able to bring her lover home to meet her parents, Sophie is able to experience erotic pleasure with her new body, and, as noted below, bondage experiences help Jake to make his peace with the Amish community.

Sex educator Madison Young's description of how it feels to play the submissive role has clear relevance for Mennonite literature. Young writes that "in order to find my true self [as 'queer' and other identities that she names], I must give in [to my Dominant]" (298). This language echoes Mennonite descriptions of surrendering oneself to Jesus, a similarity strengthened in her observation that when she submits she obtains a "clarity in which I feel that I am exactly where I am supposed to be, full of purpose and with an internal stillness that exists only in absolute surrender" (302–03). An important difference between a submissive's surrender and a religious one is that the former is a choice consistently taken with pleasure, instead of one that can feel forced in a religious context, often made with the hammer of guilt and the threat of eternal damnation hanging over one's head. This is how it feels to Jess and Jake; they feel no sense of liberation in their religious experiences. This is not to say that one cannot find the kind of peace which Young describes in religious faith, but to suggest that new models and language for discussing this fealty in the Mennonite community are necessary, and may be found via BDSM.[14]

In one of the very few Mennonite discussions of BDSM,[15] Di Brandt analyzes a bondage pictorial from *Penthouse* to argue that bondage echoes the same patriarchal values found in traditional Mennonite theology, "which depends on the language of submission and obedience to define the nature of faith" (*Dancing Naked* 54). I agree that this language is hurtful within the context of religious community, but I also agree with Taormino and Califia that oppressive real-world uses of authority can be subverted via BDSM role playing. Brandt's concerns notwithstanding, it is a maxim in the BDSM community that the submissive is actually the one in power because she or he sets guidelines for what the Dominant can do to him or her. This reversal is only one example of how BDSM interrogates power structures. Take, for example, the case of *boneyard,* in which bondage occurs between two men. This context introduces power dynamics different from those in Brandt's *Penthouse* example of bound women, and the bondage happens in the flesh rather than with an outside viewer in the Dominant position and an anonymous submissive captive on the page. The intimacy of a real-life bondage scene offers the radical liberating possibilities described by Taormino and Califia, which are less available in pornography.

Experiences with bondage help Jake to work through his difficult relationship with the Amish community that results from his desires to continue his education and explore his sexuality. Bondage is one of *boneyard*'s major themes, with over two dozen passages that reference it in some way, ranging in length from a few words to several pages.[16] It helps Jake to move toward healthier interactions with religious authority as he initially rejects the Amish community, but then is able to rejoin the group at the end of the novel after learning from the world via his sexual experiences. This narrative arc fits the traditional Amish *Rumspringa,* or sowing of wild oats before joining the church, but what a unique *Rumspringa* it is! Having an Amish boy tell a story this sexually explicit is the epitome of a subversive queering act. Its purpose is not to titillate or shock but to invite readers to rethink their own views of the taboo, of othered sexual practices.

The most significant way in which experiences with bondage help Jake to work through his difficulties with his Amish upbringing is in how they redeem the language of "submission" for him. He has always been attracted to men but tells us that he had no outlet for this desire during his childhood aside from looking at the "pictures of half-naked men" in bondage from the *Martyrs Mirror* (Beachy 191). This book, which held a place of honor second only to the Bible in Mennonite and Amish families from the 1700s well into the twentieth century, was originally compiled by Thieleman J. van Braght in 1660 and contains the stories of early Anabaptists who were killed for their faith. It includes over fifty illustrations, many of which depict people being gruesomely tortured or on their way to such a scene. *boneyard* reproduces several of these pictures, including the one of Louwerens Janss Noodtdruft that Jake finds arousing. Noodtdruft is about to be burned at the stake, but his picture is akin to something that we might see today in a Calvin Klein ad: shirt half open, showing his defined pectoral muscles, and standing defiantly (van Braght 1055). The *Martyrs Mirror* illustrations are "pornographic" in the sense of being gratuitous, but Jake names their erotic element as well. They teach him about himself but in a way different from what van Braght intended. *boneyard* queers the *Martyrs Mirror* as a way of questioning its perplexing examples of submission. On the one hand, van Braght's book positively epitomizes how literature can help to build community because of its traditional status as an essential text for Mennonites and Amish;[17] on the other hand, numerous contemporary Mennonites find its ethic of extreme self-sacrifice problematic. Jake rehabilitates its fetishization of bondage and torture by making it relevant to his own subversive desires. He gets joy from it and from his experiences with bondage, so the practice becomes life affirming instead of threatening and violent. BDSM helps Jake to live a healthier life both physically and spiritually rather than turning him into a monster, thus belying his church's fear that a loosening of its authority will lead to its destruction.

The protagonists in *Somewhere Else, boneyard,* and "Other Women" are queer Mennonites, with their queerness being the most prominent aspect of their hybrid identities, though they also cannot escape their Mennonite (or, in the case of Jake, Amish) roots. The identity chooses them rather than vice versa, and, because they attempt to make their peace with it instead of fighting it, they offer hope that their presence will make the larger Mennonite community a less oppressive one. But this is not an act of acquiescence to either Mennonite or societal homophobia. In her essay, Braun claims the hybridity that Jess says is an oxymoron in *Somewhere Else,* powerfully asserting that "I am a queer Mennonite" ("From" 71). Her statement, echoed in the experiences of Jess, Sophie, and Jake, shows that the community of queer Mennonites does exist, and that it refuses to be ignored. It manifests itself in part through the pieces of queer Mennonite literature that keep appearing. Those of us privileged enough to be literary critics must acknowledge this presence in our scholarship and share it with the broader literary community.

NOTES

1. Further examples of recent Mennonite literature with significant queer elements include David Bergen's *The Retreat,* Jessica Penner's *Shaken in the Water,* and several pieces in the 2013 *Mennonite Sex* issue of *Rhubarb,* guest-edited by Di Brandt, Andreas Schroeder, and Armin Wiebe. See also Plett's short-story collection, *A Safe Girl to Love.* Although a bit older, Lynnette (Dueck) D'anna's novels are essential queer Mennonite texts as well, especially *RagTimeBone* and *Belly Fruit.*

2. That is, criticism of texts that can be considered "Mennonite literature," or work by writers with some form of Mennonite background, whether these texts involve Mennonite subject matter or not. This criticism is not necessarily written by critics with Mennonite connections, though much of it has been.

3. Most Mennonite literature has aesthetic value, too, but I focus on its activist elements here because they are where it seems to be most compelling to make connections with other literary/critical traditions.

4. I realize that, as a literary critic who does not work for a Mennonite institution, I have more freedom to be transgressive in my work than some others. But my basic point is that the

field has things to learn from "the world" just as it has things to teach "the world." Holding the After Identity: Mennonite/s Writing in North America symposium at a state-owned institution rather than at a Mennonite college is an apt symbol for this potential dialogue.

5. I offer this chapter as a model of this type of criticism, but the task is too large for one critic alone. It is necessary for others to join me. Mennonite literary critics have been increasingly conversant with non-Mennonite literary themes, and this chapter is meant as one suggestion for how this trend can continue.

6. Works by John J. Fisher, Jeff Gundy (especially chapter 6), and David Wright illuminate this activism.

7. Much of Janet Kauffman's fiction, especially *The Body in Four Parts* and *Characters on the Loose,* could be considered queer in this sense.

8. Di Brandt examines some of these transgressive roots in chapter 8 of *So this is the world & here I am in it* (especially 114–21).

9. By this term, I mean Mennonite Church USA and Mennonite Church Canada and their previous institutional incarnations.

10. The violent ending of Rudy Wiebe's *Peace Shall Destroy Many* and Nomi's experience in Miriam Toews's *A Complicated Kindness* are two well-known examples.

11. Although the Mennonite communities in the texts at hand have much to learn from the queer concept of community, there are some historical similarities between the Mennonite community and the queer community. Kay Stoner examines these commonalities and how they have led to rituals that are surprisingly alike. Although my primary focus here is on Mennonite literature rather than theological Mennonitism, it is important to note that the contentiousness in the queer concept of community is also present in the North American Mennonite community via organizations such as Pink Menno and the Brethren Mennonite Council for LGBT Interests that advocate for LGBT rights within the church. However, these organizations are still refused official recognition and denied space at denominational conventions.

12. This chapter is one example of how Mennonite literary critics need to respond to this new openness by exploring it in our criticism.

13. Similarly, Piontek writes that BDSM "demonstrates that it is possible to have *bodies without orientations* and bodily pleasures that are not predicated on clear-cut sexual identities" (94).

14. BDSM theory could also be helpful in analyzing the use of corporal punishment in the Mennonite community. There is a sexual element of this violence whether or not the perpetrator acknowledges it. Patrick Friesen's "pa poem 4: naked and nailed," which describes a whipping, recognizes this element in both its title and its subject matter. The speaker wishes that his father could have explored his body via dancing, "leaping / on your long narrow feet howling / and sweat flying from that fine muscled chest" instead of taking out his physical aggression through violence (40). It is possible that the traditional suppression of sexuality in the Mennonite community plays a part in the hurtful expression of passion in punishing one's children, who are supposed to be submissive to parental authority.

15. D'anna offers fictional representations of BDSM throughout *Belly Fruit, fool's bells,* and *vixen.*

16. These passages include pages 32–35, 38, 42, 47, 51n, 59–60, 63, 66–69, 72, 85, 113–14, 138–39, 179–81, 184, 191, 214, 216–18, 222, 227, 235, 257, 274–75, 279, 288, and 290.

17. Even a young, rebellious, twenty-first-century Mennonite such as Jess is familiar with it (Braun, *Somewhere Else* 28).

WORKS CITED

Beachy, Stephen. *boneyard.* Portland: Verse Chorus, 2011.

Bergen, David. *The Retreat.* Toronto: McClelland and Stewart, 2008.

Brandt, Di. *Dancing Naked: Narrative Strategies for Writing Across Centuries.* Stratford, ON: Mercury, 1996.

———. *So this is the world & here I am in it.* Edmonton: NeWest, 2007.

Brandt, Di, Andreas Schroeder, and Armin Wiebe, eds. *Mennonite Sex.* Spec. issue of *Rhubarb* 32 (2013).

Braun, Jan Guenther. "From Policy to the Personal: One Queer Mennonite's Journey." *Journal of Mennonite Studies* 26 (2008): 69–80.

———. "Re: I Just Read *Somewhere Else.*" Message to the author. 3 Oct. 2012. Email.

———. *Somewhere Else.* Winnipeg: Arbeiter Ring, 2008.

Califia, Pat[rick]. *Public Sex: The Culture of Radical Sex.* 2nd ed. San Francisco: Cleis, 2000.

A Call to Affirmation, Confession, and Covenant Regarding Human Sexuality. 1987. Web. https://www.goshen.edu/campuslife/counseling/sexuality/purdue/. 2 Apr. 2013.

D'anna, Lynnette. *Belly Fruit.* Vancouver: New Star, 2000.

———. *fool's bells.* Toronto: Insomniac, 1999.

———. *RagTimeBone.* Vancouver: New Star, 1994.

———. *vixen.* Toronto: Insomniac, 2001.

Fisher, John J. "Making Something Happen: Toward Transformative Mennonite Peace Poetry." *Mennonite Quarterly Review* 82.1 (2008): 27–42.

Friesen, Patrick. "pa poem 4: naked and nailed." 1984. *Blasphemer's Wheel: Selected and New Poems.* Winnipeg: Turnstone, 1994. 40–41.

Gundy, Jeff. *Walker in the Fog: On Mennonite Writing.* Telford: Cascadia, 2005.

Kauffman, Janet. *The Body in Four Parts.* St. Paul: Graywolf, 1993.

———. *Characters on the Loose.* St. Paul: Graywolf, 1997.

Penner, Jessica. *Shaken in the Water.* Tipp City, ON: Foxhead, 2013.

Piontek, Thomas. *Queering Gay and Lesbian Studies.* Urbana: University of Illinois Press, 2006.

Plett, Casey. "Other Women." *The Collection: Short Fiction from the Transgender Vanguard.* Ed. Tom Léger and Riley MacLeod. New York: Topside, 2012. 91–121.

———. *A Safe Girl to Love.* New York: Topside, 2014.

Reimer, Douglas. *Surplus at the Border: Mennonite Writing in Canada.* Winnipeg: Turnstone, 2002.

Stoner, Kay. "How the Peace Church Helped Make a Lesbian out of Me." *Mennonot* 3 (1994): 10–12.

Sullivan, Nikki. *A Critical Introduction to Queer Theory.* New York: New York University Press, 2003.

Taormino, Tristan. "'S is for . . .': The Terms, Principles, and Pleasures of Kink." Taormino, ed. 3–32.

———, ed. *The Ultimate Guide to Kink: BDSM, Role Play and the Erotic Edge.* Berkeley: Cleis, 2012.

Tiessen, Hildi Froese. "Homelands, Identity Politics, and the Trace: What Remains for the Mennonite Reader?" *Mennonite Quarterly Review* 87.1 (2013): 11–22.

Toews, Miriam. *A Complicated Kindness.* 2004. New York: Counterpoint, 2005.

van Braght, Thieleman J. *The Bloody Theater or Martyrs Mirror of the Defenseless Christians Who Baptized Only upon Confession of Faith, and Who Suffered and Died for the Testimony of Jesus, Their Saviour, from the Time of Christ to the Year A.D. 1660.* 1660. Trans. Joseph F. Sohm. Scottdale: Herald Press, 1950.

Wiebe, Rudy. *Peace Shall Destroy Many.* Toronto: McClelland and Stewart, 1962.

Wright, David. "The Beloved, Ambivalent Community: Mennonite Poets and the Postmodern Church." *Mennonite Quarterly Review* 77.3 (2003): 547–58.

Young, Madison. "Submissive: A Personal Manifesto." Taormino, ed. 297–308.

9

Toward a Poetics of Identity

JEFF GUNDY

I

I have visited the nature preserve just outside Bluffton many times. Recently I found my binoculars and rode out on my bike after supper on a lovely spring day. The trees were just starting to leaf out, and I saw ten species of birds I could identify in half an hour of wandering, from three starlings in a cluster to lone goldfinches and redwing blackbirds. Two swans loitered on the ponds, not deigning to notice the noisy geese, and two kingfishers flew one by one and arrow straight from the shore to the little island, where they disappeared into a tree.

I saw other birds flying but didn't get a clear look at them; I heard others I never saw. Without the binoculars, most of them, except for the swans and the geese, would have been only dark shapes in the branches.

If I'd run through on the trails, as I sometimes do, I'd have missed most of the birds. I might have seen more if I had stayed longer, but it was getting dark. When the trees leaf out, it'll be harder to get a clear look. Knowing the names is no more than a beginning.

What do I know about the identities of those birds, of that pond, of that small knot of "nature"? We might talk about such identity in any number of ways: a catalog of species, detailed descriptions of behaviors, webs of relationships, patterns of appearances. If I were hungry, I might concentrate on which things were good to eat and how to catch or harvest them. Or I might take some photographs, or paint the place, or count its creatures, or measure them by height or weight, or analyze its soil. I could describe it as filled with signs of God's presence, or as emblematic of the "fallen" world, red in tooth and claw.

All of these ways of reading identity might be useful, depending on the situation, but surely none of them would be definitive or exclude others, and all imply some particular agenda and point of view. To do most of them thoroughly would require extensive, if not exhausting, study and more background knowledge than I have now.[1]

While we're multiplying possibilities, here's one of the dozen or more poems I've written at the nature preserve. Which sorts of identity does it involve and investigate?

Day at the Pond without Geese

A good day for late wildflowers—daisies and burrs
leaned out into the path for a better view, brilliant

blue somethings with tiny blooms on tall stalks.
A good day for a young dog's yapping, the splish

of a muskrat, thin gold of poplar leaves screening
the low sun. At the end of a lush summer, not much

has changed. The latest suicide bomber was nearly
done with law school. The enemy shot her brother.

Afterwards her head was found on the floor
of the restaurant in Haifa, black hair still flowing.

Like most men in such times, I want to give advice.
The pond is pretty in its small way, trees still green,

a bank of cattails, water echoing blurry greens and sky,
for once no geese to harry and complicate things.

Two quiet wrens, that dog yelping stupidly,
and a crow way off to the east. Like most men,

I think I'm smarter than most men. I dream of women
even when I'm awake. If I sit long enough, the trees

> or the water will surely tell me something. A woman
> passes, explaining to her cell phone as she walks.
>
> As far as I can see, everything is calm as Eden.
> Her black hair, flowing like the night. (*Spoken* 65–66)

The speaker of this poem (who is a lot like me) finds his attention divided between the calm and lovely landscape and the troubling news from Haifa about the young woman turned suicide bomber. That violence and the bucolic scene intersect in his contemplation, and, though his masculine and geographic privilege insulates him from the violence, its presence will not be easily dismissed. He broods on how little use his privilege is to others and records his grief, a little obliquely, mixed with his hapless appreciation of human and natural beauty. Of course, without his being, the poem would not happen; someone has to write it, and no one else would write it just this way. But the real locus of the poem, at least as I see it, is the mystery of a world where such beauty and such violence constantly commingle. I suppose one could read the poem as a meditation on my "identity," and even trace its ecological and peace concerns to my Mennonite commitments, and not be wrong, but (once again) that would surely not exhaust the poem, much less the set of concerns and references that are entangled in its brief space.

II

Mennonite critics have been investigating and interrogating questions of identity for many years. Other chapters in this volume trace that critical history more fully; here I note only that, as the body of Mennonite/s writing becomes ever larger and more diverse, the reality of that work strengthens my own long-held position that we should be cautious about attempting to fit it into any single, simple narrative (*Walker* 25 and passim). A geography of modern Mennonite/s writing would have to include Chortitza and Steinbach and Winnipeg, Goshen and Big Valley and Fresno and Waterloo (just for starters). A chronology of key publications might seem to be easier, but where one starts and stops, and which works seem to be truly crucial, might well depend on which side of the border one inhabits or whether one is most interested in novels or poems or memoirs. To trace the web of influences on any single writer would be useful but challenging, for all of the major Mennonite writers have been deeply affected not only by each other but also by other, far more diverse, sources and influences. Thematic approaches might explore any number of issues and oppositions: individual and community, female and male, Swiss and Russian, country and city, *Russländer* and *Kanadier,* Canadians and Americans, rebels and orthodox, poetry and prose. . . . And every one of these binaries itself deserves interrogation if not multiplication or erasure. This reality creates both a rich field of opportunities for critics and, to say the least, many complications.

In this chapter, I mainly set aside such work of analysis and critique, valuable and necessary as it is, and offer some perhaps contentious ideas about identity from my perspective as a poet who has also often been drawn into writing both creative and critical prose and who has been deeply engaged with "Mennonite/s writing" without ever thinking of myself as simply or singly a "Mennonite writer."

A long time ago I wrote a dissertation, very little of it published and most of it forgotten even by me, on "versions of the self in modern poetry." There was little if any mention of Mennonites in those pages, but I was already puzzling over problems of self-representation and self-location in poetry and in writing in general. And then as now I was drawn to writers who complicated and resisted simple notions of self and identity—T.S. Eliot, Charles Olson, William Stafford, among others—and toward sorts of writing that are not, in the curious but evocative phrase of Jay Gatsby, "just personal."

Of course, many of the writers I love most were hardly self-effacing. Blake insisted he must create his own system or be enslaved by someone else's, Thoreau allowed that he would not write so much about himself if he knew anyone else as well, and Whitman's egotism is legendary, though complicated in ways I cannot pause to examine here. Yet none of these writers was especially interested in straightforward autobiography—all were intensely and deeply engaged with the world outside themselves and with creating texts that foreground imaginative creation and exchange between author and world (which includes other people and texts as well as the things of the physical world). In the two centuries and more since Blake, the poets I love most have offered a brilliantly, bafflingly rich variety of strategies for placing the "self" in the poem—sometimes with apparent transparency and sincerity, often with a wide variety of maneuvers for complicating the relationship between poet and poem.

Even a cursory anatomy of those maneuvers would constitute a book in itself. Here I can offer only this hasty summary of what I have come to believe: writing takes place when a being and the world intersect in a particular body, in a particular moment, in a way that brings forth something new made out of language. Writing is always entangled with a particular self, but it is also inextricable from the larger world in which that self has its being.

III

Mostly, as I have suggested, I am quite content these days to leave discussions about Mennonite identity, before or after, to those with a different sort of patience than I have. In some moods, I enjoy wrangling over such questions, and I am happy enough to be "a Mennonite" if the alternative is "an American" or "a white man," troubled as those identifiers are. But at least according to my willful yearnings, I would claim first to be a poet, and so my first calling is to bring new and beautiful things made of words into the world.

If the ground of poetry is *embodied* identity, then the body of poetry is to be found in its tangible language, in image, song, narrative, and metaphor. My own body and being incorporate things Mennonite, and abstract notions such as identity, but despite the claims of John Howard Yoder and generations of worthy churchmen it will no more be enclosed, defined, or contained by Anabaptism or Christianity than the prairies I grew up on can be enclosed by a church building.[2]

Poetry weaves in and out among human doctrines and orders the way the wind weaves among leaves and branches, the way birdsong dances above and through houses, streets, and automobiles. Its work is to encounter and engage all of reality, tragic and transcendent, brutal and lovely, tangible and intangible, all the manifestations of time and matter and the imagination.

In a poem flatly titled "Vocation," William Stafford claims this unexpected one: "Your job is to find what the world is trying to be" (102). His spacious vision of the writer's vocation looks not toward fussy definitions of self in relation to some overdetermined version of community and discipleship but toward the broad possibilities of the world and language. A committed and active pacifist, Stafford found friends and fellow travelers all over the world, scattered among many literary, religious, and activist communities, but he danced among sectarian, literary, and other identities, resisting any as conclusive. His son Kim reports his father once boasted "I outflanked all of Dorothy's relatives by joining the Brethren Church" (231).[3]

IV

The three scholarly books that have most influenced my thinking in recent years have the provocative titles *Becoming Divine: Towards a Feminist Philosophy of Religion* (by Grace Jantzen), *Becoming Animal: An Earthly Cosmology* (by David Abram), and *The Weakness of God: A Theology of the Event* (by John D. Caputo).

From very different perspectives, each offers a radical critique of long-standing Christian and Western assumptions about God, the natural world, and human society—and, at least by implication, all also question our standard notions of personal and literary identity.[4]

We've been all wrong about what it means to be Christian, says Jantzen: we must lose our patriarchal fixation on death, abstract belief systems, and the afterlife. What matters is to live here and now, in this world, so that beings of all kinds can flourish. "Whereas with the metaphor of salvation God is seen as the saviour who intervenes from outside the calamitous situation to bring about a rescue, the metaphor of flourishing would lead instead to an idea of the divine source and ground, an immanent divine incarnated within us and between us" (161).

We've been all wrong about the physical world, says Abram: it is not an alien place where our immortal souls live as temporary refugees but the very ground and essence of our beings. The abstracting, distancing effects of language have made us almost forget we are, and will remain, animals, thoroughly embedded in the tangible, material world, however thoroughly we have altered it. "Human awareness could not exist without a human body, true, but it could no more exist in the absence of ground, leaf, and falling water. Mind arises, and dwells, between the body and the Earth, and hence is as much an attribute of this leafing world as of our own immodest species" (111).

We've been all wrong about God, says Caputo: God's main attributes are not power and might but mystery and secrecy. God is a voice, a call, a direction we might follow, not a gray-bearded father issuing peremptory commands from above the clouds. "The kingdom of God is a domain in which weakness 'reigns,' where speaking of a 'kingdom' is always an irony that mocks sheer strength. The kingdom is not the simple weakness that lacks the power of faith or the courage for action, but the provocative and uplifting weakness of God, a sublime weakness that, however weak, should not be underestimated because it is a divine force, capable even of inflicting a divine trauma" (14).

V

My recent literary thinking has mainly had to do, on the one hand, with the lofty-sounding enterprise of "theopoetics" and, on the other, with a long effort to reckon, explore, and tease out the multiple layers of experience and significance of my 2008 Fulbright experience in Salzburg and eastern Europe. Both of these projects have been deeply informed and influenced by my Mennonite roots, interests, and commitments, but neither has much to do with stock Mennonite identity markers and thematic obsessions. There are no bonnets, no buggies, and very little worrying about salvation or church membership or boundary maintenance in these texts, at least so far. (I have not been able to resist entirely the general Mennonite obsession with the *Martyrs Mirror,* but even there I find myself drawn more toward the canny survivors than the earnest victims.)

As one who has long described my own situation as a sort of odd but not uncomfortable interior exile, in the church but not entirely of it, I must admit I am left cold by the "missional" exhortations of bureaucrats and their claims to know what is "spirit led" and what is not. The long-running and complex Amish experiments in cultural resistance are more interesting to me intellectually, but (several generations removed from my own Amish ancestors) I am not about to go that route either.

Some of the many high-profile Mennonite literary texts of recent years moved me deeply, but I must confess I initially reacted to some of them in ways that now seem to be more complicated than kind. I grew up among the thinly scattered Mennonites of rural Illinois, where we are far enough removed from our Amish roots that I did not even hear of them until I was fully grown, and have lived for nearly thirty years among the educated and diffident Mennonites of northwest Ohio. Both of these communities have their own failings and pathologies, but compared with the more enclosed villages of southern Manitoba or the valleys of central Pennsylvania their boundaries are relatively porous, their authority structures more flexible, their patriarchies less entrenched. So (like many other Mennonites) I encounter texts such as Miriam Toews's *A Complicated Kindness* and Rhoda Janzen's *Mennonite in a Little Black Dress* from a strange insider/outsider perspective, sometimes hearing the name of my people used to define communities very different from my own, even when the narratives and voices themselves are entirely compelling and when I am moved by the human truths they express.

But of course this dance of likeness and difference is at the heart of identity. If I grew up among gentler patriarchs than some, if my parents sent me off to college anxiously but freely, if my teachers at Goshen College—mostly men—prepared me to learn, eventually, from a whole series of strong women who continue to instruct me about my blind spots and capacity for unwitting blunders, then all those things reflect privileges that should not make me discount or ignore those other voices, no matter how tempting it can be to do so.

My own sense of location is curious in other ways as well. My privileges are easy to tick off as a tenured white man with a lengthy list of publications and connections. It would be equally easy for my hungry ego to tick off another list of the things I have *not* accomplished, the status I have *not* achieved, but to do so would offend both the Swiss tradition of humility and the pragmatic side of my ego, which wants me to quit whining and get back to work.

The way these conflicting narratives mingle and cohabit leads me to a point that might seem obvious but that I want to make with some urgency: Mennonites, Americans, Canadians, human beings need both to keep generating narratives and to resist the impulse to view any of them as final or conclusive. This temptation, I think, operates at all levels; even highly personal, even quirky narratives such as *A Complicated Kindness* and *Mennonite in a Little Black Dress,* if they sell enough copies, come to be viewed both by their fans and (even more problematically) by their critics as something like master narratives of their own curious sort—though surely neither Toews nor Janzen wrote them with that purpose in mind.

This syndrome only heightens my own long-standing (and equally subjective) skittishness about epic tales and narratives on the scale of Rudy Wiebe's more ambitious novels. I have no literary or intellectual justification for this resistance, though support could clearly be found in postmodernism; I suspect it stems more directly from the lack in my own life of dramatic narrative tension and commercially viable story arcs. What compels me toward writing are local, particular encounters that invite, even demand, contemplation, embellishment, and elaboration—though I must also admit my impulses toward humility and *Gelassenheit* must often coexist with various and excessive presumptions. It may even be true, as J.C. Hallman says, that "in order to write a book you have to have a combination of profound hubris and crippling insecurity."

And so, much belatedly, I offer this thesis: a poetics of identity might be constructed of many small pieces, not one grand narrative; might be built of multiple realizations and epiphanies and minor encounters rather than sweeping generalizations; might contain a welter of small claims and recognitions and puzzlements rather than a few global pronouncements. It might look, in short, more like a book of poems than a novel or memoir, much less a creed or confession. It might be explicitly autobiographical at some points, elusive or fictional or downright fantastic at others. It might well break the rules I find myself unwittingly offering again. It might well contradict itself.

Such a version of identity will still be entangled, clearly, with the so-called real world and the "personal" in innumerable ways and make use of all the resources the blooming, buzzing world provides to us, including our particular stories, traumas, and relations. We all read for the sense of a particular connection with another human being, but I have read too many dull poems and tedious memoirs written by interesting people to think the *life* matters to the text. It's the *writing* that matters. Simply telling our stories may be of interest to our relatives, but (as many writers will testify) finding the particular story arc, the specific narrative details, or the precise voice the text requires is rarely simple or easy.

I *am* interested in (1) trying to make the planet a place where humans and other creatures might live and flourish and (2) thinking and writing about our lives as we actually live and imagine them, and our relationships with God as we live and imagine them, in ways that make the first point more likely. This field of interests draws me in many directions, from deep mysticism to deep ecology to politics to cosmology, from economics to everyday behaviors to the service of beauty. In the realm of Mennonite writing, I find myself drawn to adventurous experiments of many sorts, some of which resonate immediately and personally with me, others of which make me (as Gerard Manley Hopkins said of the classics) want to "admire and do otherwise" (291). So I am content to leave the writing of tales of dysfunctional villages and families, gay husbands, and Mennonite "popes" in the capable hands of others, even while I wholly endorse Toews's canny reflections on her own Mennonite and Canadian identities. "The only legitimate role of a writer, regardless of her community or nation, is to tell the stories that are truly hers," Toews writes. "The imagination is inherently subversive and cannot be mandated." Even among writers, I suspect, it is sometimes easier to claim this subversive freedom for ourselves than to grant it to others—for who can promise we will not end up subverting each other's narratives as well?

VI

So . . . after identity? What does it matter, on the one hand? I am a human animal sliding into the future at a terrifying pace, bound into my place and time by materiality, capable of reflection and (apparently) certain minor agential acts, but entirely aware of how much is outside my control. Aside from getting myself fed, watered, and exercised, what matters most to the part of this animal that thinks beyond the moment is making things out of words that a few others might find beautiful, useful, or both. In this process, my friends, guides, and fellow travelers are many, dead and living, and a wildly diverse group, some of them Mennonite and many not, some Christian and others not. Neither of those categories has much to do with my subjective human affinities, what William Stafford used to call the "understanding from sympathy" that draws me to some but not others. I'm often startled to hear people use the terms "Christian" and "Mennonite" as if they actually define something crucial about people, or establish some kind of meaningful boundaries.

Identity is personal and cultural at once, as is memory, as is desire. In the hypermediated, multilayered world I inhabit, it seems to be sentimental if not foolish to imagine an identity defined in terms of a single, neatly delineated tradition. (I suspect that it's always been more or less this way, though technology makes it more evident.) Maybe an Anabaptist Swiss peasant on some high alpine farm actually could live a simple life, but I suspect the sickly glow of nostalgia makes us underestimate the complications even those good folks faced. Thoreau—one of my chief heroes and surely deserving of honorary Mennonite status—also instructed us to "simplify," but his own life was enormously complicated by his reading, by his attentive immersion in the natural world, by his prickly relations with the people of Concord, by his concerns for social justice, by the vast and mysterious yearnings that echo through the sentences of *Walden.* All this was pressing enough on him, it seems, that he never managed a plausible sexual relationship,[5] but for many of us, certainly, family life adds another rich layer of complication.

Can a writer, an artist, do without complications and multiplicity of one sort or another? Why would we want to? "Problems are a comfort," writes Donald Barthelme (488). Stephen Beachy's novel *boneyard,* discussed in more detail in Daniel Shank Cruz's contribution to this volume, brilliantly explores the problems of being gay and Amish (and, I must note, large parts of it are actually written in the sort of "Anabaptist Surrealist" mode I advocated in a manifesto some years ago) (*Walker* 261 ff.).[6]

VII

> The way [to live a more fruitful writing life] is to make both the practice of writing and the work itself less about ourselves. To thrive, we must be mindful of our motives and our attachment to desired outcomes.
>
> —Dinty Moore, *The Mindful Writer*

Dinty Moore speaks here primarily of memoir, his preferred genre, which is by definition about "ourselves." His perspective might startle those who think of memoir precisely as "writing about ourselves," but I agree with him.[7] Writing dominated by an authorial ego anxiously explaining and justifying itself almost always strikes me as tedious and without enduring interest. We can stipulate, surely, that both the literal "I" of the author and the "I" of the written page are constructions; the questions that should concern us, then, have to do with *how* the "I" of the page might be constructed. Recent scandals and controversies have brought these questions front and center, especially for those invested in memoir and nonfiction. Although I stand with those who believe nonfiction should indeed be as truthful as the vagaries of memory allow, and invented materials ought to be signaled as such, I also find myself drawn to writing that does more than claim to offer a simple account of "what really happened."

"Identity has always been a fragile phenomenon," reads section 84 of David Shields's provocative recent *Reality Hunger: A Manifesto* (33). One must consult the appendix (which Shields recommends removing from the book with a knife or box cutter) to discover that this sentence was written by Lauren Slater, whose own books, though published as nonfiction, often "exaggerate," as she herself admits. *Reality Hunger* is constructed largely out of bits of others' texts, shaped and arranged into a quite coherent argument for writing that disrupts tidy narratives and story arcs, for the sorts of nonfiction and memoir that have more kinship with lyric and poetry than with the novel, and for the *made* quality of all writing.

Reading Bob Dylan's memoir *Chronicles: Volume One*, I was struck by how little Dylan worries about being "true" to a tradition he was born into, or being "creative" by doing something unprecedented, sprung from some sense of innate genius. When, as a young man, he made his famous trek to New York City to become a musician, the problem he set about solving (not even entirely consciously, as he tells it) was akin to what Ezra Pound called "gather[ing] a live tradition from the air," though the tradition Dylan discovered and claimed as his own was not much like Pound's. It was thoroughly but not exclusively American, heterogeneous, and polyglot, drawing on folk traditions and high culture, poetry and popular music, rednecks and black people, contemporaries and historical figures. Beyond Woody Guthrie, a famous influence, there were also Clarence Ashley, Rimbaud, and many more; a key passage describes his discovery of Nina Simone's intense 1964 recording of Kurt Weill and Bertolt Brecht's "Pirate Jenny," which in her version becomes a spooky, moving civil rights anthem.

Dylan, especially in his early days, was famously protean (was he a folk singer? a writer of protest songs? a rock and roller? a born-again Christian?). In the 1973 movie *Pat Garrett and Billy the Kid,* he played a character named Alias, and that seemed fitting. In the more recent biographical film *I'm Not There,* his character was played by a half-dozen actors, including the young black actor Marcus Carl Franklin; the one who resembled him most closely was Cate Blanchett, who also played the elf queen Galadriel in *Lord of the Rings.*

His hundreds of songs are likewise widely varied in subject matter, style, and form (and, even diehard fans like me would admit, quality).

Not every artist takes such a shape-shifting path—many stick much closer to a single identity, a single mode. But there's something wonderful about Dylan's shape changing, however nervous it makes those who would prefer what Emerson called "a foolish consistency." Part of its attraction surely is the sense that the shifting masks, the resistance to labels and ideologies, is not a put on or series of phony gestures but based on fidelity to some deeper, more obscure sense of purpose, of loyalty to something that resists the labels of critics and fans alike. It has to do with the constant search for the next song, the next poem, the next way of drawing on the resources at hand to shape something both new and not new at all. We might call it art.

VIII

Although it's tempting (and sometimes necessary) to focus on our own lives and traumas, it seems to me that the problem of "the world" is the most pressing one we face—Mennonites, yes, but everybody else too. Many Mennonites participate readily in the ritual Christian abuse of the world, by which we usually mean pretty much whatever aspects of human culture disgust us. For some that means TV and sleazy pop music; for others it means violence and abuse on any number of levels; for still others it means "gay rights," abortion, birth control, and whatever threatens patriarchal control of all things sexual. No less than identity, the world is a hard thing to pin down.

In a memorable essay in the anthology *A God in the House: Poets Talk About Faith,* poet and Anabaptist convert G.C. Waldrep heaps something just short of scorn on both mainline Protestants and what he calls "acculturated Mennonites," saying that both are "vacuous," given to "postures" and living fractured lives, now as consumers, now as workers, now as churchgoers or occasional activists (186, 195). Fair enough, perhaps. But what if the path toward unifying our splintered lives involves not only bringing the "profane" into the sphere of the Christian but also beginning to recognize the manifold ways the profane, the worldly, the "unholy" are already filled with the presence of God? That the trees and the mud and the bullfrogs are not merely "the Creation"—something made and then ruled over or (worse) given over to the Fiend—but also the habitation of God, the place where God dwells, the place where we must meet God if anywhere at all?

It's more praise of the world that we need, I think—more loving attention to the creation that (of course) includes each other. More reverence and a deeper awareness that the world *is* our home, that the Platonic claim that reality is off elsewhere, in some ultimate region of forms, some heaven, is at best something for a later time and at worst a fantasy, a deeply harmful one. Even the realm of the mind and the imagination, where I dwell during many of my best hours and days, is not separate from the physical world but deeply grounded in it, accessible only through it, through my breathing, sweating, demanding body.

Many days it seems there's no real language for this need—or, if there is, it's not the language of prose and abstraction but the language of poetry, grounded in the actual, physical being of actual, physical beings. "Just because we have birds inside us, we don't have to be cages," writes Dean Young in "Instant Recognition between Strangers" (86). The impoverished Greek notion of an immortal soul trapped in a transient and untrustworthy body has been the cause of much grief, but surely we are not bound to it forever, any more than we are bound to the harsh rules of Leviticus.

Yes, to deepen one's inner perceptions is necessary, but for many years I have written from the conviction that my "self" is not especially interesting, except as it gives me a vantage point on a world far more complex and worthy of attention than my mostly conventional experiences as a privileged white American man. Of course, I pay attention to my inner thoughts and feelings, the currents that course unpredictably—and sometimes all too predictably—within the awareness that is mine for this time. Yes, I have contemplated at some length the inescapable particulars of my life and the opinions, biases, views, intentions, leanings, and aspirations that I present to the world as "me." Many days I feel some kind of harmony among all of this, other days not so much.

Yet, after all of this, do I "know" my "self"? I have learned to maneuver among the various aspects of my being, many of them still partly or fully hidden even now from the intentional, volitional self that leads "me" through the world. I have tried to lure the aspects of my self that inhabit the lower levels out into the open and to listen as they speak things the everyday self would never speak. Those things mostly have to do with the ways the world outside, with its miraculous, horrifying beauty and misery and complexity, resonates within me, calling forth a voice I recognize as belonging only partly to my self but also to the larger networks, social, physical, spiritual, in which I live and move and have my being.

In an early poem, Rainer Maria Rilke put it this way:

I live my life in widening rings
that spread out over the things of the world.
Maybe I will not accomplish the last
but I will try.

I circle around God, around the oldest tower,
and I have been circling for thousands of years.
And I don't know yet if I am a falcon, a storm
or a great song. (my translation)

Like the search for God, like our drive to "know" the world or any other being, the search for ourselves is not to be concluded in this world. Like our language for God, our language for things and our identities is necessarily full of metaphor and image; we can no more name others, or ourselves, fully and clearly than we can see beneath our skin or name all the intricate, patient, furious processes that go on there every instant we live. That is why, after so many poems and stories and images and songs, we continue to need more. "Inside human beings," Rilke wrote in "Just as the Winged Energy of Delight," "is where God learns" (175). Perhaps all of these poems and stories and images and songs are God's way of learning as well as teaching, very slowly, what it is that the world is trying to be.

NOTES

1. Pattiann Rogers offers a series of varied descriptions of a poplar outside her window and muses on its inexhaustible reality: "In one poplar in one moment are a million poplars in a million moments and a million places, places within a place, each singular, each forbearing, each emphatic, all simultaneous in their contradictory and mutually exclusive natures" (18). David Abram also speaks eloquently of the limits of our perceptions: "No matter how long I linger with any being, I cannot exhaust the dynamic enigma of its presence. It is this reticence, the inexhaustible otherness of things, that enables them to hold my gaze, to sustain themselves in my awareness. I can never plumb all the secrets of even a single blade of grass—cannot fathom every aspect of its interior composition, or the totality of the relations that it sustains with the sky and the air. . . . And why not? Because I am not a pure spirit. . . . Because, finally, I am a thing myself, and hence have only a finite access to the things around me" (45).

2. Yoder: "Insights which are not contradictory to the truth of the Word incarnate are not denied but affirmed and subsumed within the confession of Christ" (32–33). Cf. Kasdorf: "This park closes at dusk, a sign warned. // How can a mowed field close against the sky?" (18).

3. It might be worth contemplating that Stafford left behind ninety-some books and 20,000 pages of daily writing, but after his early memoir of life in the Civilian Public Service

camps, *Down in My Heart,* he never wrote another memoir or even a long essay; his later prose books are all accumulations of short essays, reviews, interviews, aphorisms, and poems.

4. None of these writers is Mennonite (though Jantzen had roots in the Mennonite Brethren). Although each has a certain reputation, as far as I know I might be the first person to cite all three in the same paragraph. My book *Songs from an Empty Cage: Poetry, Mystery, Anabaptism, and Peace* includes more extensive discussions of all three authors.

5. For a useful critique of Thoreau's blindness concerning mothers, and family life in general, see Rogers (8–12).

6. Through Facebook, I made contact with Jake Yoder, the possibly fictional protagonist of *boneyard.* He responded warmly on 18 June 2013: "Jeff Gundy has written a Manifesto of Anabaptist Surrealism, or Surrealist Anabaptism, which is like a map of at least one of my minds (as a multiple personality, I have several)."

7. Here I am clearly leaning in a direction different from that of Ann Hostetler when she writes that, in one sense, "The only subject of literature is the self," though I agree with her advice that writers should "go inward" until "the boundaries of your little self begin to dissolve into the big self" (39) and with her call for a more open, less anxious cultivation of the self by Mennonite writers.

WORKS CITED

Abram, David. *Becoming Animal: An Earthly Cosmology.* New York: Pantheon, 2010.

Barthelme, Donald. "Not-Knowing." *The Art of the Essay.* Ed. Lydia Fakundiny. New York: Houghton Mifflin, 1991. 485–98.

Beachy, Stephen. *boneyard.* Portland: Verse Chorus, 2011.

Caputo, John D. *The Weakness of God: A Theology of the Event.* Bloomington: Indiana University Press, 2006.

Dylan, Bob. *Chronicles: Volume One.* New York: Simon and Schuster, 2005.

Gundy, Jeff. *Songs from an Empty Cage: Poetry, Mystery, Anabaptism, and Peace.* Telford: Cascadia, 2013.

———. *Spoken Among the Trees.* Akron: University of Akron Press, 2007.

———. *Walker in the Fog: On Mennonite Writing.* Telford: Cascadia, 2005.

Hallman, J.C. "Both Always Ever." Blog. *From the Vortex: On Reading and Writing.* By the Faculty of the Bennington Writing Seminars. 24 May 2013. Web. 25 June 2013.

Hopkins, Gerard Manley. *The Letters of Gerard Manley Hopkins to Robert Bridges.* Ed. C.C. Abbott. London: Oxford University Press, 1955.

Hostetler, Ann. "The Self in Mennonite Garb: Or, Where Does the Writing Come From?" *Mennonite Quarterly Review* 87.1 (2013): 23–40.

Jantzen, Grace. *Becoming Divine: Towards a Feminist Philosophy of Religion.* Bloomington: Indiana University Press, 1999.

Kasdorf, Julia Spicher. *Poetry in America.* Pittsburgh: University of Pittsburgh Press, 2011.

Moore, Dinty. *The Mindful Writer: Noble Truths of the Writing Life.* Boston: Wisdom Publications, 2012.

Pound, Ezra. "Canto LXXXI." *Poetry Foundation.* Web. 12 Mar. 2015. http://www.poetryfoundation.org/poem/241054.

Rilke, Rainer Maria. "Ich lebe mein Leben in wachsenden Ringen." *Das Stunden-Buch.* Leipzig: Insel-Verlag, 1918. 4–5.

———. "Just as the Winged Energy of Delight." *Selected Poems.* Trans. Robert Bly. New York: HarperPerennial, 1981.

Rogers, Pattiann. *The Grand Array: Writing on Nature, Science, and Spirit.* San Antonio: Trinity University Press, 2010.

Shields, David. *Reality Hunger: A Manifesto.* New York: Vintage, 2010.

Stafford, Kim. *Early Morning: Remembering My Father, William Stafford.* St. Paul: Graywolf, 2003.

Stafford, William. *The Way It Is: New and Selected Poems.* St. Paul: Graywolf, 1998.

Toews, Miriam. "A National Literature." International Festival of Authors, Toronto, 25 Oct. 2012. Edinburgh World Writers' Conference. Web. 18 June 2013.

Waldrep, G.C. "Not a Butler to the Soul." *A God in the House: Poets Talk About Faith.* Ed. Ilya Kaminsky and Katherine Towler. North Adams, MA: Tupelo, 2012. 180–201.

Yoder, John Howard. *The Priestly Kingdom: Social Ethics as Gospel.* Notre Dame: University of Notre Dame Press, 1984.

Young, Dean. *Fall Higher.* Townsend, WA: Copper Canyon, 2012.

10

Question, Answer

JESSE NATHAN

for my mother

Any discussion that moves from identity to art quickly becomes confusing. This is because art forced to serve anything but itself struggles to retain the essential quality of freedom that makes it art. Nonetheless, artists are human beings, and human beings have commitments, and so the questions persist. Does it matter if a poem is written by someone who is a pacifist, an environmentalist, a libertarian, . . . or a Mennonite? Do these things somehow register formally in the work? How?

In 1974, two years before John Ruth delivered a series of lectures at Bethel College (Kansas) calling for a literary movement simultaneously Mennonite and artistically serious, Elmer Suderman published a chapbook titled *What Can We Do Here?* Suderman was an Oklahoma Mennonite, fifty-four years old, a product of Mennonite education, and a literature professor for a time at Bethel, among others. *What Can We Do Here?* is striking for its repeated, abject questioning. The collection is filled with inquiries. Whole poems are just strings of questions. Some of the questions are rhetorical, all are earnest, most go unanswered. Five of the poems' titles are questions betraying a sense of great doubt, often veering into sheer lostness: the poem "What Can We Do Here?" is followed, for instance, a few poems later by "Why Had We Come?," which echoes off the later poem "Which Way?"

Ruth, a little younger, was trying to answer similar questions for his generation of Mennonites, this small Anabaptist religious group whose not-so-distant ancestors had immigrated to the United States from Europe and Russia to preserve their cultural and religious freedom. Ruth recounts attending a conference on the role that Anabaptist history does or should play in present-day church life. He was startled by "catatonic imaginations that evade certain basic questions: Who are we? How did we join the discussion? Where are we? How did the questions we are answering become formulated? Where did we join the discussion? Where are we going? What *is* the past we are pronouncing irrelevant? Have we ever made imaginative contact with it?" (55). The Harvard-trained literary scholar spent a year revising these lectures, and published them in 1978 as *Mennonite Identity and Literary Art.* He titles the first two lectures in the form of questions—"Where Is the Story?" and "What Are the Scruples?"—directed, ostensibly, at English-speaking Mennonites trying to figure out who they are and where they came from, and how this identity might fuel a meaningful literary artistic effort. Ruth opens with etymology: "The Latin root of the word I am employing—'identity'—derives from the concept of 'the same,' suggesting a continuity of experience made conscious by the repeatedness of recognition" (9). His definition of *identity* is thus grounded in repetition, and in a literary context, repetition is a formal device. The titles Ruth chooses for his first two lectures, as well as Suderman's question-riddled chapbook, point to the thesis I want to develop here: the question, and the accompanying implication of—or hope for—an answer, became for late twentieth-century American Mennonite writers a site for "experience made conscious by the repeatedness of recognition." The form—question, answer—appears across Mennonite poetry, wielded in very different ways and culminating, I think, in the recent poem "A Catechism" by Jean Janzen. A faithfully questioning stance, intrepid and earnest, is the river beneath this territory, a common trace identity leaves on form.

In Suderman's case, though, there are no direct references to form. There are poems like "What Can We Do Here?," which comprises three questions, ending desolately with:

> What can we do but walk,
> walk, walk on and on
> breaking sod no man
> has ever broken before? (1)

In "Which Way?" Suderman sees a boy, David, who sees "a sunflower-bordered trail" and wonders "Where it will lead? / To or away from the Mennonite village?" (27). Doubt—if not despair—infuses both questions, though they seem less rhetorical than terrifying (for the speaker) to answer. It is no secret what the author thinks the answers are. He fears that whatever "Mennonite" meant in the past, its identity-connotations will be swallowed by a new, assimilated future. The next generation "will no longer learn / to ride with oxen . . ." (17). "Who will tell us our name?" asks one poem (1). "Why had we left Russia?" asks another (17). The questions become melancholy inquisition; Suderman's decision to leave dangling question marks suggests that the *idea* of a response has come into a state of existential uncertainty. The universe is filled with silence.

Who in past ages—in the Old World village life of, say, the nineteenth century—provided Mennonites with sure answers? God. The Bible. The church. The colony. But by 1970 these institutions were under increasing scrutiny. David—the boy in "Which Way?"—has the same name as Suderman's father-in-law, one generation closer to the family's immigrant moment, to the old ways ("Obituary"). David, of the generation that actually lived in and remembers the Old World, will spend most of his adulthood in the new homeland. The unanswered question, in Suderman's poetry, becomes a figure for the loneliness of this transition from a time and place of perceived stability to a time and place in which even God might no longer exist. God, like formerly certain answers to the great existential questions, has left the human universe, retiring into metaphor. This divine evaporation, and the now unanswerable questions, were literally and formally still obsessing Suderman years later in 1979, when he published "Some Questions for God" in *Christianity and Literature.* The poem's form is again a string of unanswered questions, but the string is longer than anything in *What Can We Do Now?* One of the first questions is "Why can't theology do more / than show your vanishing footprints?" In a poem in which "your" is lowercased and "rumor" and "somewhere else" are applied to God in the final three lines, every question mark becomes a miniature devastation, enacting the absence of divine coherence in the coincident formal absence of answer. Instead of closure, we meet in these questions the exhilaration and terror of an open-ended, non-teleological metaphysics. The answer matters, but it matters mainly because it—like God the white-bearded father figure who answers prayers—has absconded or been dethroned. Maybe better to say that the absence is what matters. When coupled with the literal representation of a lost answer, Suderman's earnest affect throughout—no trace of irony, to my ears—effectively undermines the stability of the dialectic form composed of a question and then an answer. Suderman has no answers. He seems to be giving up on them. At best, he is troubled and impatient with the silence; at worst, despairing.

Despair, though, is not the only possibility. Dallas Wiebe, in contrast, sometimes offers a wry answer or simply a parade of ironic queries. *The Kansas Poems,* published in 1987, includes, for instance, the ten-line poem "Alexander

Kipnis in Kansas," in which the speaker recalls hearing—in the "dirty" Newton High auditorium—the great Ukrainian bass sing Goethe's "The Song of the Flea" (10). Kipnis, born in 1891 in Zhytomyr, capital of Volhynia (in modern-day Ukraine), became an American citizen in 1931; Wiebe was born in 1930 in Newton. Many Mennonites had lived in Volhynia in the nineteenth century. Goethe's fabulist narrative poem "The Song of the Flea" ends by celebrating the knowledge of what to do when pricked by a flea: "But we, when we are bitten / Know how to scratch and kick!" Wiebe responds to hearing those lines. "We clapped," says the speaker of his poem,

> and said,
> "Why are we plowing fields?
> Why are we baling hay?
> Why are we gathering eggs?"

And there the poem ends—with three lines of questions. The poem's meaning does not resolve neatly. The Goethe song seems to have triggered a rebellion in the minds of the Kansas—Mennonite?—audience. The rebellion's target, though, remains strangely vague. Who is being compared to a flea? Who should be kicked? Who—or *what*—makes this "we" plow fields, bale hay, and gather eggs? And why is the image pitched slightly to the comical? Wiebe's humor here feels self-deprecating, an incredulous tone seems to lace his questions: how could *we* be so *duped?* This feeling, articulated aloud or in the minds of people who are dutifully or enthusiastically clapping, offers a tragicomic sensibility in contrast to Suderman's more earnest pessimism. For Wiebe, the terrible question needs to be asked, but the lack of an answer seems more strictly rhetorical, delivered with a twinkle in the eye. Wiebe uses the question mark to undermine orthodoxies with a side of irony. Here is one of his "Tornado" poems, three lines long, delighting us with petulance: "God never spoke to us / out of the whirlwind. / Or did He?" (45).[1]

Whether absent, parodied, stripped of its conventional logic, or snubbed as irrelevant, the *answer,* for Suderman and Wiebe, has been problematized. In Jeff Gundy's hands, meanwhile, the answer expands Whitmanically. Gundy's "Inquiry into Faces, Light, the Guilt of Metaphor" appears in a collection called *Inquiries* (31).[2] The poem comprises five one-line questions, starting first with "And so what is a face?" The answers are sometimes twenty lines long, occurring after each question. The last question is a variation on Suderman's original—*What Can We Do Now?*—asking in pop-Christian language "And so what would you do?," which Gundy answers, not only with a wryness akin to

Wiebe's, but also with a pronounced, impish sincerity, channeling the voice of Lear's fool:

> I would gather and sort and shape
> and make something. From faces
> I have studied, terrorized, ignored,
> from light falling casual and burning
> as sun on the garden in July, from tomatoes
> and bindweed groping for water
> they can push on into their seeds,
> from these and my guilty selves:
> to make a child whose face will blind me. (32–33)

The pattern that Gundy holds to in this poem, and in several other "inquiries" in the book, consists of relatively short questions (from six to eleven words) followed by relatively lengthy answers (from three to eighteen lines). This gives each poem a billowing, prose feel. But it is the assurance of form—the repetition of question-answer, question-answer—that controls the apparent straying into streaming narrative or flash fictions.

Later appearances of the question-answer in American Mennonite poetry suggest a greater and greater ambivalence toward answers. Keith Ratzlaff's 2005 book *Dubious Angels* features ekphrastic poems inspired by Paul Klee's angel drawings. "Doubting Angel" is one of the last in the book (63). It begins, as Gundy's questioning did, with the word "and" followed by an inquiry, as if the reader is dropping into a conversation begun some time ago. Ratzlaff references Rilke—essential poet of the earnest and emotionally charged inquisition of angelic hosts—and in doing so invites in a much wider canon, reaching beyond Mennonite traditions. Writes Ratzlaff,

> And if I cried out
> who would hear me?
> (Prayer is just
> a thickening of the air.)

Rilke's "Duino Elegies" begin, in Stephen Mitchell's translation, "Who, if I cried out, would hear me among the angels' hierarchies?" (3). Ratzlaff's version puts the voice in the angel, who is wondering to whom *he* should call. It is funny but also sad because no great elegy follows. The parenthetical emphasizes the exhaustion with prayer, dismissed here in the rhetorical space typically allotted for an answer. Prayer, like the hope of answers, is no more than "a thickening of the air." "And if I listened / what would I hear?" continues the second quatrain: "The music of a dog / dragging his chain." A flat description of an animal creating "music" unwittingly from the tool of its constraint. It would seem light if it were not so melancholy, this use of question to pitch toward idealism and answer to hurl us into bleakness. And if it weren't clear enough that any possible answer won't be sufficient, Ratzlaff turns the screw in the poem's final six lines:

> And whatever blessing
> I gave would only be
> the world's usual stutter,
> the space between notes,
>
> the silence already
> tied in my hair.

Questions are answered but only with a "stutter" and "the space between notes" and "the silence" that one "already" has.

Ann Hostetler dramatizes a similar stutter in "Unexpected Ghost." Hostetler, an English professor at Goshen College, depicts a child asking her mother about the world as the child is pulled along by bicycle. "'Momma, what are eyes?'" "'They are for seeing.'" There is a sing-song quality to the back-and-forth that develops, mother pedaling forward into the world and creating a dynamic of instruction and guided exploration. The questions and responses continue: "'Can you have eyes and not see?' / 'Then you are called blind.'" In the penultimate stanza, the exchange devolves into incoherence, as incidental as it is unsettling:

> "What is it called when you have ears but can't hear?"
> "Deaf."
> "Death?"
> "Deaf-f-f."
> "Death?"

It is a beautiful dark display of language sliding around, words and meanings blurring unexpectedly. The child and mother are no longer moving, and the mother at this point simply gives her daughter a kiss and sends her on her way. So the answer, and the instructive current of question-answer, dissipate abruptly for Hostetler into a mistransmission collapsing into a kind of joke, leaving us with "'Death?'" Neither the "question" nor the "answer," nor the form of question-answer, is dead for Mennonite poets, but these things did not live through the past fifty years unbruised.

So does it matter if a poem is written by someone whose identity is, in one way or another, wrapped up in Mennoniteness? I have been trying to discern a Mennonite tone that I think emanates from the handling of the question-answer structure as it has appeared in various poems by Mennonite-affiliated writers over the last five decades. Now I want to make explicit the leap from form to identity that I've been developing in this chapter. I make this leap in search of something beyond fetishization of the word *Mennonite,* in search of ramifications of the sensibility behind that word, ramifications that might translate into something that we could call a "value," detectable in the form. Does a certain identity produce certain formal tendencies? What remains after *Verenike, Borscht,* and Dutch Blitz are forgotten in the sweep of generational change, what then will the word *Mennonite* mean? What *could* it mean? These days fewer than a third of all Mennonites globally live in North America. The European Mennonite cultural line continues, but it is a smaller and smaller portion of the larger Mennonite body. Stripped of nostalgia, stripped of all subculture-specific signs, is there a metaphysics distinctly Mennonite, one that might matter to Mennonites anywhere at any point in history? So when even the name of our small, principled band fades away—when we are just humans, or Nigerians, or Californians, or Europeans, or Guatemalans—what values might remain? I think something emergent, but very old, distills, even if all else becomes vapor: for European-descended, Mennonite-connected, American poets at least, it is a stubbornly earnest, irreverent, faithfully questioning spirit.

Catechesis, a sequence of performed questions and answers, is an invention predating the development of Mennonite identity by at least a thousand years.[3] A teacher delivers queries. A new convert, prior to baptism, gives the answers, which have been predetermined. The scripted series of questions and answers was developed by early Christians and designed to be a performance demonstrating the new convert's mastery of the ideological program. When written down as a kind of script, the exercise is called a catechism.

In Christianity's early days, catechesis would have played a key transmissive role because of its didactic lucidity, its affect of plainspoken, confident truthfulness. It is the kind of performance persecuted early believers would have needed to cement communal ties, armor individuals against the trials of being a religious minority, and inseminate the specifics of belief. Catechesis provides an interactive, ritualistic, and lovely simplicity in its binary unity—a prescription of questions followed by perfect answers.

When church and state merged in the fourth century, programs of catechesis lingered mainly in the background as other practices—infant baptism and holiday rituals—ascended to prominence. More than a thousand years later, during the Reformation, catechesis again became important. The elegant question-answer dance suggested, as it did for early Christians, induction into a community defined by the simple but conscious embrace of a set of principles. It was a demonstration of faith by an adult believer, an unadorned intellectual declamation of principle that must have appealed greatly to reformers.[4]

Catechism's history for Anabaptists begins with the radical German Christian reformer Balthasar Hubmaier's *Ein Christennliche Lehrtafel, die ein yedlicher mensch, ee vnd e rim Wasser getaufft wirdt, vor wissen solle* (A Christ-Like Instruction: What Every Person Should Know Before Being Baptized with Water), published in Nikolsburg in 1526. Hubmaier stages a doctrinal conversation between Leonard and son Hans von Liechtenstein. It proceeds like the Socratic method. These questions are not open ended, and the son learns from the father by regurgitating doctrinal positions. Catechesis is always the weird child of dogma and inquiry: a form that *appears* to be inquiry but in fact is a form of indoctrination. Hubmaier's embrace of the practice at the very birth of Anabaptism seems to me to suggest the importance of this particular question-answer structure in the creation and deployment of a new ideological vision.

Anabaptist Mennonites, however, did not produce a catechism—a written document—until 1690, at Danzig.[5] *Kurze Unterweisung aus der Schrift* (Brief Instruction from Scripture) had thirty-six questions and thirty-six answers, and was very popular: it was reprinted many times, first appearing in English in 1857 in Lancaster, Pennsylvania, and in Spanish in 1927 in Argentina. Overwhelmingly, though, the most popular Mennonite catechism was published in German in Elbing, Poland, in 1778. It was translated into French and English and by the nineteenth century had become the primary catechetical document for Amish and Mennonite congregations on both sides of the Atlantic.[6] In the Elbing catechism, each answer comes with a biblical reference, tying prescriptions directly to the word of God. It might be something like this: a catechumen feels God's very language flow out of one's mouth as one's own.

Why was it so popular? Probably because it worked. The Elbing catechism covers many aspects of life in plain language, easily carried in one's mind. It is a how-to for being a good Mennonite, a promise made by a convert to a community of fellow believers. A flowing momentum develops with each question generating and spilling into the next, teasing out an idea's dimensions while building up an inspiring energy in the back-and-forth:

Is it necessary that we should know good?
Yes: but knowledge without the proper application of it in our lives
puffeth up: charity edifieth. (1 Corinthians 8:1)

In what spirit should we possess all knowledge?
We should be humble and unassuming; for if a man thinks himself
to be
something, when he is nothing, he deceiveth himself. (Galatians 6:3)

What benefit do we derive from knowledge?
We must know the will of God, that as children of the light we may
walk
after God in righteousness and true holiness.
(1 Thessalonians 6:4, Ephesians 4:17–32, & II Timothy 3:15)

Does mere knowledge then not suffice?
No: we must be doers of the word. (James 1:22) ("Elbing Catechism")

One could digress at length about the layers of meaning that develop around a formalized indoctrination on the topic of knowledge and its insufficiency. But to early church leaders, the Elbing catechism likely meant a way to solidify communal and theological identity. Order—and catechesis is a highly ordered form—seems essential to this community working. And the ascension of the Elbing document meant, in any case, that thousands of young Mennonites, for several generations, held these particular words in their minds and mouths, felt them on their tongues, absorbed belief through this question-answer form.

Jean Janzen's poem "A Catechism" appeared in her 2008 collection *Paper House* (59) and is seventeen lines clustered into seven couplets, finishing with one tercet.[7] A villanelle's smooth repetition pervades the poem, along with an awareness from the beginning—established by the title—of the poem's sharpened sense of form.[8] Here is "A Catechism" in full:

What is the definition of Glory?
    It is the fire at the center of pain.

Where does it live?
    Everywhere in this world.

Why does Glory exist?
  To make us whole.

How does it work?
  It draws us to the water.

What does water do?
  It washes the pain.

Does the Glory die?
  No, the fire cannot be put out.

Does the pain die?
  No, because it is Love.

Can Love make us whole?
  Yes, because the fire
  and the water are one.

The poem's clean visual presentation is striking: each question's answer is slightly indented; the inquiries are concise—six of the eight questions are only four words long—and the answers direct. Few words in the poem have more than two syllables; many are one syllable, imbuing phrases (e.g., "To make us whole") with plainspoken sureness, just this side of brusque. The questions suggest a speaker eager to get to the point, but patient; this inclination feels heightened by the couplets that enclose and isolate the units of question-answer. This chiseled simplicity aligns the poem with Mennonite catechetical goals: to be plainspoken, direct, and brief.[9]

Janzen has long been concerned with Christian forms generally and the rhetoric of the question specifically. Her debut volume, published in 1984, is *Words for the Silence,* a title that takes the stance of a response ("words") to an emptiness or provocation ("silence"). The longest sequence in the book is "Reflections on the Beatitudes," a sequence of beatitudes quoted verbatim followed by lines of poetry interpreting the biblical language (19). It is almost Talmudic. It is a less fully realized reinterpretation of a biblical form than her catechism, in my view, but it does show Janzen's longstanding interest in "transfiguring" (Ruth 44) communal religious forms and words. In her 1992 collection *The Upside-Down Tree,* Janzen includes "Questioning the Cold," in which a speaker reminisces on summers in Saskatchewan, how she never knew her grandfather, and how she is alive beholding the "colored light-bands / flick their icy tongues" across the sky, eventually finding her way to an Elmer Suderman–like finish: a series of earnest questions left unanswered, ending with "Can holy be warm? Was Job right / about the flesh?" (20).

In "A Catechism," published sixteen years later, Janzen features roughly four types of questions, and none goes unanswered. The first two types seem informational. "What is the definition of Glory?" asks the opening line. The answer is a one-syllable noun, "fire," said to exist "at the center of pain." This locational specificity is also the kind of information sought by the second question: "Where does it live?" the line asks of Glory. The answer constitutes line four of the poem, and the sense of two disembodied voices speaking to one another—a classic element in a written catechism—has become pronounced. "Everywhere in this world" is where Glory lives. This kind of grand, encompassing language—"everywhere" and "world"—suggests the confident knowledge of a believer, but here it is yoked to much vaguer spiritual language. The answerer is faceless, completely abstract, coming from anywhere. Who is this answering the poem's questions? And who, for that matter, is asking them? Is it the self asking the self? The self to the divine? The divine testing the self? This ambiguity rather efficiently overturns the Christian form in which the questioner is known as an authority on a specific set of religious tenets and the answerer is known to be a convert to those tenets. All specific religious reference has been erased, and the words—Glory, for instance—are universal to the point of a beautiful blandness, simple and not necessarily Christian.

The second type of question occurs only once in the poem, at lines six and seven, and it is the powerfully interpretive question "Why does Glory exist?" The "why" here is actually a veiled kind of "what for," but in using "why" Janzen leaves open the possibility that the answer is more than a functional kind of information. To ask "Why do we die?," for instance, is rarely to ask for a biological explanation of death. It asks for meaning. In the case of "A Catechism," the question invites an answer that speaks to the meaning of Glory and its metaphysical potential—this is the "why." The answer—made up of four one-syllable words, including two that are two letters—is another sweeping statement: "To make us whole." I know exactly what that means, and I have no idea what that means, so delicately does it verge on the brink of platitude. Janzen's feat—simplicity that does not quite collapse into cliché—is one of silvery minimalism. At this point in the poem, there are no images more specific than "the fire," and there are concepts and nouns as capacious as "world" and "pain." "To make us whole" suggests a concrete function for this still largely undefined Glory concept—to fashion human beings back together after becoming somehow broken—but it also suggests the next step in the theological construction that the poem is building. That is, it tells us "why" this thing, Glory, this thing that is "pain" and is burning and is "everywhere," exists. "To make us whole" inaugurates the Glory into a purpose.

A third type of question focuses on mechanics. "How does it work?" asks line seven. The verb in the answer describes one thing working on another: "It *draws* us to the water" (emphasis added). Magnetic pull. Glory, "the fire at the center of pain" that lives everywhere "[t]o make us whole," is at this point a force leading us "to the water." In *The Elements of Faithful Writing,* Janzen has chapters on fire and water, and in the chapter on water she quotes Terry Tempest Williams: "Desire begins in wetness. We are born out of longing, wet, not dry. We can always return to our place of origin. Water. Water music" (20). Janzen notes that in her own surveys of her work she's surprised at how often water comes up. In "A Catechism," Glory has become a thirst. It has facilitated desire, "draw[ing] us to the water."

And what Glory does is connected to the next question, also of a mechanical bent, in line nine: "What does water do?" is an inquiry into the functional, and the answer is practical: "It washes the pain." The practicality and the diction remain simple and spare through ten lines, the last six of which are composed primarily of one-syllable words. A calmness in the tone develops; it's the assured voice of knowledge and—because confidence can be evidence for the believer—faith. Faith in what, specifically? Well, the *mysterium tremendum* is mighty as ever.

The vision remains steadily abstract and grandiose throughout the poem, but if the final kind of question seems to be rooted in the functional, too, it feels distinctly more speculative than any previous. "Does the Glory die?" in line eleven begins the poem's final stretch into a theological conclusion. The answer to this question is ambiguous, equal parts prediction and mechanical working. "No," is the reply, "the fire cannot be put out." Is this a statement of belief? Or is it a statement of neutral fact? The verb is not *will* but *can.* This statement's faith is plain and unwavering as it becomes, in the grammar and tone of the catechism, a statement of fact. At this point in Janzen's poem, though, I float between what I can imagine real and what I can know empirically. Which is to say, if you need further proof that we are in the realm of the metaphysical, the land of the transcendent, the districts of the fantastic and mythic, look no more: these are waterproof flames.

Line thirteen asks for another wager on what will happen: "Does the pain die?" The poet uses the verb *does* rather than *will,* and thus makes the catechist's question softer, more tentative. At line fourteen, and for the second time in the poem, comes an answer that's a denial, "No." "No, because it is Love." Love is the second capital-lettered conceptual element introduced into the ecology of this poem, along with Glory, the thing that the poem aims to define. Line fifteen folds Love into Glory, connecting them in the idea of "mak[ing] us whole." Love becomes glory, glory becomes a precipitate of love. "Can Love make us whole?" is answered, in lines sixteen and seventeen (which, by the way, comprise the poem's only two-line answer, the only answer layering one line onto another, folding like waves), with a decisive "Yes." And here, in the poem's final couplet, "the fire / and the water are one." That waterproof fire is also water. The back-and-forth of the catechism form has found wholeness by uniting two antithetical elements that, in fact, turn out not just to need each other but to be each other.

These final two lines unite Janzen with a wider poetry canon, the way that Ratzlaff's riff on Rilke does for Ratzlaff. In her poem's last line, Janzen modifies the last line of T.S. Eliot's "Little Gidding": "And the fire and the rose are one" (39).[10] Janzen pushes the line back to the elements, back to the conventional fire and water, the bookends of love—desire leads to love, which leads to new birth, to the next iteration. If the rose is the pure romantic symbol for Eliot, Janzen is replacing it with an older, more primal image, one just as involved with love (to her mind, via desire and birth) but perhaps with more fundamental force: water. Meanwhile, union as a point of intersection seems to be important here for both poets, the way that a thing passes from one state to another, a beginning to an end, a fire into a rose, fire into water, water into fire. Janzen titles a section of *The Elements of Faithful Writing* "Fire and Air: Breathing the Light." "The original fire of creation," says the poet, "of love, of the Gospel, and of truth is what we long for as artists and writers. Sometimes that means destruction of what exists. Fire and wind can mean cleansing and regeneration" (37). And when she describes this process as "the wild love which destroys for the sake of the new" (37), I think of Eliot in his theological voice: "In my beginning is my end" (11).

And there is a circularity that the question-answer structure implies, the circularity of the chain. The catechism preserves this. That is, question flows into answer which leads to question producing answer and so on. But Janzen innovates in ways that undermine, complicate, and celebrate the catechism form specifically, and the idea of question and answer generally. The first innovation is the most direct: Janzen overthrows the predetermined answers usually found in catechesis. Catechesis is a closed system; it has the appearance of oral spontaneity, but it is always a performance that follows a prescribed script. There is something vaguely troubling about this aspect of the form—for the problem of catechism is the problem of dogma, which itself is a problem of order and authority. Janzen rewrites the script, replacing biblical prescriptions with those of her own imagining. "In the Mennonite catechisms, Bible references have always been listed with each question since our faith is based on the Bible," writes Paul Shelly in an introduction to one recent catechism (3). This particularly Mennonite element of the form—featuring answers proof-texted by scripture—has been eliminated in Janzen's poem. In this sense, Janzen has made the form less Mennonite, but only in an obvious way. I perceive her to have dispensed with Mennonite notions in one respect even while amplifying them in the very act of this revision: she is taking the inherited form and reimagining it, challenging it but not abandoning it, faithful to it even as she is recasting it, just as the original Anabaptists were with the Christianity they inherited. Not only does Janzen omit the biblical references, but she also omits words like *God* or *Jesus* or *heaven* or *salvation.* It's hard to say if the poem is even Christian, yet the form is a Christian invention.

What does Janzen replace the predetermined Christian answers *with*? Her poem is a constructive act, after all—a testing of an old form and a re-envisioning of it.[11] She uses language that mirrors the original in simplicity, and retains a sense of directness and lucidity even into high abstraction. She fills the space originally holding Mennonite-specific lines with lines of maximum universality, so that her stance is one speaking to inherent human conditions, like pain. "Where does [Glory] live? / Everywhere in this world." Still, some of these universals become inscrutable riddles with seemingly secret answers. The clarity that the original catechisms sought seems contravened because the poem is not necessarily "clear," to use Shelly's word (3). Lines thirteen and fourteen, for example: "Does the pain die? / No, because it is Love." It is not self-evident that pain is love, though I detect a truth in this somehow. This sense of truth is the psychological result, I propose, of the form's design of simple, accessible instruction—crossed in Janzen's poem with words abstract and elegantly vague. Lines fifteen, sixteen, and seventeen: "Can Love make us whole? / Yes, because the fire / and the water are one." Secrecy of meaning is planted within the openness of simplicity and plainspoken diction. Then again, a sense of mystical secrecy is an essential element of much scripture, and is present in the Elbing catechism: "No, we must be doers of the word" is the answer therein to "Does then mere knowledge not suffice?" What, precisely, is a "doer of the word"? How does one know if one is a good "doer"? What constitutes "mere knowledge," and what constitutes the other stuff? These are questions of interpretation. Janzen, in her poem, has replaced predetermined answers but has retained the catechistic locus of mysticism in the metaphors. She has widened the interpretive possibilities of material appearing in this particular form. For Frank Kermode, the wideness of possible interpretation marks literature that endures, and is part of why some biblical poetry holds up—generates new meaning, remains strange and fresh—after centuries of rereading.

Even so, there seems to me something especially unspecific—more than in the Elbing catechism—to lines in Janzen's poem like "Yes, because the fire / and the water are one" or "Everywhere in this world." Shelly describes the Elbing text as "a guide" and characterizes it by saying that "questions are direct and answers are specific. Bible references to specific answers will open the door to satisfying Bible reading and study" (4). Twice this word, *specific*. Satisfaction, framed as a function of specificity. "Everywhere in this world" seems an explosion in the other direction, toward encompassing wideness and generality. Janzen's lines pop; generality does not make them slack. But Janzen argues in broad terms, celebrating a faith in love that heals and a sense of pain as honorable because human.

Catechesis seems in some ways to be an antipoetic form: the original idea is not an aspiration to lyricism, but an effort at "clarity." These two goals—lyricism and clarity—are not opposed, but they do not necessarily overlap. Catechesis is plodding, not dazzling or heady or swirling or hallucinatory—and this is the astonishing animation that Janzen performs, imbuing a fairly rote and functional church tool with poetry and a dreamy wisdom. "How does it work?" asks line seven about Glory, to which the next line responds, "It draws us to the water." Janzen works within a simple, dogmatic—and in this sense perhaps less poetic—form, making lovely plain song. Her revisions to the form constitute an Anabaptist act, and, because many of her primary existential commitments are, in a historical sense, to an American Mennonite milieu, this act can also be thought of as an American Mennonite act.

Writing in 1997, Jeff Gundy suggested that "it would be too strong to call the recent emergence of American Mennonite poetry . . . an explosion or even a renaissance" ("U.S." 6). Whether by now it can be called "an explosion or even a renaissance" is not a question I'm prepared to answer. I'm not sure what the word *Mennonite* means when placed in front of the word *poet.* I can't even clearly define *Mennonite.* And I realize that this talk of "Mennonite" and "essences" flirts with essentialism: the literature is Mennonite because it is Mennonite.

So does it matter if a poem is written by someone with a connection to Mennonites? It does in the sense that many poets with those ties, at least European-descended North Americans, share some larger goals, and this is visible in the myriad but—to my eye—metaphysically aligned ways in which they use the question-answer form. And the fact *that* they use the question-answer form. This is how, at any rate, poetic form might help us think about identity, that "continuity of experience made conscious by the repeatedness of recognition" (Ruth 9). If there is a Mennonite *inflection* or *accent*[12] to their handling, it is in the way that these poets rewrite the answers and transfigure the inherited forms. They keep asking questions. There is no closure, and there is the embrace of this lack of closure. There is despair at the silence, but not only that. There is the invention of new answers, surreal answers, parodic answers, paradoxical answers, confessional answers. There is a dogged faith in inquiry, in the anti-nihilism of curiosity. There is a fidelity to revision. It is the fidelity of Jacob to the angel he wrestled. Writes Ruth:

> In fact, our particular story may not be tellable in terms of the stylistic cadences of the stories currently in vogue. Our imagination must be our own, and its limitations must not be blamed on external factors. The depth of our art does not depend on the ability to employ some one particular mode that our age has pronounced correct—or salable. . . . The question is: are we in touch, have we wrestled, with the angel of our covenant-identity? Do we know, have we felt, its soul-issues? Are our dreams, our personal memories, our impulsive confessions, our involuntary historicizing—in short, our imaginative life—organically intertwined with the dialectic of our covenant-soul? (52)

I am working to answer these grand questions myself. I can say that poetry, for the European-descended Mennonite community, seems to have become one forum where this wrestling can and does take place. Poems carve space for Mennonite ideas of life to be invested and tested. An interrogatory stance is strong in these poets' writing, and perhaps represents something we might call a Mennonite "value," an "essence," though surely only one among many. It does, at the least, constitute one of the traces that identity and form leave on one another.

In 1975, Victor Davies addressed central questions of Mennonite identity in his film . . . *and When They Shall Ask.* Under these words on the soundtrack recording, an earnest little girl crouches, peeking out from between the spokes of an enormous wagon wheel. Shoved beneath her is a rag doll, its face dirty. The girl wears a head covering in the style of some of the older Mennonite traditions, and the more I look at her the more I understand that this girl is not just sad and scared, but waiting. She has asked her question. She is the future speaking to the past. She hopes for answers. What is it that she has asked? Maybe the same questions John Ruth and Elmer Suderman were asking. Who are we? What did we come from? What does it mean to live? To what should we be saying no? To what should we be saying yes? "O How Shall I Receive Thee" is one of the Mennonite hymns featured on the soundtrack. Line four in Janzen's "A Catechism" offers a sidelong answer to that question: "Everywhere in this world."

NOTES

1. In Wiebe's later work, such as the numerous "sayings" of the fictional Abraham Nofziger, the poet uses the question mark more plaintively, calling with more earnestness into the silent void. Some of the "sayings" are in fact unanswerable questions that seem to be meant as unironically as anything Suderman published: "102. Why must our lives be guilt-ridden?" (*Sayings* 19). Or Wiebe will answer the unanswerable question with a riddle that is really another unanswerable question: "172. Why are the dead important? For the same reasons that the living are important" (*Sayings* 22).

2. A number of the poems begin "Inquiry into. . . ."

3. This section draws heavily on several sources worth looking into for much more on catechism. See Koop; Kreider; Reimer; and Snyder.

4. Martin Luther published *Kurze Form der Zehn Gebote, des Glaubens, des Vaterunsers* (A Condensed Form of the Ten Commandments, the Creed, and the Lord's Prayer) in 1520, a series of questions and answers on the meaning of the Ten Commandments, and published two more catechisms in 1529. The Roman Catholics, not to be outdone, produced one in 1535, the Anglicans in 1604, and the Presbyterians in 1646.

5. It is hard to say why this temporal gap exists between the creation of Hubmaier's catechism and the one produced at Danzig. The editors of *The Mennonite Encyclopedia* write that "the obvious non-use of the catechetical method and non publication of a catechism by Anabaptist-Mennonites in any country for the first century and a quarter of their history poses the question as to whether catechisms are an importation, foreign to the genius of Anabaptism, whose use indicates a spiritual decline of the brotherhood and departure from its original character and type of piety, or whether it was actually a fruitful adaptation from the outside, useful and beneficial throughout the long history of its use in the Amish and Mennonite churches of Germany, France, Prussia, Russia, Holland, and North America" ("Catechism"). I don't think it matters much. The catechism is much older than Mennonites, so it is clearly an "importation." But does that make it "foreign to the genius of Anabaptism"? Anabaptists have been attracted to the form since Hubmaier, and for more than two centuries the Elbing catechism has been massively popular in Mennonite congregations.

6. The Elbing catechism first appeared in North America in 1824 at Ephrata, Pennsylvania, and was translated into English in 1849 under the title *The Catechism: Or Simple Instruction from the Sacred Scriptures, as Taught by the Mennonite Church.* Today, when catechisms are used (and they are still used in many mainstream Mennonite congregations across the United States), the Elbing version is most common, according to *The Global Anabaptist Mennonite Encyclopedia Online.*

7. As an object, *Paper House* is oddly proportioned. It's just five inches wide, but nine inches tall. The conventional size for contemporary poetry collections (and for Janzen's other

books) is something like six by nine inches. Both the 1963 and the 1995 editions of the *Mennonite Confession of Faith* are five inches wide and a little over seven inches tall. This means that *Paper House* is the width of a confession but as tall as a typical poetry book. It might be entirely coincidental, but "A Catechism," in its own narrowness and tallness, matches *Paper House*'s format perhaps more perfectly than any other poem in the collection. The forms and formats of these artistic and religious documents seem to mingle freely in Janzen's book.

8. Janzen, who comes from a Mennonite Brethren background, is adapting a form about which her own church community, more so than any other Mennonite denomination, has been ambivalent. "It has been the policy of the Mennonite Brethren Church to reject all catechism and catechetical instruction from its beginning in Russia, in favor of an emphasis on evangelistic preaching and conversion" ("Catechism").

9. Mennonite religious forms and semantic endeavors seem to prioritize directness and clarity, often laudably associated in these communities with a no-nonsense functionality and restraint. In the foreword to the 1963 *Mennonite Confession of Faith,* the drafting committee comments that they "sought to prepare a statement which was Biblical in character, rather than theological; positive, rather than polemical, and simple, rather than technical or philosophical." In the introduction to *My Christian Faith: A Catechism,* Paul Shelly, chairman of the Catechism Revision Committee of the General Conference Mennonite Church, offered that their revised version—published in 1962—"does not change the basic ideas which are found in the first Elbing Catechism. The purpose of this revision is to make the eternal truths found in the Bible as clear as possible." In the catechism's next section, "How to Use This Book," the pamphlet is named a "guide," a "dictionary," and a "resource." "Questions are direct and answers are specific. . . . This book will help you to ask the right questions and find specific answers drawn from the Scriptures as understood by the Mennonite Church" (3, 4).

10. For the record, Janzen told me in person in early November 2013 that she was not aware of creating an Eliot reference, that the nod was unconscious.

11. Gordon Kaufman, a Mennonite theologian, called for a reconstruction of Christian forms and stories in light of the present, arguing that a drastic transfiguring is necessary to save an ailing planet from human degradation. His lifelong effort at a constructive theological revision is most powerfully outlined in *Jesus and Creativity.* John Ruth exhorted Mennonite artists to "test" the tenets, ideas, stories, and rhetoric of the tradition (48).

12. Magdalene Redekop helped greatly in the formulation of certain aspects of this chapter. Thanks are due to her for the idea of a Mennonite "inflection" or "accent."

WORKS CITED

"Catechism." *Global Anabaptist Mennonite Encyclopedia Online.* Ed. Christian Neff and Harold Bender. 1953. Web. 28 Feb. 2013.

Davies, Victor, dir. . . . *and When They Shall Ask.* Winnipeg: Mennonite Media Society, 1975.

"Elbing Catechism (Mennonite, 1778)." 1778. *Global Anabaptist Wiki.* Web. 28 Feb. 2013.

Eliot, T.S. *The Four Quartets.* New York: Harcourt, Brace and Company, 1943.

Gundy, Jeff. *Inquiries.* Huron, OH: Bottom Dog Press, 1992.

———. "U.S. Mennonite Poetry and Poets: Beyond Dr. Johnson's Dog." *Mennonite Quarterly Review* 71.1 (1997): 5–41.

Hostetler, Ann. "Unexpected Ghost." *Bluestem* Mar. 2013. Web. 1 Oct. 2013. http://www.bluestemmagazine.com.

Hubmaier, Balthasar. *Ein Christennliche Lehrtafel, die ein yedlicher mensch, ee vnd e rim Wasser getaufft wirdt, vor wissen solle* (A Christ-Like Instruction: What Every Person Should Know Before Being Baptized with Water). Nikolsburg, 1526.

Janzen, Jean. *The Elements of Faithful Writing.* Kitchener, ON: Pandora Press, 2004.

———. *Paper House.* Intercourse, PA: Good Books, 2008.

———. *The Upside-Down Tree.* Winnipeg: Henderson Books, 1992.

———. *Words for the Silence.* Fresno: Center for Mennonite Brethren Studies, 1984.

Kaufman, Gordon. *Jesus and Creativity.* Minneapolis: Fortress Press, 2006.

Kermode, Frank. *The Genesis of Secrecy.* Cambridge, MA: Harvard University Press, 1979.

Koop, Karl. "Catechisms in the Mennonite Tradition." *Vision* 4.2 (2003): 28–35.

Kreider, Alan. "Baptism, Catechism, and the Eclipse of Jesus' Teaching in Early Christianity." *Mennonite Quarterly Review* 72.1 (1998): 5–30.

Kurze Unterweisung aus der Schrift (Brief Instruction from Scripture). Danzig, 1690.

Luther, Martin. *Kurze Form der Zehn Gebote, des Glaubens, des Vaterunsers* (A Condensed Form of the Ten Commandments, the Creed, and the Lord's Prayer). 1520.

Mennonite Church. "Mennonite Confession of Faith, 1963." *Global Anabaptist Mennonite Encyclopedia Online.* 1963. Web. 25 Mar. 2015.

The Mennonite Encyclopedia. Scottdale: Herald Press, 1996–2013.

"Obituary: Norma M. Suderman." *Free Press* 4 June 2012. Web. 1 Oct. 2013. http://www.mankatofreepress.com.

Ratzlaff, Keith. *Dubious Angels: Poems After Paul Klee.* Tallahassee: Anhinga Press, 2005.

Reimer, A. James. "Why Give Them Stones? Catechesis as Imaginative Apologetics." *Vision* 4.2 (2003): 36–44.

Rilke, Rainer Maria. *The Selected Poems of Rainer Maria Rilke.* Trans. Stephen Mitchell. New York: Random House, 1982.

Ruth, John L. *Mennonite Identity and Literary Art.* Scottdale: Herald Press, 1978.

Shelly, Paul R., ed. *My Christian Faith: A Catechism.* Newton, KS: Faith and Life Press, 1962.

Snyder, Arnold. "Modern Mennonite Reality and Anabaptist Spirituality: Balthasar Hubmaier's Catechism of 1526." *Conrad Grebel Review* 9.1 (1991): 39–51.

Suderman, Elmer F. "Some Questions for God." *Christianity and Literature* 28.3 (1979): 99.

———. *What Can We Do Here?* St. Peter, MN: Daguerreotype Publishers, 1974.

Wiebe, Dallas. *The Kansas Poems.* Cincinnati: Cincinnati Poetry Review Press, 1987.

———. *The Sayings of Abraham Nofziger II: An Enchiridion for the Pious.* Cincinnati: Self-published, 2007.

11

"Is Menno in There?"

The Case of "The Man Who Invented Himself"

MAGDALENE REDEKOP

If Sander Gilman was right in arguing that identity is not something optional but a necessary part of how we perceive anything, then our assigned topic—"after identity"—is a contradiction in terms, a conundrum related to the old riddle about the Cretan who pronounced that all Cretans are liars. Poet E.F. Dyck puts a Mennonite spin on the problem: "The ethnicity that is called Mennonite is figured by a paradox called *plain style*" (36). Despite our claim to being a plain-speaking people, the liar paradox has been in Mennonite history from the beginning. Imagine a present-day writer called Menno in the position of Menno Simons in one of the trickster stories about how he escaped martyrdom. Let's say our Menno is on a book tour, "riding up front, up high with the driver," on a stagecoach that contains all his baggage, the cultural stuff we all lug around with us. When accosted by a reporter who asks "Is Menno in that coach?" Menno turns around and yells into the coach, "Is Menno in there?" Others shout back, "No, he's not in here." So Menno tells the reporter, "They say Menno's not in there." As Ervin Beck notes, using terminology coined by Erving Goffman, the fugitive "does nothing at all. He merely observes his opponent placing the wrong 'frame' on his experience" (Beck 88; Goffman 217). The technology is different now (with profound implications to which I will return), and the stakes are not so high, but such survival lies (known in sixteenth-century Holland as *Menniste leugen*) are familiar to every writer who has been confronted by a reporter with questions about his or her ethnic identity.

I begin with this updating of an old story as a thrifty way of introducing my dialogic approach. Like Robert Stam, who speaks of "ethnic dialogism,"

I find Bakhtin's theory helpful as a way of countering "naïve formulations of realism" (Stam 252). The Mennonite conferences I have attended have convinced me that Plato was right to associate good dialogue with local hospitality (Redekop, "Mother"). The word *symposium* comes from the Greek meaning "drinking party," and Plato's symposium was hosted by a poet called Agathon. It is not known how Agathon reacted to Plato's banishing of poets from his ideal republic since none of his work has survived. Luckily, this is not our situation. We have poets aplenty, and many of them are willing to talk *about* literature when they are not writing poetry. Unlike Plato, I believe we should be listening to the poets. William Butler Yeats wrote, "We make out of the quarrel with others, rhetoric, but out of the quarrel with ourselves, poetry" (29). He was using the word *rhetoric* in its pejorative sense, as bombast. A knowledge of rhetoric in the classical sense, however, is precisely what is needed in order to "listen" to poetry. I will argue here that we should pay close attention to the language of particular literary texts, keeping in mind how it is inflected by local context (in this case Mennonite) while considering how it resonates within larger aesthetic traditions. Before I can proceed with this task, however, I need to define the problem as I see it—to ask what it is that stops us from listening to the poets.

Poet Robert Kroetsch (a non-Mennonite observer) was asked to chair the closing panel at the 1990 conference at Conrad Grebel College in Waterloo. He began by describing the discussion as a "ferocious family quarrel" and asked us to consider questions about rhetoric and genre (Kroetsch et al. 226). These questions fell by the wayside because of a quarrel about mirrors. Rudy Wiebe expressed concern that "talking about Mennonite writing" is a form of "navel-gazing" and that the imagination is not necessarily stimulated "by sitting and looking in a mirror" (229–30). When it was my turn, I referred to "the Holbein picture of the non-fool looking into the mirror and the fool looking out at him." Wiebe interrupted with "Oh the mirror, you can't talk about the mirror and the shadow and all that stuff." To which I replied, "I can't? I just did." Wiebe then asked, "[W]hy are you always writing about looking in the mirror? Stop it. Your soul is O.K. Go on. You don't need to be redeemed." Not surprisingly, the discussion that followed was lively. Patrick Friesen noted that "In Zen Buddhism to not see yourself in a mirror is actually a triumph" (233). For my part, I stubbornly returned to Holbein's fool.

We never did get around to responding to Kroetsch's questions about genre and rhetoric. Indeed, our frustrated efforts in 1990 to get to a place "after identity" played out a version of the dilemma we face now. When the wheels on the stagecoach go round and round, they could be making progress. The chapters in this volume attest to a shared sense that the wheels are not making progress—that they have been spinning. When our family car—a '53 Ford—got stuck in Manitoba gumbo (a glue-like mixture of clay and water peculiar to the region), there was always that moment when the wheels would start to spin and my father would get out of the car to assess the problem. If only we could step out of the vehicle now to see what is blocking us, what is keeping us trapped in this circular quarrel about identity. As Marshall McLuhan would have it, we are all trapped inside, able to see only what is reflected in the rear-view mirror. Gerald Noonan was right when he pointed out in 1988 (as a non-Mennonite invited to speak at a conference on Mennonite identity) that McLuhan was not thinking of a "Mennonite buggy . . . with the driver looking back at the Anabaptist ruts" and that, "the more un-buggylike" and invisible the technology, the more likely we are to end up in what McLuhan called a "Narcissus trance" (260–61).

McLuhan's hope that the electronic media would liberate us was sadly mistaken. The numbing effects of mass media are nowhere more apparent than in the reproduction of stereotypical images of ethnic groups. Identity remains an issue for people in minority groups if for no other reason than because *they* keep making fun of *us.* Consider, for example, a cartoon by Stephan Pastis, part of the comic strip "Pearls Before Swine," in which the bust of an Amish man pops up from a "catch-all drawer." In the cartoon, Rat concedes to Pig that the Amish man is an example of something "a bit unusual." The cartoon illustrates a problem that W.J.T. Mitchell once identified when he noted that there is "no representation without taxation" (21). As Robert Weimann glosses that inimitable phrase, there is no representation of any person without "loss in the shape and presence of the represented" (196). The tax is high in the Pastis cartoon. Do we laugh when the bust pops up? That depends on who "we" are. Never underestimate interethnic protectiveness. It can be fierce when those among your "people" who are being attacked are less educated or cultured than you suppose yourself to be or when you are the one who can "pass" while they pay the price of being a visible minority. Caught up in such strong feelings, we quickly lose sight of the fact that the cartoon is satire—a particular kind of art.

As cultural critics examining our own culture, we are participant observers, each with a particular bias, but we do have to try to take a critical distance. The Mennonite critical gumbo that I see from where I stand is related to the fact that we tend, as Dyck notes, to see plain style not as a style but as "a moral imperative" (41–42). The result, as I suggested earlier, is a strong preference for "naïve formulations of realism" (Stam 252), accompanied by an ethical emphasis. Not that our problem is unique. Perhaps it is because I am aware that our besetting sin is self-righteousness that I have developed an aversion to the moralistic tone that now saturates even the most abstruse literary theory. A turn away from literature itself has been a feature of literary criticism for far too long. Like the vehicles of other groups, our wheels are mired in a muck of theory. To make matters worse, we have harnessed the cart before the horse—putting the writing of theory before the reading of literature. The horses might be thirsty from running on the spot, but, as the old proverb goes, you can lead a horse to water, but you can't make it drink. You can make twenty photocopies of a poem for twenty scholars in a room, but you can't make a single one of them read the poem. Anxious that the text in our hands might be stale-dated, we hop onto a different bandwagon, rushing to keep up with the latest fad.

These problems are accentuated when the art being studied is made by people who are part of a minority group, caught up in what Charles Taylor has called "the politics of recognition" (38). My studies have left me wary of approaches to "minority literature" that conceive of a Mennonite literature set apart to go with "the people apart." I am not saying that the political issues around minority literatures do not matter, but I believe that the best way to make them visible is to work to do justice to the achievements of artists coming out of minority groups. Too often literary critics are lured into joining the interviewers who run alongside that hackneyed stagecoach, repeatedly calling "Is Menno in there?" How many different ways are there of answering that question? Patrick Friesen answered it plainly in a 1985 interview: "I'm not a Mennonite writer. I'm a Mennonite and I'm a writer and you must differentiate" (Reimer and Tiessen 253). It is what Philip Roth has said repeatedly about being Jewish, and it reflects the efforts of artists everywhere to protect their freedom to create. Some might think that Miriam Toews and David Bergen (two major "Mennonite" writers who emerged in the 1990s) have achieved such a wide reception because they are writing "after identity." To be fair, however, one would have to add that they have benefited from the writers who preceded them in the 1980s. A major joint achievement of that time was the creation in Canada of the category "secular Mennonite." Again and again various writers have urged us to respect the difference that Friesen articulated so simply. If we keep pestering them with questions about their Mennonite identity, then we should not be surprised if they come up with increasingly bizarre answers. Nor is it fair to blame them for the fact that we, the critics, are mired in identity issues.

The consolation is that, when all is said and done, we have the art left over. There is no Mennonite buggy large enough to contain the amazing art that has been produced. The 1980 publication of Patrick Friesen's *The Shunning* was the beginning of a decade of astonishing ferment in southern Manitoba that saw publications (many of them literary debuts) by E.F. Dyck, Sandra Birdsell, Lois Braun, Anne Konrad, Sarah Klassen, Audrey Poetker, Al Reimer, Douglas Reimer, Andreas Schroeder, David Waltner-Toews, John Weier, Armin Wiebe, and others. Confronted with an embarrassment of riches marked by heterogeneity, we have long relied on Hildi Froese Tiessen to do invaluable interim reports on the "state of the art." Our problems might be compounded, however, if we expect these reports to be accounts of literary progress. In a recent essay, Tiessen claims that "identity politics and essentialism" have been left behind in a "new Mennonite literature" that is no longer concerned with the "communal memory" of a "homeland." "In the new Mennonite writing," she continues, "history and tradition are no longer authoritative" ("Remains" 13). Tiessen expresses concern about a future time when "the Mennonite text is in effect no longer recognizable as a 'Mennonite' text," when it no longer "'identifies me to myself.'" What if, she asks, this "new 'Mennonite' literary text were to prove to be simply, utterly *everyone's* text" (14)? By implication, her argument assumes the existence of an "old Mennonite writing" in which identity was essentialized and tradition was authoritative. However, the body of her own writing—her appreciations of the earlier writers—exposes her distinction between "old" and "new" as a false dichotomy. This illusion—that literature makes progress—is tied to the nineteenth-century model of literary history that underlies the accepted account of the origins of the Manitoba Mennonite phenomenon. According to this account, the story begins in Russia with the "commonwealth" that developed there after the departure of those Mennonites who came to Manitoba as immigrants in the 1870s—the *Kanadier*. The cultural leaders of the group that came to Manitoba as refugees in the late 1920s—the *Russländer*—worked hard to reconstitute in Canada the renaissance that had happened in Russia. As Al Reimer notes, they had "a concept of ethnic identity [that] was to a large extent modelled on the German concept of *Volk* and *Kultur*" (17).

The first step in any response to the dilemma I have described is acknowledgment of bias. Unacknowledged bias is often the source of confusion since non-Mennonites lack knowledge of the complexities of interethnic Mennonite conflicts. My bias as a woman from the *Kanadier* group means that I am used to dealing with experiences that do not fit the old stories. What Tiessen describes as a "new" kind of text is something that, from my point of view, happened in Canada before the *Russländer* culture developed. Paul Hiebert's *Sarah Binks,* published in 1947, is an example of a text that is "simply, utterly *everyone's* text." It "identifies me to myself" not because it is about a lost homeland but because I now hear a Mennonite aesthetic accent in Hiebert's ironic play with plain style. I did not always hear it. It was the new fiction and poetry written by members of my own group, the *Kanadier,* that emboldened me, in "Escape from the Bloody Theatre," to begin formulating new questions. Let's see what happens, I asked myself, if we look at the literary phenomenon going on in Manitoba not as defined only by the trauma experienced by the *Russländer.* What if we try not to collapse that story into the martyrdom story and concentrate instead on the aesthetic tricks of the crafty ones—from all the groups—who got away? These questions led me inevitably into interdisciplinary territory since the Manitoba literary phenomenon was accompanied by new developments in the visual arts.

This chapter is an offshoot of a larger study in which I consider particular art by Mennonites with attention to local material context as well as to the larger context of the history of art since the Reformation. I have found representation studies to be a helpful theoretical context, and I think it no coincidence that the 1980s, when the flowering began in Manitoba, was also the heyday of postmodernism, when representation was questioned in ways that echoed early modern conflicts (Hutcheon 119–21). I have learned to listen for a Mennonite aesthetic accent—not simply in the literal sense of those flattened vowels but also in the broader sense of noticing what is *accentuated.* The accent is marked by a heightened awareness of the self/other and us/them distinctions. This is familiar enough as a result of the Mennonite history that has been written. Is there a conflict more central to our peculiar history than the tension between individual identity that results from choice (Anabaptism) and communal identity that results from covenant (the people apart)? More difficult to study—and more necessary for those of us who want to push past the thematic level—is the anxiety about representation that I see as a part of the Mennonite aesthetic accent. The almost complete lack of Mennonite scholarship in the area of art history is astonishing, given the central importance of the Reformation to the history of Western art. Even the flowering of Mennonite art that happened during the time of Rembrandt has received almost no attention. Theologian Philip Stoltzfus laments a "475-year 'drift'" during which "philosophical *ethics*" has triumphed in Mennonite culture because of a "self-induced aesthetic masochism" (77) and notes that the "cultural journey" of Mennonites has happened "largely without the benefit of a broader analytical and critical perspective" (76).

From the body of art by Mennonites, I have extrapolated a working aesthetic that has helped me take on this daunting task. Far from being focused on the kind of identity that longs for a homeland and looks for *Lebensraum,* or "living space," the implicit aesthetic that I see at work in all of the major artists is a search for *Spielraum,* or the affirmation of a "play space" that has porous boundaries and is shared with artists from all ethnicities. It is possible and often useful to make out distinct aesthetic accents that vary with ethnicity in the *Spielraum.* Novelist Ashok Mathur describes the "voicing of identity-location" in our time as "lost in an echoey chamber" (144–45). In her "theory of resonance," however, Wai Chee Dimock describes the literary text as "an echo chamber" in a more positive context (1062). She celebrates a "primarily aural and primarily interactive" quality in texts. Texts endure, she argues, not because of some timeless content but because they are "touched" as they travel, "causing unexpected vibrations in unexpected places" in "readers on different wavelengths" (1061).

Dimock's theory lays the groundwork for an approach to echo on several levels: as an acoustic phenomenon and a character in classical myth but, most importantly, as a rhetorical device. My focus here is on a tension between story and song at the heart of Mennonite culture. It is reflected in Rudy Wiebe's insistence that the prairie can only be represented by the laying of "great black steel lines of fiction" and that "No song can do that" (131). In the poem on which I focus here, Patrick Friesen deploys echo in a way that moderates the competing claims of story and song. Here is the poem in its entirety.

the man who invented himself

1.
I remind you of the man who invented himself
out of clay and spit amino acids if you will
out of photographs and dreams
out of the right hand of god and baptism he invented himself

he thought as a young man he would read palms in the pub
or display his memory for the names of spanish poets
he writhed in fevers of justice saw they weren't just
and was almost lost in a map of emotions

the man who invented himself
failed to explain it all to himself
no matter where he left a distinct impression
he walked toward obscurity

2.
after splashing for a while my son sits quietly in the bath
examining his fingers how they wrinkle
his feet his penis and whatever else he can reach

3.
in 1977 I sat in the northern square of the golden cathedral
when lawrence came to guadalajara he saw this cathedral first
from a distance hills between this dome glowing in the west
I remembered reading that in one of his travel books
I walked back to my hotel a shadow on mexican stones

4.
'I once was lost/but now am found'

the man who invented himself didn't write that
but he heard it the day he was born and couldn't forget it
you might say that line was the true mystery for him
it gave him something to do
you could hear him humming between drinks
or laughing or mocking or posturing
and more than once he turned the line around

the man who invented himself invented mirrors
though he was told it had been done before
you can imagine how upsetting that was
to be such a fool caught with his foot in the door
but he knew his history and everyone was wrong
he knew it hadn't been done before

5.
I thought just now how to continue
the life and times of this devious man
how to keep your interest in one I hardly know myself
a man not particularly interesting
who likes to believe he invented himself
and longs like all his kind for the grave

my son interrupts me
calling to share yet another anatomical discovery
you and me dad he confides it's kind of touching
the only real solidarity I've ever felt

as I leave the bathroom I turn to the mirror
and for an instant see myself turn toward myself

6.
you're always where you've been
said the man who invented himself
you're always where you're going
(I remember him as a child)

7.
'there's going to be a meeting/
in the air' he sang he liked the tune
imagining the invention of selves
remembering the streets of towns and cities
the songs 'amazing grace' on home street
or 'green river' in guadalajara from a shortwave radio

songs that reminded him of other songs
sidewalks that recalled other sidewalks and other towns
in the evening a bath then out drinking with the others
and always singing in his heart 'I once was found' (37–39)

Music is central to the impact of any poem by Friesen. The rhythmic complexity of his poems derives from the fact that they variously absorb the rhythms of rock, blues, jazz, and hymns, as well as classical music. "the man who invented himself" is a poem that shows how identity becomes fluid and dialogic—alive—if you open your ears to song. Echo is a form of allusiveness that "does not depend on intention," and our memories of songs are often involuntary (Hollander 64; Redekop, "Haunted" 243). In this poem, echo works in conjunction with conscious allusions and quotations to set up a humming and a whispering that feel oddly dissociated from the visual scene—as if a cinematic image and a soundtrack are slightly out of sync.

The ancient story of Narcissus and Echo resonates as a subtext in the poem. Ovid's version goes like this. Once there was a beautiful nymph called Echo, who falls in love with a beautiful youth called Narcissus. Sensing the pursuit of Echo, Narcissus shouts, "Anyone here?" To which Echo replies, "Here!" Narcissus says, "Come this way!" To which Echo replies, "This way!" But when Echo tries to embrace him, Narcissus rejects her and says, "I'll die before I yield to you." To which she replies, "I'll yield to you." As Echo wastes away from unrequited love, Narcissus is lured to a pool, where he falls in love with his own reflection, and he too wastes away. In some versions, he drowns (62–63).

As John Hollander points out, echo is "a powerful mocker," and "the role of questioning is crucial in the literary device of the echo song or text" (12). The questions travel across time and result in revisions of our old ways of seeing. The major revision of Ovid's tale in Friesen's poem is that Narcissus does not reject the embrace of Echo. The central reversal in the poem is a moment of attraction to and repulsion from the image in the mirror, but echoes are what break the frame of the poem itself. The poem swings on a hinge, going back and forth between reflections by and about "the man who invented himself" and the simple scene of a father watching his son identify the parts of his body in the bathtub.

The poem is divided into seven numbered sections linked to each other by a fugue-like repetition of phrases. The first four lines are shaped by anaphora (the initial repetition of "out of") and epistrophe (the closing repetition of "invented himself"). Blasphemy, explicit in the title of the poem, is a recurring feature of Friesen's poetry, often creating a tension between Bible stories that threaten to trap and songs that liberate and comfort. The repetitions in these opening lines strike a chord that will, in a sense, allow Friesen to "take on" the biblical story of salvation, salvaging from it a kernel of goodness that resonates like the *Kernlieder* that our people have sung for centuries. The ambiguity of the first line is crucial to this effect. "I remind you of" could mean "Let me remind you of. . . ." It could also mean "Do I remind you of the man who invented himself?" The "you" in "amino acids if you will" is unmoored from any specific referent. *I* and *you* are like markers where readers can enter the interactive process.

The next two sections make clear that the biblical creation story will not be replaced by the mystique of the poet as some kind of superior or prophetic being. The speaker is a father taking care of his son. The present tense—"my son sits quietly in the bath"—works with the economy of the words to bring us, so to speak, down to earth. As the boy examines his fingers, "how they wrinkle," we intuit the father's sense of his own mortality. It is in the fourth section, the middle of the poem, that Friesen alludes to the salvation story: "I once was lost/but now am found." One touch, one carefully selected fragment, is all that is needed for the line to resonate with familiar stories such as the parable of the prodigal son. The words are set apart with single quotation marks, which emphasize them as a printed fragment, but common or hymn meter can be felt as an iambic beat. The music that enters the poem has a life of its own beyond the printed words. The familiarity of the song ensures that most readers will hear an understood echo: "Amazing Grace." The effect of the quotation is to open the poem to choric voices, but these voices work in ironic counterpoint to the individual lyric voice. As he puzzles over the "true mystery," the man turns away from the communal voices, distances himself from the song, and parades his own ego. The result is predictable. Pride goes before a fall. He is "a fool caught with his foot in the door."

In section 5, we take in the implications of this self-knowledge as the voice is flattened again, becoming "plain" and everyday. The speaker confesses that he is wondering how to keep the poem going, how to keep our interest. Here, at the point where a traditional religious turn would steer the poet away from his own ego and toward God the Father, who created him, Friesen takes us back to earth, to the father-son relationship. In a startling moment, the child speaks—"you and me dad"—and then the father speaks to us: "it's kind of touching." Earlier in the poem, the boy touched "his fingers," "his feet," "his penis," and "whatever else he [could] reach," but he sat quietly and did not speak. His excited discovery now suggests that the unnamed body part is not the penis but the navel. The conclusion is plain. Both father and son are born of women, not invented by either a father god or themselves. It is only after reaching this solid ground, the "only real solidarity," that the voice moves us to anagnorisis, or recognition: "as I leave the bathroom I turn to the mirror / and for an instant see myself turn toward myself." Repetition of the reflexive pronoun "myself" is the point in the poem where it is clear that the visual, by itself, is a dead end, like the wasting away of Narcissus. The presence of the mirror, however, tells us that the aural, by itself, is also a dead end—like the wasting away of Echo. The interaction of eye and ear in this poem is inseparable from the interaction of *I* and *you* that creates dialogic identity.

The brief penultimate section of the poem offers a four-line encapsulated "message." Its tone is mock authoritative, not unlike the speech of the urn in Keats's "Ode on a Grecian Urn." Like that speech, this one is a tautology. It collapses time past, present, and future in a mock prophetic vision that threatens to make nonsense of it all. The voices draw us back from that collapse with the parenthetical line "(I remember him as a child)." The line is bracing, but within those brackets the ambiguity of the pronouns keeps the text open to invasion. Who is *I,* and who is *he,* and who is the *child?* The poem has a "tendency to fall apart," to use Dimock's image (1064), and each time it does the reader is drawn into the interactive process.

In the last section of "the man who invented himself," the rhythms reach a crescendo. Where the earlier line from "Amazing Grace" introduced an iambic beat, the last section begins with a quotation that introduces an anapestic beat and an increase in tempo: "'there's going to be a meeting / in the air' he sang he liked the tune." Even as some readers will be humming along, hearing the rest of the song and thinking of the "sweet by and by," the allusions multiply. As the speaker imagines "the invention of selves" and remembers "the streets of towns and cities," other songs come to mind: "'amazing grace' on home street / or 'green river' in Guadalajara from a shortwave radio." The poem is like a script for participation in a dialogic process that is exhilarating but that varies from reader to reader. Some readers will know that "Green River" is a 1969 song by Creedence Clearwater Revival. Others will not. A few readers might even pick up on an allusion to a 1981 song by Robyn Hitchcock that ends "He's the fellow, the man who invented himself." The poem is not a self-contained artifact. It is, rather, a place where our senses respond to the resonance of the text.

It is this open-ended dialogue that is celebrated in the last lines of the poem. The final quotation, inverting the phrase from "Amazing Grace," might seem like a too-neat closed ending. To read it that way, however, is to think of the poem as a static artifact. In the context of the dialogue in the poem, it is an inversion that enacts the earlier "posturing" of the man who boasts that "more than once he turned the line around." The irony of the last phrase puts the emphasis not on the man but on the songs themselves and on "the others" who sing along. Even as we sing along, we feel our own identity as fleeting, like a "shadow on mexican stone."

Poems remind us of other poems. Friesen's poem reminds me of Robert Frost's "Directive," which also affirms the experience of being "lost enough to find yourself." Like the speaker of Friesen's poem, the speaker of "Directive" is wary of gospel truths. His "broken drinking goblet like the Grail" is "Under a spell so the wrong ones can't find it, / So can't get saved, as Saint Mark says they mustn't." Also like the speaker in Friesen's poem, the one in Frost's poem is looking for a place to play: "(I stole the goblet from the children's playhouse)." There are many differences, of course. Frost ends his poem with two lines of clear, albeit ironic, statement: "Here are your waters and your watering place. / Drink and be whole again beyond confusion." Friesen's ending is open—fragments of voices drifting to us while we are "out drinking with the others." But all of the differences happen on common ground and in a common *Spielraum.* In these two voices—one writing the folksy plain speech of

New England and the other the plain speech of southern Manitoba—can be heard the nuanced variations of different aesthetic accents as they play with "the paradox called *plain style*" (Dyck 36).

If "the man who invented himself" is "simply, utterly *everyone's* text," then is there anything to be gained by asking the question "Is Menno in there?" Perhaps we should stop directing that question at the authors and begin by taking the answer for granted. A straight-talking Miriam Toews recently instructed an interviewer to do so: "I'll always be a Mennonite, there's no denying it and no need to deny it" (43). What happens if we direct the question at the text instead? Does the *poem* have a Mennonite aesthetic accent, and, if so, does it matter whether or not the reader hears it? Do we need to know details about the life of the author in order to make that accent audible? If the text has an accent, then does it mean that the text has an ethnic identity? I hope I have made clear that my answers to all of these questions would begin with a rejection of monologic definitions of identity that lead to reductive interpretations of art. The fact that Friesen "like so many other Mennonites both loves and hates his roots" (Lenoski 131) is surely no more unusual than the fact that William Faulkner both loved and hated the American South. If the question is heard as part of a playful dialogue, then I think it is still worth asking. Is Menno in there? Now you see him. Now you don't. Whether or not you do will depend, at least to some extent, on whether or not you are a Mennonite. How could it not? Because I am a Mennonite, I relate to the fear of pride that is palpable in the Friesen poem and that John Ruth long ago described as one of our primary scruples (37). When the speaker recoils from his image in the mirror, I feel the ambivalence about self-representation close to the bone. If I linger, however, in that place where I "see myself turn toward myself," then I will be like "a fool caught with his foot in the door." If I stop there for too long, then I might waste away like Narcissus. I have tried to show here that the dialogic identity that Friesen celebrates in this poem revises this sad ending by embracing Echo. The voices that meet in the air of this echo chamber are not only Mennonite, and we have no more right to sing about "the sweet by and by" than the people who parade at a jazz funeral in New Orleans. Singing the same song, however, does not eliminate the historical differences among ethnic groups. I hear a Mennonite aesthetic accent in "the man who invented himself." It is there in the inescapable ironies of "the paradox called *plain style*," in the awareness that the repudiation of pride can itself be an act of pride. The integrity of Friesen's voice results from fidelity to his particular local experience. Friesen once observed, "In a curious way, it makes more sense for me to be considered a 'Kleinegemeinde' writer than a Menno writer" (qtd. in Enns 51).

Non-Mennonite readers will be on different "traveling frequencies" and have different associations, but a good poem will resonate just as deeply with them. We make a mistake, furthermore, if we assume that non-Mennonites cannot see through our *Menniste leugen* and hear the accent that betrays a Mennonite identity. How is it, for example, that the abstract art of both Warren Rohrer and Wanda Koop is ignored by most Mennonites and yet has led secular art critics to ask questions about Mennonite attitudes toward representation (Koop 95; Rosenberg 12)? Biographical context remains useful as long as we do not use it to kill the poem with reductive interpretations. The major achievement of Patrick Friesen has not yet been recognized, partly because a thematic focus on *The Shunning* has acted to obscure the range and depth of his poetic craft.

Good questions lead to other questions, and I make no claim to be able to answer all of the questions that I have stirred up. This chapter is an *essay* in the original sense of that word, meaning "a trial" or "an attempt." I am the descendant of pioneering Mennonites, the group that built sod houses on the Manitoba prairie. I think of them as I attempt to break new ground and build my provisional structures. Always I come back to the mystery and magic of art. It escapes all containers. As Roland Barthes put it, "the work *escapes*" because it is "*something else* than its history, the sum of its sources, influences, or models" (54–55). The work of art escapes because it is not a commodity. It is a gift. The single most important feature of a gift, according to Lewis Hyde, is that it must be passed on: "*the gift must always move*" (4). Unlike the exchange of commodities, gift exchange "establishes a feeling-bond between two people" (56). Hyde relates this bond to the concept of "mutual aid" (76), which he traces back to Anabaptists (87–88). In the intensity of Friesen's poetry, I feel an affirmation of this value that lies so deep in the heritage of our people, a value described by Hyde as the "erotic life" of a gift. Hyde speaks of the labor of gratitude required to pass a gift along (47). It is enough for me if my labor here has succeeded in passing on the gift of at least one poem.

WORKS CITED

Barthes, Roland. *On Racine.* Trans. Richard Howard. New York: Octagon, 1977.

Beck, Ervin. "Trickster Tales." *MennoFolk: Mennonite and Amish Folk Traditions.* Scottdale: Herald Press, 2004. 76–95.

Dimock, Wai Chee. "A Theory of Resonance." *PMLA* 112 (1997): 1060–71.

Dyck, E.F. "The Rhetoric of the Plain Style in Mennonite Writing." *Mennonite/s Writing in Canada.* Ed. Hildi Froese Tiessen. Spec. issue of *New Quarterly* 10 (1990): 36–52.

Enns, Victor Jerrett. "The Missing Mennonite Cabaret: Excerpts from the Correspondence of Patrick Friesen." *Patrick Friesen.* Spec. issue of *Prairie Fire* 13.1 (1992): 45–52.

Friesen, Patrick. "the man who invented himself." *Unearthly Horses.* Winnipeg: Turnstone Press, 1984. 37–39.

Frost, Robert. "Directive." *Selected Poems of Robert Frost.* New York: Rinehart, 1963. 251–53.

Gilman, Sander L. *Difference and Pathology: Stereotypes of Sexuality, Race, and Madness.* Ithaca: Cornell University Press, 1985.

Goffman, Erving. *Frame Analysis.* New York: Harper and Row, 1974.

Hiebert, Paul. *Sarah Binks.* Toronto: Oxford University Press, 1947.

Hitchcock, Robyn. "The Man Who Invented Himself." *Black Snake Dîamond Röle.* Armageddon, 1981. CD.

Hollander, John. *The Figure of Echo: A Mode of Allusion in Milton and After.* Berkeley: University of California Press, 1981.

Hutcheon, Linda. "Afterword: Postmodernism's Ironic Paradoxes: Politics and Art." *Remembering Postmodernism: Trends in Canadian Art, 1970–1990.* Ed. Mark Cheetham. 1991. Don Mills, ON: Oxford University Press, 2012. 113–36.

Hyde, Lewis. *The Gift: Imagination and the Erotic Life of Property.* New York: Vintage, 1979.

Koop, Wanda. "The Transformative Art of Wanda Koop." Interview by Robert Enright. *Border Crossings* 5.4 (1986): 94–104.

Kroetsch, Robert, et al. "Closing Panel." *Acts of Concealment: Mennonite/s Writing in Canada.* Ed. Hildi Froese Tiessen and Peter Hinchcliffe. Waterloo, ON: University of Waterloo Press, 1992. 223–42.

Lenoski, Daniel S. "The Sandbox Holds Civilizations: Pat Friesen and the Mennonite Past." *Essays on Canadian Writing* 18–19 (1980): 131–42.

Mathur, Ashok. "How Writers of Colour Became CanLit." *Trans.Can.Lit: Resituating the Study of Canadian Literature.* Ed. Smaro Kamboureli and Roy Miki. Waterloo, ON: Wilfrid Laurier University Press, 2007. 141–51.

Mitchell, W.J.T. "Representation." *Critical Terms for Literary Study.* Ed. Frank Lentricchia and Thomas McLaughlin. Chicago: University of Chicago Press, 1990. 11–22.

Noonan, Gerald. "Seeing Oneself in the Mirror of Art." *Mennonite Identity: Historical and Contemporary Perspectives.* Ed. Calvin Redekop and Sam Steiner. New York: University Press of America, 1988. 259–63.

Ovid. *Metamorphoses.* Trans. A.D. Melville. Oxford: Oxford University Press, 1986.

Pastis, Stephan. "Pearls Before Swine" [cartoon]. *Go Comics* 21 May 2012. Web. 20 Nov. 2013.

Redekop, Magdalene. "Escape from the Bloody Theatre: The Making of Mennonite Stories." *Journal of Mennonite Studies* 11 (1993): 9–22.

———. "Haunted by Hymns: The Fate of Melody in 'Mennonite' Poetry." *Sound in the Lands: Mennonite Music Across Borders.* Ed. Maureen Epp et al. Waterloo, ON: Pandora Press, 2011. 243–70.

———. "The Mother Tongue in Cyberspace." *Center for Mennonite Writing Journal* 1 (2009). Web. 1 Aug. 2013.

Reimer, Al. *Mennonite Literary Voices: Past and Present.* North Newton, KS: Bethel College, 1993.

Reimer, Margaret Loewen, and Paul Tiessen. "The Poetry and Distemper of Patrick Friesen and David Waltner-Toews." *Visions and Realities: Essays, Poems, and Fiction Dealing with Mennonite Issues.* Ed. Harry Loewen and Al Reimer. Winnipeg: Hyperion Press, 1985. 243–53.

Rosenberg, Susan. *Warren Rohrer: Paintings 1972–93.* Philadelphia: Philadelphia Museum of Art, 2002.

Ruth, John. *Mennonite Identity and Literary Art.* Scottdale: Herald Press, 1978.

Stam, Robert. "Bakhtin, Polyphony, and Ethnic/Racial Representation." *Unspeakable Images: Ethnicity and the American Cinema.* Ed. Lester D. Friedman. Urbana: University of Illinois Press, 1991. 251–76.

Stoltzfus, Phil. "Performative Envisioning: An Aesthetic Critique of Contemporary Mennonite Theology." *Conrad Grebel Review* 16.3 (1998): 75–91.

Taylor, Charles. "The Politics of Recognition." *Multiculturalism: Examining the Politics of Recognition.* Ed. Amy Gutmann. Princeton: Princeton University Press, 1994. 25–73.

Tiessen, Hildi Froese. "What Remains of What Does Not Remain?" *Rhubarb* 30 (2012): 12–15.

Toews, Miriam. Interview by Rosmarin Heidenreich. *Rhubarb* 30 (2012): 42–43.

Weimann, Robert. *Authority and Representation in Early Modern Discourse.* Ed. David Hillman. Baltimore: Johns Hopkins University Press, 1996.

Wiebe, Rudy. "Passage by Land." *Writers of the Prairies.* Ed. Donald G. Stephens. Vancouver: UBC Press, 1973. 129–31.

Yeats, W.B. *Per Amica Silentia Lunae.* New York: Macmillan, 1918.

12

After Identity

Liberating the Mennonite Literary Text

HILDI FROESE TIESSEN

This chapter begins with a number of assumptions: (1) that critics of Mennonite literature are in the company of a vast number of scholars who have determined that the literary-critical approaches of recent decades—in which critics (and writers) found themselves "in deep conversation with their historical contexts and the social worlds or publics they engage" (Edwards 232)—are inadequate as interpretive strategies; (2) that, even though scholars of Mennonite literature do not share all the concerns (about race, nation, etc.) of a range of literary critics focused on other minority culture literatures in North America, they might be richly informed by the stimulating critical conversations about "identity" and "after identity" occurring in fields such as Jewish American literature or Asian American literature, for example; and (3) that any discussion of identity issues relative to Mennonite/s writing remains a vexing matter not least because concerns about identity in general continue to challenge the complexly layered landscape of Mennonite communities across North America and beyond.

It is worth observing, at the outset, the diversity of people who identify themselves as Mennonites and the heterogeneous nature of the tag "Mennonite," routinely used to identify people by creed and culture first but most often qualified by distinguishing identifiers such as "Canadian" and "American," or by epithets such as "Swiss" and "Russian," or in terms of migratory groups such as *Kanadier* and *Russländer,* or by denominational divisions such as Mennonite Brethren, Bergthaler, Kleine Gemeinde, and many others. (Margaret Loewen Reimer's *One Quilt Many Pieces: A Guide to Mennonite Groups in Canada* lists a few dozen denominational groups in Canada alone, quite apart from the many distinctive language-based clusters among them: German, French, Hispanic, Chinese, Vietnamese, Korean, Arabic, Punjabi, and others.) Furthermore, when literary critics speak of Mennonite literature, they tend to refer to writing produced only by individuals identified with certain groups within the North American Mennonite community, which itself, even in its immense diversity, represents barely 30 percent of the world's 1,775,000 Mennonites.[1] Moreover, other sorts of modifiers, such as "ethnic" or "secular," are much more readily acknowledged as appropriate descriptors of Mennonites in Canada than they are of Mennonites in the United States, where Mennonites are generally regarded as a religious group, and where the word *ethnic* has troublesome resonances not generally detected by most Canadian Mennonites, who have long seen themselves—and have been seen in the public eye—as belonging to both religious and ethnic communities.

This chapter barely begins to explore one aspect of an emerging subject for the literary critic interested in Mennonite/s writing: Mennonite literature "after" (i.e., "apart from" or "in pursuit of" or "regarding" or "subsequent to") "identity." This subject doggedly confronts anyone working in the field, in particular the editors of the two journals at present devoted exclusively to Mennonite/s writing: *Rhubarb* magazine and *CMW Journal* (online), in which editorial declarations concerning "who is a Mennonite writer" and "of what does Mennonite writing consist" might include statements such as this one from the frontmatter of *Rhubarb,* asserting that the magazine accepts work "by non-Mennonites about Mennonites" as well as by writers "who self-define as Mennonites, whether practicing, declined, or resistant," or this announcement from the editor of *CMW Journal,* which describes the "emerging writers" of a recent issue simply as "those who have spent formative years with or who have chosen to hang out with Mennonites."[2]

What would it mean to edit a journal or magazine devoted to "Mennonite" writing, or to compile an anthology featuring Mennonite work, or to convene a conference on Mennonite/s Writing if none of the work presented or discussed made any explicit reference to things Mennonite or none of the writers self-declared as Mennonite? What does the multiply inflected term "Mennonite/s writing" signify? How is the term useful? How does it serve writers or readers? What would it mean to define it in relatively exacting ways? In what manner do we need to retain some version of it? What if it disappeared altogether? Do any of these questions have any import for anyone beyond the relatively few who make it their business to ask?

This chapter acknowledges the rich diversity that exists within the ever-expanding panorama that is Mennonite/s writing—a range of work much of which in no palpable way addresses distinctive ways of "being Mennonite," work including the eclectic range of poems and fictions published in specialized and mainstream magazines, journals, and anthologies. That valuable work poses a particular range of identity questions within the field of Mennonite/s writing. What concerns me here is one thing in particular: the ways in which any literature that has been, and continues to be, encompassed by the circle of Mennonite/s writing has been or might be affected, inflected, refracted, or infected by what critic Wai Chee Dimock refers to as "literary causality" derived from "a territorial [or territorialized] jurisdiction" (*Through* 3) generally identified, in this case, by the descriptive moniker Mennonite—and the sorts of illuminations and new possibilities that might proceed from this investigation.

This chapter (which borrows language and insights from outside the Mennonite circle) urges us not to abandon identity issues in Mennonite writing altogether but to probe them vigorously—especially as the work of more and more writers who self-identify as Mennonite appears in print—and to explore avenues of interpretation that would foreground perspectives other than those rooted in identity categories. The chapter applauds the direction proposed by those who have urged the critics of Mennonite/s writing to move in new directions; to open up the conversation; to liberate the texts, the writers, the readers, and the critics themselves from a propensity to foreground referential knowledge and historical situations that have often tended to precede and guide—and limit—the accessibility of texts and reader response.

During the era of identity politics and multiculturalism, the idea of identity in large measure "structured the field imaginary"[3] of any number of minor or major literatures, including Mennonite/s writing, in which deeply held assumptions about the relationship between literary texts and their contexts prevail. Although Mennonite writing continues to flourish in both Canada and the United States, introducing a vast range of voices and narratives, not only in novels and other major works but also via little magazines in print and online, critical responses to Mennonite literature—especially those written by commentators of Mennonite heritage—have tended to work with the tacit assumption that identity categories will, in large measure, continue to direct the reading and to condition the experience of Mennonite literary texts. Only recently have scholars begun to reframe the critical discourse related to Mennonite/s writing in Canada and the United States, to move beyond the familiar conventions of identity-based criticism and launch new conversations that a 2013 symposium identified as critical conversations about Mennonite/s writing "after identity."

Critics of Mennonite/s writing are by no means alone among literary critics looking for fresh ways to talk about the relationship between literature and identity or seeking ways to discuss literature without referring to matters related to identity. From the encouragement of French literary theorist Pascale Casanova, who, in the context of what she calls "the world republic of letters," advocates the abandonment of "habits of thought that create the illusion of uniqueness and insularity" (5), to the exhortation of Americanists such as Brian T. Edwards, who has observed that "the relationship between text and context needs to be reconsidered: the link is too stable when the text is understood as the translation of historical context and vice versa" (233), the call has gone out for critics across the spectrum of local, national, and world literatures to invent new critical discourses, to dislocate texts from their original contexts, to disturb notions of "national" or ethnic authenticity, to abandon what Michael P. Kramer refers to rather roughly as the "critical narcissism" whereby context precedes and guides reading ("Critical").

Mennonite literature is a small player in a vast landscape of writing that has "come of age" in recent decades and now finds itself in an era in which that anchoring concept, "identity," is spoken of in terms of exhaustion (e.g., Palumbo-Liu 765; Roof 1; Millner 541) and abandonment (Lee passim); it is referred to as a concept "under erasure" and "no longer serviceable" (Hall 1–2). Resisting the urge to abolish identitarian categories even while recognizing that notions of identity have left critics with a range of vexing questions, Stuart Hall and others suggest that critics might make the effort to reconceptualize identity (2). Inspired by Dimock's assertion that the "'immortality' of literature must be understood . . . as the continual emergence of interpretive contexts" ("Theory" 1065), the Mennonite reader and critic could be informed and enlightened by considering what it might mean to ease the Mennonite text away from its context, and by exploring what it might mean to dislocate and relocate it, and so, as Judith Roof has remarked in her commentary on "post-identity," to offer, in the world of Mennonite/s writing, "a glimmer through a tear in what once seemed to be the very fabric of culture" (5).

Because the critic of Mennonite literature would not be alone in exploring various means of escape from what Casanova calls the "intrusion of history" (xiii) and Paul Giles refers to as "the magic circle between text and context" (263), a consideration of the concerns and commentaries of other critics of literatures grounded in identity might be instructive here: the thinking of Benjamin Schreier, for example, who has composed a range of responses to what he identifies as the "fraught relationship between historiography and literary practice" in American Jewish literature ("Editor's" 1), or the stimulating commentaries offered by Asian American literary critics who have challenged in recent years "the assumed coherency if not the ultimate efficacy of Asian Americanness [for example] as a viable subject category" (Chen 186). These critics and many others are engaged in exploring, in various guises, the question that draws our attention here: how do we speak of a body of writing that has been identified, as Dimock (as I have already observed) puts it, by an adjective "derived from a territorial [or territorialized] jurisdiction" that has turned it into "a mode of literary causality" (*Through* 3)—while abjuring references to its identity?

It might be useful to pause briefly here to make it clear that throughout this discussion I use the term "identity" as a concept closely related to notions of context and historicity. Among those who have tried to clarify the concept is French philosopher Paul Ricoeur, who has observed that the concept of identity tends to have "two major uses" (115). The first use refers to identity in the way that I, and most of the critics whom I refer to here, make use of it—to suggest sameness, or (Latin) *idem,* or (German) *Gleichheit.* When we speak of identity in this mode, we refer, according to David J. Leichter, in his commentary on Ricoeur, to the external projection of identity over the course of time; static and reductive characterization; "the habits, *ethos,* or ideology that defines an individual or a group"; or the norms, traditions, and practices through which a community might be identified (for a more expansive discussion, see Leichter 120–21). Ricoeur's second distinctive use of the term "identity" refers to identity as selfhood, or (Latin) *ipse,* or (German) *Selbstheit:* inner identity, the fluid and indeterminate self that persists despite changes in habit or opinion or desire (see Leichter 120). These two forms of identity, in the simplest terms, answer two questions: "What are you?" and "Who are you?" The apparent propensity of readers of identity-based texts to conflate or confuse these two conceptions of identity has created the kind of circumstance that has compelled many a writer of Mennonite heritage, for example, to balk at being identified as Mennonite because she observes that such identification can confine or conceal her as a writer, as a dynamic individual, and relegate her to a fixed type. I have heard many a Mennonite writer declare, in exasperation, a version of Philip Roth's frequently cited self-description, suggestive of Ricoeur's two forms: "I am not a Jewish writer; I am a writer who is a Jew" (qtd. in Wisse 11). One would not have to search far to discover any number of interviews with or articles by Mennonite writers (the novelists Rudy Wiebe, Miriam Toews, or David Bergen, for example) who address—sometimes sympathetically and sometimes irascibly—what it means for them to be known as Mennonite writers. One could trace, of course, among members of the Mennonite community, a propensity of both writer and reader alike to represent each other as "types."

Some commentators on matters of identity in literature, without reference to Ricoeur, have implicitly equated the two forms of identity that he identifies with two paradigmatic approaches to the literary text. They have urged critics to attend to the variable internal structures of a text (to engage in a form of close reading that, if they were to adopt his model, would be equivalent to a form of inner identity) and thus to avoid the pre-emptive constraints of context and historicity—a text's external structures, equivalent, these commentators might observe, to the static and reductive qualities associated with what Ricoeur identifies as *idem,* sameness, *Gleichheit.* As long as Mennonite writers and readers insist on *identifying* each other—corraling each other's being and sensibility by invoking sameness and stability—each might pre-empt the response of the other and perhaps limit the potential scope of the literary texts that span the spaces between them.

Vexing questions about identity have drawn the attention of American studies critics for a few decades now, including Edwards, who recently observed that placing texts (we'll say Mennonite texts) "in deep conversation with their historical contexts and the social worlds or publics they engage" has resulted in the construction of "a formidable framework." He continues, "Yet that critical structure has outlasted the conditions within which it was created" (232). Indeed. One could make the case that a number of large literary gestures in the landscape of Mennonite writing fairly directly address the very matter that Edwards identifies. Central characters in works as diverse as Wiebe's *Sweeter than All the World* or Toews's *A Complicated Kindness,* for example, among others, investigate the troubled and troubling relationship between historical "givens," or the "formidable framework" of which Edwards speaks, and contemporary conditions that belie their relevance—or even their palpable presence—for citizens of postmodern North America. Such a disjuncture between apparently moribund, or simply disappeared, social and religious understandings and the conditions that confront a character finding him- or herself compelled to negotiate the postmodern world lies at the heart, also, of Rhoda Janzen's bestselling American memoir, *Mennonite in a Little Black Dress,* in which the principal character literally travels back into a past context so incongruous with her modern worldly life that it appears quaint at best and ridiculous at worst.

So what does one speak of when one purports to address the issue of context/historical identity relative to Mennonite/s writing? A description of the social context in which Canadian Mennonite writing in particular emerged (the historical trajectory of American Mennonite history and American Mennonite/s writing, in many senses, is another matter altogether) could be borrowed from commentators who observe that the Jewish artist in America, for example, arose "at a time of crisis" and "during the transition from religious tribalism to worldliness."[4] Or from Irving Howe, who, observing in 1977 that "the tensions of immigrant life" and "the tug-of-war between tradition and assimilation" (qtd. in Kramer, "Art" 306) no longer dominated the Jewish American experience, feared that Jewish literature had lost its subject and would disappear. Howe was wrong, but his comment is worth our attention. How do we speak of Mennonite writing in Canada now that virtually all members of the Mennonite community have moved well beyond the sorts of conditions to which such commentaries might refer?

How do we speak of Mennonite writing—and how do writers write Mennonite—now? A provocative proclamation by Schreier in his essay on Philip Roth, if we could apply it to Mennonite writing, might be illuminating here: "It is not that Roth's characters do not want to be Jews; it is that they do not know how to describe themselves as Jews" ("Failure" 107). This observation, adapted for use in the world of Mennonite writing, seems to me to strike to the heart of the matter. It is not that characters in Mennonite fiction, for example (or, for that matter, the writers of Mennonite prose and poetry themselves), do not want to be Mennonite; the challenge that confronts fictional and real characters alike is how to identify, describe, or represent the Mennonite in the twenty-first century in North America. Ah, how to both embrace certain treasured aspects of Mennonite identity and escape its imperatives at the same time?

How do Mennonite writers describe their "people"? The task appears to have been relatively straightforward for Julia Spicher Kasdorf when she made the attempt in 1992, in her oft-anthologized poem "Mennonites," which begins, "We keep our quilts in closets and do not dance. / We hoe thistles along fence rows for fear / we may not be perfect as our Heavenly Father" and continues "We love Catherine the Great and the rich tracts / she gave us in the Ukraine," and "We love those Nazi soldiers who, like Moses, / led the last cattle cars rocking out of the Ukraine," and so on. Or for Jeff Gundy a year later, when he composed a tongue-in-cheek companion piece, "How to Write the New Mennonite Poem," which begins

> Choose two from old Bibles, humbly beautiful quilts
> Fraktur, and the *Martyr's Mirror* in Dutch.
> Get the word "Mennonite" in at least
> twice, once in the title, along with zwiebach,
> vareniki, borscht, and the farm,
> which if possible should be lost now. (86)

It is interesting to note that both Kasdorf and Gundy implicitly conflate "Swiss" and "Russian" Mennonite experiences here (as well as American and Canadian experiences); in a former paradigm it was convenient and acceptable to do so, when, in Ricoeur's terms, writers and readers tended to be driven in their thinking by *idem* identity: focusing mostly on fixity and sameness. As writers, readers, and texts move beyond relatively stable notions of identity in discussions of Mennonite/s writing, each moves in the direction of foregrounding what Ricoeur calls *ipse* identity: identity that is fluid and indeterminate. We speak here of loosening the hold of a rigid sort of historicist thinking on a field. As we liberate the field, of course, we also liberate texts and writers, many of whom have felt confined by the *idem* identification that in effect has challenged their claims to a certain kind of autonomy. So a younger generation of Mennonite writers, including the authors of many of the kaleidoscope of poems gathered in Ann Hostetler's anthology *A Cappella: Mennonite Voices in Poetry*—Shari Miller Wagner and Keith Ratzlaff and Barbara Nickel, for example—and others, including Cheryl Denise and Becca J.R. Lachman, both assert a particular perspective on accepted common stories of Mennonite heritage and introduce new narratives. In the process, they become, in effect, strikingly comprehensive in their particularity.

But we dare not suggest that identity-based readings of Mennonite poems and fictions are only limiting. Perhaps no one has taken greater pleasure in the texture and light that they have offered than have I. The identity-based critical understandings that have served as prisms for critics and writers alike leave us in a condition perhaps best described by Stuart Hall in an essay aptly subtitled "Who Needs Identity?": identity is "an idea which cannot be thought in the old way, but without which certain key questions cannot be thought at all" (2). So critics of Mennonite writing are left both with readings that have illuminated texts that have seemed to belong to a certain history and sensibility and with a desire, a need, for a new critical language, to freshen and inform the prisms through which they read—perhaps to disrupt, disturb, trouble readings of existing texts structured on notions of ethnic authenticity—and to remove constraints that might inhibit their responses to new literature being composed by a new generation of writers whose work, for the most part, addresses issues substantially different from the issues that earlier generations of writers found most compelling. I have observed elsewhere, in a similar vein, that a new generation of Mennonite writers and their readers are asking questions different from those foregrounded in Mennonite literature in the past. Many of the writers whom we encounter in *Rhubarb* magazine, for example, or in *CMW Journal*, are "less interested in origins than in milieus; less concerned with group history than with individual becoming; less compelled by essential identity than by multifaceted identifications. . . . taken less with traditional notions of community than with . . . 'multiple ecologies of belonging.'"[5] Neither disturbed nor distracted by notions of displacement or exile or deterritorialization, they embrace the freedom to locate themselves in a "worldly" present ("Homelands" 15).

It is not the lives of writers alone, of course, that are inflected by the texture of the postmodern world. Most of their Mennonite readers (critics included) share with them the conditions and concerns of a new generation, though (of course) among them are many for whom the concerns regarding identity and immigration and ethnicity and various forms of "otherness" that many Mennonite texts gave expression to at the height of the era of identity politics remain of substantial interest. The propensity to invoke a sense of historicity persists nevertheless, for example in the theme for an international conference on Mennonite/s writing in Fresno, California, in 2015. The theme, "Movement, Transformation, and Place," while not precluding readings that might circumvent matters of identity, clearly invokes a consideration of matters central to most deliberations that defined the era of identity politics: migration, borders, location, home, and belonging.

What does it mean to speak of Mennonite writing "after identity"? Any determined examination of the landscapes within which this body of work emerged, and continues to exist, will surely reveal that the question has resonances and implications well beyond texts, writers, and critics. Laurence Roth, commenting in a compelling essay on his father's Jewish bookstore in Los Angeles, observes that a people's literature is not only constituted "by authors and texts" but exists also "within social space" (293). Yes. A similar kind of social space was evident in Waterloo, Ontario, during the winter of 2012, when I convened a series of readings and lectures at Conrad Grebel University College at the University of Waterloo, celebrating "the first fifty years" of Mennonite/s writing, "mostly in Canada."[6] Every Wednesday evening, for nine weeks of a Canadian winter, over a hundred readers of Mennonite literature, most of them Mennonites themselves, gathered seemingly with what Morris Dickstein describes as a "sense of communal pride" (325) to listen to and hear about Mennonite writers. Dickstein uses the term "communal pride" derisively; I do not. I speak here of a generation of readers who have paid particular attention to the historicity of the Mennonite texts of the first decades because those texts tended to illuminate worlds that they comprehended collectively and individually in terms of what Alison Landsberg has named "prosthetic memory": that is, like other members of their generation of Mennonites in Canada, they had been informed and affected by narratives in the context of which they were nurtured or, as Landsberg would say, by "memories of events through which [they] did not live" but took on as their own (1). These memories, it seemed, were challenged and confirmed, elaborated and enlarged in the literary texts that lent them weight and substance—texts embraced by a generation of readers who in various ways might make the claim to be familiar with the religious and cultural topography of their people's texts: to have "been there."

Many Mennonite texts have invited certain limited interpretive approaches—have carried within them what Kasdorf refers to in this volume as "ethnographic announcements": most notably, perhaps, Wiebe's *Peace Shall Destroy Many,* with its explanatory foreword, or Toews's *A Complicated Kindness,* with its comic documentary commentary, offered by Nomi Nickel early in her narrative: "We're Mennonites. As far as I know, we are the most embarrassing sub-sect of people to belong to if you're a teenager. Five hundred years ago in Europe a man named Menno Simons set off to do his own peculiar religious thing [. . .]" (5). So the literature itself announced the nature and scope of the prism through which it was to be read, or at least it offered access through a particular framework of understanding.

In one of his several stimulating articles on American Jewish literature, Schreier asks, rhetorically, do Jewish readers read a Jewish writer for his or her Jewishness? (see "Against" and "New York"). Do Mennonite readers, I wonder, read a Mennonite author for his or her Mennoniteness? (And which "Mennoniteness" would that be?) To some degree at least, I have taken pleasure in the fact that Wiebe's work (as I have put it in the past, citing Canadian critic Clara Thomas) "identifies me to myself." That is, I recognize his characters and the typical gestures of their lives; they are familiar to me. I have shared their meals and heard their singing. The German phrases that they use are immediately legible to me, on several levels. Their history, the structure of their families, and their conflicted piety resonate with my own. Chapter 6 of *The Blue Mountains of China* tells the story of my parents' escape from Stalin's Russia in 1929 more clearly and evocatively than I have ever read or heard elsewhere.

Having grown up as a Mennonite in a culture in which all the public stories, it seemed, belonged to the (apparently) Anglo-Saxon Canadian majority, I learned to embrace Robert Kroetsch's dictum that "stories make us real," and I remember the enormous pleasure that I took when the early work of Mennonites writing in English appeared in Canada: Patrick Friesen, Sandra Birdsell, and Di Brandt, for example. I must add, in this context especially, that I do not mean to suggest that any other reader—Mennonite or not—would share my experiences or my readings of them or of the texts that evoked them.

When I first started teaching Mennonite poetry and fiction in southwestern Ontario in the 1980s, my students would often include Mennonite readers, some of whom, by virtue of their being either or both American and "Swiss," for example, declared themselves to be at a substantial remove from the mostly prairie-based, often markedly unsophisticated, characters presented by Canadian Mennonite writers. Some of them expressed shock at the portraits of writers and characters whom they were unable to recognize as Mennonite; the matter of those literary texts (which depicted cultural landscapes so familiar to me) bore no resemblance to their Mennonite experiences.

It is interesting that in the winter 2012 reading/lecture series, even the new, under-forty writers and critics—Darcie Friesen Hossack and Carrie Snyder and Robert Zacharias—failed to draw a younger crowd. The findings of Franco Moretti's rather unconventional literary history came to mind: that literatures tend to remain in place "for twenty-five years or so" and that almost "all genres active at any given time seem to arise and disappear together according to some hidden rhythm" (20). Why? Because the audience changes; the readers vanish. Commenting on the literature of the United States in the middle of the past century, Robert E. Spiller declared that each generation "should produce at least one literary history" because "each generation must define the past in its own terms" (vii). Long before that, Ralph Waldo Emerson had observed, "The books of an older period will not fit this" (88). Mennonite literature seems to be in no danger of vanishing, but the conditions that sustained its origins and the early critical readings of it no longer compel many who have an interest in the field. Much of the new Mennonite writing is a different thing altogether: vibrant and fresh and worldly.

Although Mennonite literature has tended to be monitored and commented on mostly (though by no means exclusively) by critics who are Mennonite, it is worth observing that in Canada, at least, this literature (the principal writers of which are national figures functioning in the top ranks of Canadian literature) did not emerge as a sectarian literature. Almost all of Canadian Mennonite literature has been published by public presses (Turnstone Press is notable here, along with McClelland and Stewart, HarperCollins, and many well-established small publishers and little magazines). The first conference on Mennonite/s Writing took place on a public university campus; it was initiated and sponsored by *The New Quarterly,* the literary magazine based at the University of Waterloo. The conference was attended by a number of prominent Canadian literary scholars, some of whom played significant roles; the conference proceedings were published by the University of Waterloo Press, as was the first collection of Mennonite short fiction: *Liars and Rascals: Mennonite Short Stories* (see Tiessen, ed.). If those who work in the field are to illuminate one of the paths to Mennonite literature "after identity," then they would do well to continue to invite literary critics outside the Mennonite circle to join (or remain in) the conversation.

When I began to anticipate what it might mean to speak of Mennonite writing "after identity," I was compelled to consider, first of all, the fact that the term "Mennonite writing" contains and conceals a tangle of relations. I wondered whether scholars might do well to dislocate particular "classic" Mennonite texts from the contexts in which they have been written and received (in which they have, in large measure, served as what Jeff Karem calls "objects of desire for . . . reading publics" [213]) and relocate them to allow new readings to emerge. Inspired by Dimock's warning against "analytic domain[s] foreclosed by definition" (*Through* 3), I wondered about the impact, for a small but powerful literary movement that we have come to identify as Mennonite, of investigating what might happen if critics were to focus their attention on alternative, non-Mennonite tropes and traces in seminal (and assumed to be seminally Mennonite) works such as Rudy Wiebe's *Peace Shall Destroy Many* (haunted by the shadow of Big Bear and, as Paul Tiessen reveals in this volume, shaped in some measure by its first central Canadian, Anglo-Canadian readers), some of the lyric poetry of Patrick Friesen (in which he adopts as muse the great Russian and Soviet modernist poet Anna Akhmatova), Di Brandt's early poems (richly infused with feminist critical theory) or her late verse (a feast for the ecocritic), the Tante Tina poems of David Waltner-Toews (the roots of which are in the work of Ugandan poet Okot p'Bitek), or the fiction of Dallas Wiebe (influenced and informed by the satire of British modernists). I mused about exploring how critical responses to Mennonite works that engage traces and territories "after identity" might liberate texts and creators and inspire readers to revisit these texts without the lingering distraction of what Karem calls "the romance of authenticity." Can this literature, I wondered, survive such abandonment?

Any number of critical trajectories that eschew the issue of identity might result in very interesting readings of the Mennonite texts referred to here—and others. Dimock, in her "theory of resonance," offers further encouragement in this vein, asserting that a text is "continually interpretable": "[S]tretched by a growing web of cross-references, often to the point of unrecognizability, a text cannot and will not remain forever the same object" ("Theory" 1061, 1062). If we are to "liberate" the Mennonite text, we could do worse than to take direction from Dimock. Like some of the other critics cited here, she offers valuable perspectives that encourage us to explore and exploit the fact that Mennonite literary texts extend well beyond their originating circumstances.

Such a "liberation" might require some qualification. Some critics of "minoritized" literatures that embody issues of race and/or politics that extend well beyond anything that Mennonites have had to encounter, for example, have suggested that, to emerge safely on the other side of conversations about identity, we might need to consider doing away with the minority subject as a category (e.g., see Chuh; Lee). Mennonite writers in North America have not been compelled to deal with matters of race (even though there are many Mennonites of color in North America, no prominent Mennonite literary voices have emerged, so far, among them), and Canadian Mennonites especially have not tended to trouble themselves about how the Mennonite fits into the broader culture; in fact, with a few notable exceptions (e.g., the issue of conscription in the Second World War, addressed in *Peace Shall Destroy Many*), Mennonite characters in fiction tend to be much more interested in their places within their own communities than in their situations in society at large. This is not to say that there are no national or racial resonances in their work; Sandra Birdsell was sharply criticized in the *Globe and Mail* by fellow Canadian (i.e., Ukrainian Canadian) novelist Janice Kulyk Keefer for her dismissive treatment of Ukrainians in *The Russländer*, for example. And Rudy Wiebe's treatment of Canada's Native peoples has not been universally applauded. Perhaps centuries of willed isolation from "the world" and things "worldly" have left at least Canadian Mennonites relatively comfortable expressing a separatist sensibility; nevertheless, issues of nation, race, and ethnicity as they are treated in Mennonite literary texts might bear some further investigation.

It is by no means imperative that critics of Mennonite writing abandon all notions of identity; in fact, as Tina Chen, citing Paula Moya, observes in another landscape altogether, "it is imperative that ethnic studies scholars develop theoretical models for demonstrating how identity is still an indispensable category of inquiry, a site of investigation" (192–93). Moya is speaking here of the need for critics to attend to matters especially of political agency. Chen cites her in the context of a discussion in which she observes that "poststructuralist conceptions of identity (and their accompanying emphases on the impossibility of coherency, the suspicion of realism, and the naïve idealism and essentialism of identity politics) have been embraced in the academy at precisely a moment when minorities are claiming for themselves the right to speak as subjects and agents" (192). Even for Mennonite writers—almost exclusively, until now, North Americans of white European ancestry (though this too is changing, as it should, given the change in Mennonite demographics)—Chen's observations and their implications resonate; after all, the discourses developed and sustained by the identity politics of decades past have offered opportunities for a vast range of minority voices to be heard, not only in the culture at large, I might add, but also within any given minority community itself. The most appreciative and engaged readers of minority literatures in North America, it could be argued, are members of the minority cultures that have produced the liminal texts that in large measure serve to identify their members to themselves.

The challenge, then, is not to forget about identity altogether but to refuse it the front seat that it has occupied for so long in Mennonite literary discourse, to invite new—possibly disruptive—readings; perhaps to abandon the desire to read texts as Mennonite/Mennonites. If critics of Mennonite writing at least temporarily set aside their presumed understandings of what Mennonites are, they might clear away the noise that prevents them from hearing the individual voices in the texts who declare who they are—as individuals, not as members of a collective. Like any literary text, after all, the Mennonite literary text surely has, in Dimock's words, "a force of incipience commensurate with the incipience of humanity" ("Theory" 1064).

NOTES

1. These are numbers of baptized members (Mennonites practice adult baptism). See the World Directory of the Mennonite World Conference, http://www.mwc-cmm.org/article/world-directory.

2. Quoted from a 26 April 2013 email circulated by *CMW Journal* editor Ann Hostetler.

3. I borrow this phrase from Michael Millner on American studies; see also Pease.

4. See Greene and Peacock (91), quoting Aharon Appelfeld, commenting on the social contexts of Jewish American writing.

5. I take this expression from Rosi Braidotti (19).

6. Video recordings of the reading/lecture series are available online: https://uwaterloo.ca/grebel/events/lecture-series/menno-lit-videos-2012.

WORKS CITED

Braidotti, Rosi. *Nomadic Theory: The Portable Rosi Braidotti.* New York: Columbia University Press, 2011.

Casanova, Pascale. *The World Republic of Letters.* Trans. M.B. DeBevoise. Cambridge, MA: Harvard University Press, 2004.

Chen, Tina. *Double Agency: Acts of Impersonation in Asian American Literature and Culture.* Stanford: Stanford University Press, 2005.

Chuh, Kandice. *Imagine Otherwise: On Asian Americanist Critique.* Durham: Duke University Press, 2003.

Dickstein, M. "A Response [to Michael P. Kramer, 'Race, Literary History, and the "Jewish" Question'] from Morris Dickstein." *Prooftexts* 21.3 (2001): 324–27.

Dimock, Wai Chee. "A Theory of Resonance." *PMLA* 112.5 (1997): 1060–71.

———. *Through Other Continents: American Literature Across Deep Time.* Princeton: Princeton University Press, 2006.

Edwards, Brian T. "The World, the Text, and the Americanist." *American Literary History* 25.1 (2013): 231–46.

Emerson, Ralph Waldo. "The American Scholar." 1837. *Selected Essays.* Ed. Larzer Ziff. New York: Penguin, 1982. 83–105.

Giles, Paul. *Virtual Americas: Transnational Fictions and the Transatlantic Imaginary.* Durham: Duke University Press, 2002.

Greene, Dana M., and James R. Peacock. "Judaism, Jewishness, and the Universal Symbols of Identity: Re-Sacralizing the Star of David and the Color Yellow." *Studies in American Jewish Literature* 30 (2011): 80–98.

Gundy, Jeff. "How to Write the New Mennonite Poem." Hostetler 86–87.

Hall, Stuart. "Introduction: Who Needs 'Identity'?" *Questions of Cultural Identity.* Ed. Stuart Hall and Paul du Gay. London: Sage, 1996. 1–17.

Hostetler, Ann, ed. *A Cappella: Mennonite Voices in Poetry.* Iowa City: University of Iowa Press, 2003.

Jelen, Sheila E., Michael P. Kramer, and L. Scott Lerner, eds. *Modern Jewish Literature: Intersections and Boundaries.* Philadelphia: University of Pennsylvania Press, 2010.

Karem, Jeff. *The Romance of Authenticity: The Cultural Politics of Regional and Ethnic Literatures.* Charlottesville: University of Virginia Press, 2004.

Kasdorf, Julia Spicher. "Mennonites." Hostetler 129.

Keefer, Janice Kulyk. "Paradise lost in Russia, found in Manitoba." Rev. of *The Russländer,* by Sandra Birdsell. *The Globe and Mail* 29 Sept. 2001: D17.

Kramer, Michael P. "The Art of Assimilation: Ironies, Ambiguities, Aesthetics." Jelen, Kramer, and Lerner 303–26.

———. "Critical Narcissism and the Coming-of-Age of Jewish American Literary Studies." *Jewish Quarterly Review* 94.4 (2004): 677–93.

Kroetsch, Robert. *The Lovely Treachery of Words: Essays Selected and New.* Toronto: Oxford University Press, 1989.

Landsberg, Alison. *Prosthetic Memory: The Transformation of American Remembrance in the Age of Mass Culture.* New York: Columbia University Press, 2004.

Lee, Christopher. "Asian American Literature and the Resistances of Theory." *Modern Fiction Studies* 56.1 (2010): 19–39.

Leichter, David J. "Collective Identity and Collective Memory in the Philosophy of Paul Ricoeur." *Études Ricœuriennes/Ricœur Studies* 3.1 (2012): 114–31.

Millner, Michael. "Post Post-Identity." *American Quarterly* 57.2 (2005): 541–54.

Moretti, Franco. *Graphs, Maps, Trees: Abstract Models for a Literary History.* New York: Verso Books, 2007.

Palumbo-Liu, David. "Assumed Identities." *New Literary History* 31.4 (2000): 765–80.

Pease, Donald E. "National Identities, Postmodern Artifacts, and Postnational Narratives." *boundary 2* 19.1 (1992): 1–13.

Reimer, Margaret Loewen. *One Quilt Many Pieces: A Guide to Mennonite Groups in Canada.* 4th ed. Waterloo, ON: Herald Press, 2008.
Ricoeur, Paul. *Oneself as Another.* Trans. Kathleen Blamey. Chicago: University of Chicago Press, 1992.
Roof, Judith. "Thinking Post-Identity." *Journal of the Midwest Modern Language Association* 36.1 (2003): 1–5.
Roth, Laurence. "Unpacking My Father's Bookstore." Jelen, Kramer, and Lerner 280–302.
Schreier, Benjamin. "Against the Dialectic of Nation: Abraham Cahan and Desire's Spectral Jew." *Modern Fiction Studies* 57.2 (2011): 276–99.
———. "Editor's Introduction." *Studies in American Jewish Literature* 32.1 (2013): 1–3.
———. "The Failure of Identity: Toward a New Literary History of Philip Roth's Unrecognizable Jew." *Jewish Social Studies: History, Culture, Society* 17.2 (2011): 101–35.
———. "New York Intellectual/Neocon/Jewish: Or, How I Learned to Stop Worrying and Ignore Ruth Wisse." *Studies in American Jewish Literature* 31.1 (2012): 97–108.
Spiller, Robert E., ed. *Literary History of the United States.* Vol. 1. New York: Macmillan, 1948.
Tiessen, Hildi Froese. "Homelands, Identity Politics, and the Trace: What Remains for the Mennonite Reader?" *Mennonite Quarterly Review* 87.1 (2013): 11–22.
———, ed. *Liars and Rascals: Mennonite Short Stories.* Waterloo, ON: University of Waterloo Press, 1989.
Toews, Miriam. *A Complicated Kindness.* Toronto: Knopf Canada, 2004.
Wiebe, Rudy. *Peace Shall Destroy Many.* Toronto: McClelland and Stewart, 1962.
Wisse, Ruth R. *The Modern Jewish Canon: A Journey Through Language and Culture.* Chicago: University of Chicago Press, 2000.

CONTRIBUTORS

ERVIN BECK is the author of *MennoFolk: Mennonite and Amish Folk Traditions* (Herald Press, 2004), editor of *MennoFolk 2: A Sampler of Mennonite and Amish Folklore* (Herald Press, 2005), and, with John D. Roth, editor of *Migrant Muses: Mennonite/s Writing in the U.S.* (1998). From 1967 to 2003, he was a professor of English at Goshen College, where he helped to organize Mennonite/s Writing conferences in 1997 and 2002. Beck has published numerous articles on Mennonite literature as well as on folklore, drama, and world literature. He is also the editor of the two most complete bibliographies of Mennonite literature—one for U.S. authors, and one for Canadian authors, as well as the co-editor of the online *Journal of the Center for Mennonite Writing*.

DI BRANDT is a poet, essayist, teacher, and critic living in Brandon, Manitoba. She has taught at the Universities of Manitoba, Winnipeg, Alberta, Windsor, and Brandon, and she has given lectures and readings around the world. She has published more than a dozen books and received numerous awards, including the Gerald Lampert Award for *questions I asked my mother;* the McNally Robinson Manitoba Book of the Year Award for *Agnes in the Sky;* the CAA National Poetry Prize for *Jerusalem, Beloved;* the Foreword Gold Medal for Fiction for *Watermelon Syrup,* with Annie Jacobsen and Jane Finlay-Young; and the Gabrielle Roy Prize for *Wider Boundaries of Daring: The Modernist Impulse in Canadian Women's Poetry,* with Barbara Godard. *Now You Care* was nominated for the Griffin Poetry Prize, the Trillium Ontario Book of the Year Award, and the Pat Lowther Award.

DANIEL SHANK CRUZ grew up in New York City and Lancaster, Pennsylvania, where his family has lived since 1711. He is a graduate of Goshen College and Northern Illinois University, and he currently teaches English at Utica College. He has published articles and poems in journals such as *Rhubarb, Crítica Hispánica,* and *Journal of Contemporary Thought.* His current research interests include the intersections between ethnic minority literatures and queer literatures.

JEFF GUNDY has published six books of poetry and four of prose; *Spoken Among the Trees* (Akron, 2007) won the Society of Midland Authors Poetry Award, and *Walker in the Fog: On Mennonite Writing* (Cascadia, 2005) received the Dale Brown Award for Anabaptist and Pietist Scholarship. His most recent works are a book of poems, *Somewhere Near Defiance* (Anhinga, 2014), and a book of criticism, *Songs from an Empty Cage: Poetry, Mystery, Anabaptism, and Peace* (Cascadia, 2014). He teaches at Bluffton University in Ohio and was a 2008 Fulbright lecturer at the University of Salzburg. Recent essays and poems appear in the *Georgia Review, Sun, Mennonite Quarterly Review, Kenyon Review, Conrad Grebel Review,* and *Nimrod.*

ANN HOSTETLER is Professor of English at Goshen College in Goshen, Indiana, where she chairs the Department of English. Her scholarship on multicultural American literature has appeared in *PMLA, Mennonite Quarterly Review, Conrad Grebel Review,* and in collections by Penn State, SUNY, and the University of Mississippi Press. She is also the website editor for www.mennonitewriting.org, which hosts the *Journal of the Center for Mennonite Writing,* of which she is a co-editor. Her poems have appeared in the *American Scholar, Grey Sparrow, Literary Mama, Nimrod, Poet Lore, Valparaiso Poetry Review,* and *Washington Square,* among other venues. She is the author of a volume of poetry, *Empty Room with Light* (Dreamseeker, 2002), and the editor of *A Cappella: Mennonite Voices in Poetry* (University of Iowa, 2003). *Empty Room with Light* was a finalist for the Arlin G. Meyer Award, sponsored by the Lilly Fellows Program of Valparaiso University.

JULIA SPICHER KASDORF, Professor of English and Women's Studies at Penn State University, is the author of three collections of poetry, a collection of essays, *The Body and the Book: Writing from a Mennonite Life,* and a biographical study, *Fixing Tradition: Joseph W. Yoder, Amish American.* With Joshua R. Brown, she edited Yoder's *Rosanna of the Amish* and Fred Lewis Pattee's *House of the Black Ring.*

ROYDEN LOEWEN is the Chair of Mennonite Studies and Professor of History at the University of Winnipeg. He is the editor of the *Journal of Mennonite Studies* and series editor of the Ethnicity and Culture History Series at the University of Manitoba Press. His publications include *Village Among Nations:*

"Canadian" Mennonites in a Transnational World (2013); *Immigrants in Prairie Cities: A History* (2009), co-authored with Gerald Friesen; *Diaspora in the Countryside: Two Mennonite Communities in Mid-20th Century North America* (2006); *Hidden Worlds: Revisiting the Mennonite Migrants of the 1870s* (2001); and, with Steven Nolt, *Seeking Places of Peace: North America; A Global Mennonite History* (2012) and *Communities of Peace and Piety: A People's History of Mennonites in North America* (forthcoming).

JESSE NATHAN's poems have appeared in the *American Poetry Review, The Nation, jubilat, Oxford American,* and many other magazines. Nathan coedits the McSweeney's Poetry Series with Dominic Luxford. He has published essays and journalism in the *San Francisco Chronicle, Adbusters, The Believer, McSweeney's, Sojourners, Poetry International,* and *Tin House,* among others, and he is working on a PhD in English Literature at Stanford University. He was born in Berkeley but grew up on a farm in rural Kansas. He now lives in San Francisco.

MAGDALENE REDEKOP is Professor Emerita in the Department of English, University of Toronto. She is the author of *Mothers and Other Clowns: The Stories of Alice Munro* (Routledge, 1992). She has published numerous articles and stories on Mennonite topics, the most recent a comic memoir entitled "Farm Animals' Desertion: In Which Puss in Boots Learns that the Kota Is Full." She is at work on a book entitled *Making Believe: Mennonites Looking for Spielraum* (University of Manitoba Press).

HILDI FROESE TIESSEN has published widely in the area of Mennonite/s writing and has edited numerous literary and critical volumes of work by and about writers of Mennonite heritage. Since 1990, she has been an organizer or chair of six international conferences on Mennonite/s Writing, and recently she hosted a series of readings and lectures by and about Mennonite writers at Conrad Grebel College at the University of Waterloo, where she taught from 1987 to 2012. The series is available online at https://uwaterloo.ca/grebel/events/lecture-series/menno-lit-videos-2012. The first Literary Editor of the *Conrad Grebel Review,* she is a member of the advisory boards of the *Journal of Mennonite Studies, Center for Mennonite Writing* (Goshen College), and *GAMEO (Global Anabaptist Mennonite Encyclopedia Online).*

PAUL TIESSEN is Professor Emeritus of English and Film Studies at Wilfrid Laurier University in Canada. His most recent work on Mennonite novelists

David Bergen, Sandra Birdsell, Miriam Toews, David Waltner-Toews, Armin Wiebe, Dallas Wiebe, and Rudy Wiebe appears in *Text Matters: A Journal of Literature, Theory, and Culture*; *Journal of Mennonite Studies*; and *Mennonite Quarterly Review.* With Hildi Froese Tiessen, his most recent work includes the introductory text for L.M. Montgomery's letters to her lifelong Mennonite interlocutor Ephraim Weber (University of Toronto Press) and the art-historical text for a volume of Mennonite artist Woldemar Neufeld's Canadian landscapes (Wilfrid Laurier University Press). Tiessen has new work on spatiality, archives, cinema, and theater published or forthcoming on texts by media theorist Marshall McLuhan, playwright Wilfred Watson, and novelists Sheila Watson and Malcolm Lowry. He is on an international team of scholars editing and publishing a trilogy of 1930s–40s novels by Malcolm Lowry with University of Ottawa Press.

ROBERT ZACHARIAS is a Banting Postdoctoral Fellow in the Department of English Language and Literatures at the University of Waterloo and Visiting Scholar at the Centre for Diaspora and Transnational Studies at the University of Toronto. Assistant Editor of the *Journal of Mennonite Studies,* his publications include *Rewriting the Break Event: Mennonites and Migration in Canadian Literature* (2013), *Shifting the Ground of Canadian Literary Studies* (2012), which he co-edited with Smaro Kamboureli, and numerous articles on Mennonite writing, diaspora studies, and Canadian literature.

CREDITS

The following publishers and estates have generously granted permission to reproduce, in part or full, sections of poetry and cover art.

"Mennonite Haiku," from *Mennonite Meets Mr. Right,* by Rhoda Janzen. © 2012 by Rhoda Janzen. Used by permission of Grand Central Publishing.

Excerpts from *Sleeping Preacher,* by Julia Kasdorf, © 1992. Reprinted by permission of the University of Pittsburgh Press.

Excerpt from *Eve's Striptease,* by Julia Kasdorf, © 1998. Reprinted by permission of the University of Pittsburgh Press.

Excerpts from *questions i asked my mother,* by Di Brandt © 1987 used by permission of Turnstone Press.

Excerpts from *Agnes in the Sky,* by Di Brandt © 1990 used by permission of Turnstone Press.

Excerpts from *Unearthly Horses,* by Patrick Friesen © 1984 used by permission of Turnstone Press.

Excerpts from *Kansas Poems,* by Dallas Wiebe © 1987 used by permission of the Wiebe estate.

Excerpts from *The Sayings of Abraham Nofziger II,* by Dallas Wiebe © 2007 used by permission of the Wiebe estate.

Excerpts from *Dubious Angels,* by Keith Ratzlaff © 2005 used by permission of Anhinga Press.

Excerpts from "Unexpected Ghost," by Ann Hostetler © 2013 used by permission of *Bluestem Journal.*

Excerpts from *Paper House,* by Jean Janzen © 2008 used by permission of the author.

Excerpts from *The Upside-Down Tree,* by Jean Janzen © 1992 used by permission of the author.

Excerpts from "How to Write the New Mennonite Poem," by Jeff Gundy © 1993 used by permission of *Mennonot.*

Excerpts from *Spoken Among Trees,* by Jeff Gundy, © 2007 Jeffy Gundy. Reprinted by permission of the University of Akron Press. Unauthorized duplication not permitted.

Excerpts from *Inquiries,* by Jeff Gundy, © 1992 reprinted by permission of Bottom Dog Press.

Excerpt from "A New Mennonite Replies to Julia Kasdorf," by David Wright © 1999 reprinted by permission of the *Mennonite.*

Excerpts from *What Can We Do Here?* by Elmer Suderman © 1974 reprinted by permission of the Suderman estate.

Cover image of Rudy Wiebe's *Peace Shall Destroy Many,* designed by Frank Newfeld, used by permission of Frank Newfeld and

McClelland and Stewart, a division of Random House of Canada Limited, a Penguin Random House Company.

Excerpts from "Hold Your Piece," unpublished lecture by Rudy Wiebe, used by permission of Rudy Wiebe.

Material quoted from McClelland and Stewart archive used with permission of the estate of Jack McClelland.

INDEX

TYPESET BY click! Publishing Services

PRINTED AND BOUND BY Sheridan Books

COMPOSED IN Adobe Garamond, Avenir, Futura, Scala Sans

PRINTED ON Natures Natural